PERFORMING RACIAL UPLIFT

PERFORMING RACIAL UPLIFT

E. Azalia Hackley and African American Activism
in the Postbellum to Pre-Harlem Era

Juanita Karpf

University Press of Mississippi / Jackson

Margaret Walker Alexander Series in African American Studies

The University Press of Mississippi is the scholarly publishing agency of the Mississippi Institutions of Higher Learning: Alcorn State University, Delta State University, Jackson State University, Mississippi State University, Mississippi University for Women, Mississippi Valley State University, University of Mississippi, and University of Southern Mississippi.

www.upress.state.ms.us

The University Press of Mississippi is a member of the Association of University Presses.

Any discriminatory or derogatory language or hate speech regarding race, ethnicity, religion, sex, gender, class, national origin, age, or disability that have been retained or appear in elided form is in no way an endorsement of the use of such language outside a scholarly context.

Copyright © 2022 by University Press of Mississippi
All rights reserved
Manufactured in the United States of America

First printing 2022
∞

Library of Congress Control Number: 2021047891
Hardback ISBN 978-1-4968-3668-7
Trade paperback ISBN 978-1-4968-3679-3
Epub single ISBN 978-1-4968-3670-0
Epub institutional ISBN 978-1-4968-3669-4
PDF single ISBN 978-1-4968-3672-4
PDF institutional ISBN 1-4968-3671-7

British Library Cataloging-in-Publication Data available

To Cole, Glady, Mira, Noah, Selah, Shem, and Tosia—running free

CONTENTS

ix   Acknowledgments

3   Introduction

15   **CHAPTER ONE**—Formative Years and Early Career

39   **CHAPTER TWO**—Travel, Domestic and Abroad

71   **CHAPTER THREE**—New Thought Activism

95   **CHAPTER FOUR**—Music Education and Racial Uplift

117   **CHAPTER FIVE**—World War I Activism

137   **CHAPTER SIX**—Writing and Uplift

151   **CHAPTER SEVEN**—Chronic Illness and New Thought

161   Coda

173   Notes

205   Bibliography

221   Index

ACKNOWLEDGMENTS

Expressing appreciation for all those who have assisted me requires that I dig deep as work on this book has occupied me, on and off, for many years. I first heard about Azalia Hackley from Thomas L. Riis, one of my faculty advisors and professors during my graduate student years at the University of Georgia. Dr. Riis guided me through the, at times, intimidating process of completing a short biographical entry about Hackley, which eventually became my very first publication. The essay appeared in *Notable Black American Women,* a reference work compiled by Jessie Carney Smith (Fisk University), who proved to be an understanding, supportive, and exacting editor.

Numerous attendees at conferences and symposia where I gave papers about Hackley have offered gracious and constructive comments about my work. Unfortunately, I cannot recall the names of all these individuals, but a few come to mind: William Banfield, Adrienne Fried Block, John Graziano, Sondra Howe, Felicia Miyakawa, Lawrence Schenbeck, Catherine Parsons Smith, Jean Snyder, Judith Ann Still, and Judith Tick.

Numerous librarians, archivists, and historical society staff members have assisted me in countless ways as I searched for information about Hackley and her times. Among those I must thank are the following: Beth Howse, Fisk University Library; Esme Bhan, Moorland-Spingarn Research Center, Howard University; Mary Kearns, Castleton (VT) Free Library; Allison Gallagher, Oberlin College Library; Diane Lee, Interlibrary Loan, Oberlin College Library; Kathy Abromeit, Oberlin College Conservatory Library; Virginia Feher, Interlibrary Loan, University of Georgia Library; Stephen Toombs and Jeffrey Quick, Kulas Music Library, Case Western Reserve University; Donzella Maupin, Hampton University Archives; Melissa Samson, Charles H. Wright Museum of African American History, Detroit; DeLisa M. Harris, Special Collections, Fisk University; and Liz Allen, London (England) Metropolitan Archives. I am also grateful for the assistance of staff members at the E. Azalia Hackley Collection of African Americans in the Performing Arts and at the Library of Congress.

Friends who patiently listened to me in many conversations about my fascination with Hackley and offered sage advice include Grace Elizabeth Hale, University of Virginia; Lynne Rogers, Mannes School of Music; and Leroy Bynum, Jr., Portland (OR) State University.

Lewis Nielson, my husband, has been a patient and stalwart ally and a constant supporter of my work. The music examples in this book benefitted enormously from his expertise with notation software. I owe him immeasurable gratitude.

I also appreciate the efficiency of the editorial staff at University Press of Mississippi. The suggestions for revisions from external reviewers proved to be most helpful. My work is much better as a result of their careful reading. Any errors in, or limitations of, this book are solely mine.

To those who provided support and assistance but whose names I have not mentioned above, I apologize.

PERFORMING RACIAL UPLIFT

INTRODUCTION

"Bravo! Madam, Woman of Wonders," exclaimed Sylvester Russell, arts critic for the widely circulating African American newspaper, the *Indianapolis Freeman*.[1] Russell's exuberance came in response to a recital he had just attended, in early November 1911, presented by soprano Emma Azalia Smith Hackley. Glowing reviews, such as the one published by Russell, typified Black press reactions to Hackley's virtuosity and captivating stage presence. In addition to touring as a soloist, she conducted innumerable choral concerts and usually played her own piano accompaniments—also to critical acclaim. Her extraordinary popularity spread throughout the United States, and she earned press accolades in London and Paris as well. However, her success as both a racial uplift activist and as a nationally respected music educator ultimately defined her career.

Hackley's life (1867–1922) fits neatly into the "postbellum-pre-Harlem" era, a descriptive term for the years from approximately 1863 to the early 1920s introduced by author Charles W. Chesnutt. For his characterization of this time span, Chesnutt consciously selected demarcations that reference two momentous occurrences in African American history: Emancipation, at one end, and the initial stirrings of the Harlem Renaissance, at the other. He intended "postbellum-pre-Harlem" to convey an African American ethos; champion accomplishments in the Black arts, humanities, and literature; and promote the flowering of the racial uplift movement. Of equal significance, Chesnutt's designation stands in stark contrast to the implications of more familiar delineations of the later nineteenth and early twentieth centuries, namely, the "Victorian Age," "Progressive Era," or "Gilded Age," all of which reflect decidedly white values and socio-historical biases. So, too, the spirit of the postbellum–pre-Harlem era offers a more optimistic and prescient alternative to African American historian Rayford W. Logan's analysis of these years as the "Nadir," a period cluttered with flagging political efforts, disenfranchisement, and racist violence.[2] Hackley's career exemplified the activist yearnings of the postbellum-pre-Harlem era, during which African American achievement held forth promise to deflect and dismantle the systematic ravages of racism and segregation. With his epithet and its implications, Chesnutt also celebrated the efforts of Black intellectuals and leaders who strove to bolster race consciousness and solidarity—a dimension of uplift activism with which Hackley readily identified and tirelessly promoted.³

Performing, in various manifestations, assumed preeminence in Hackley's career, hence, the reference to performance in the title of this book carries multiple meanings. Beyond her accomplishments as a solo artist, Hackley also earned accolades as a producer and director of community music events, especially during World War I, when she originated a unique pageant genre conceived for African American patriotic celebrations. Fundraising also occupied her throughout her career, and she skillfully enticed audiences to contribute money for philanthropic and charitable causes. For Hackley, teaching became performative as well, especially as most of her instruction took place before large audiences. She was sought after, nationally, as a lecturer—another performative act—speaking to her audiences about a variety of subjects, some of them quite far removed from the world of music. She also aspired to be an author, and, as readers constitute yet another audience, I extend the meaning of performance to include Hackley's publication projects, especially as virtually all of what she wrote originated as talks she gave. And finally, Hackley "performed" what she construed to be the ideal image of African American womanhood—as an embodiment of achievement and unimpeachable morality that capitalized on elegance, fashionable attire, and respectability.

In pursuit of an activist agenda, Hackley developed a unique interpretation of uplift ideology she called "musical social uplift." However singular in its conception and implementation, Hackley's approach to uplift strategies and goals nonetheless also incorporated principles disseminated by other activists of her era. She espoused components of W. E. B. Du Bois's philosophy, such as the valorization of intellectual and artistic achievement and the support of education in the arts and humanities. In this regard, and as a college graduate and classically trained musician, she could be counted among Du Bois's "Talented Tenth"—a coterie of educated, successful, and class-conscious race leaders. If her activist strategies and prose generally lacked Du Bois's political militancy, her initiatives nonetheless brought to the fore some of the more egregious aspects of segregation, such as the humiliating treatment Blacks endured while traveling by train in the Jim Crow South. Yet Hackley also endorsed pragmatic, gradualist, and conservative uplift viewpoints as well. Like Booker T. Washington, she saw considerable virtue in the practice of personal thrift and the cultivation of a strong work ethic. In addition, she believed in the dignity of vocational training and the appropriateness of employment in a trade for many Black citizens. Self-consciousness about Black female respectability also preoccupied some conservative activists, and Hackley stressed the imperative of projecting an image of modesty in appearance, decorum, and lifestyle. However, even as she maintained a prominent public profile and pursued the status of a celebrity, she urged Black women to follow a traditional white patriarchal model of submissiveness and domesticity by aspiring to the roles of homemaker, wife, and mother. To Hackley, motherhood assumed paramount significance in the struggle for racial justice as she held mothers responsible for bringing forth subsequent generations of African Americans and raising them to be productive, law-abiding, and respectable citizens.

Ultimately, however, music making endowed Hackley's version of racial uplift with its own distinctive characteristics, its momentum sustained by pedagogical, spiritual, and artistic considerations. As her designation "musical social uplift" suggests, she combined music performance, teaching, and learning to form an activist triumvirate with which she contributed a compelling and unique methodology to the racial uplift movement. She continually reassured Blacks that they possessed considerable musical ability and that this gift could serve as a potent vehicle in the struggle to end racist humiliation and violence. In her lectures, she spoke of how music performance provided a way for African Americans to demonstrate unequivocal competence and accomplishment and thus enhance the possibility of winning the respect of more moderate, enlightened, and sympathetic whites. She envisioned music making as a social common denominator that held forth opportunities for Blacks and whites to contemplate a sense of cooperation and shared purpose and as an activity with which both races could interact cordially. The promotion of race pride among all African Americans comprised an incontrovertible component of Hackley's ideology, and she felt that music making constituted the single most effective method for its cultivation and dissemination.[4]

When Hackley performed her first solo recital and embarked on her inaugural concert tour, she faced unremitting cultural, intellectual, and artistic racism. The majority of whites in the postbellum-pre-Harlem era tended to consider African Americans as musically inferior, capable only of learning and performing race-specific styles and genres, especially those associated with blackface minstrelsy. Journalist and historian James Monroe Trotter decried this pernicious and restrictive attitude: "The haze of complexional prejudice has so much obscured the vision of many persons, that they cannot see (at least, there are many who affect not to see) that musical faculties, and power for their *artistic* development, are not in the exclusive possession of the fair-skinned race. . . . There are some . . . persons who have formed erroneous and unfavorable estimates of the art-capabilities of the colored race [italics original]."⁵ By "art-capabilities" and "artistic development" Trotter referred to classical, European-modeled music and its utility as teaching and performance repertoire. African American singers who performed and taught classical pieces, such as opera arias, choral works, and art songs, defied cultural prohibitions that not only precluded their access to this literature, but also deemed Blacks incapable of rendering appealing, legitimate and informed interpretations of such pieces. So, too, Hackley and those African Americans who followed her into the classical music milieu transcended the Jim Crowism of European cultural expression by not only performing this repertoire to critical acclaim, but did so in venues reserved almost exclusively for whites. African Americans' confident, praise-worthy and courageous participation in a world denied to them during the postbellum-pre-Harlem era offers yet another potent expression of resistance and activism.

There are many "firsts" associated with Hackley and her career. To name but a few here: As a community music educator she pioneered the use of spirituals and works by Black composers as instructional and performance repertoire. In 1914, she became the first African American concert artist to write an article series on music performance for a prominent newspaper, entitled "Hints to Young Colored Artists."⁶ Her Normal Vocal Institute, which began operations in 1915 in Chicago, became the first music school founded by a Black performer to offer teacher training to aspiring African American musicians. When, in 1916, she published her only book-length work, *Colored Girl Beautiful*, she anticipated by several years the release of similar advice and etiquette manuals dedicated specifically to the interests and needs of Black girls and women. Her dissemination of the principles of a popular form of ecumenical spirituality known as "New Thought" established her as the earliest proponent of this liberative ideology among African Americans. Finally, during the World War I years, she produced patriotic pageants in Black communities throughout the country and became the first activist to provide huge African American audiences with opportunities to participate in community-based expressions of patriotism.

I first heard of Hackley nearly thirty years ago, when I was invited to contribute a biographical essay about her to a landmark reference work entitled *Notable Black American Women*.⁷ A preliminary search through library resources uncovered frustratingly little information about her and confirmed just how far her historical reputation had slipped into obscurity. Yet, countless hours of scrolling through scratchy microfilm reels of periodicals and newspapers revealed her one-time prominence and extraordinary fame; her name was known and respected in every African American household of the early twentieth century. At this early stage of research, I stumbled upon M. Marguerite

Davenport's book-length biography of Hackley. Davenport based her narrative on information gleaned from interviews and from scrapbooks containing some of Hackley's press clippings, photographs, and personal correspondence. These materials were in the possession of Hackley's husband and sister, and Davenport was given exclusive access to them.[8] Surely, I speculated, some of these vital sources might be relatively easy to locate, perhaps housed in the archives of a historically Black institution. Such a discovery eluded me, and eventually, I was forced to conclude that these sources had, somehow, disappeared. Nonetheless, Davenport's book, published a quarter of a century after Hackley's death, was the first attempt at a lengthy account of this influential activist and musician. Unfortunately, Davenport's hagiographic, sentimental writing style detracts enormously from her book's readability and utility. However dated, her perspective on Hackley provided inspiration for a more recent biography, published by Lisa P. Brevard in 2001. Although Brevard considers Hackley in a more contemporary context, she does not offer any discussions of her spirituality, music repertoire, or teaching methodology—lacunae that I believe do a disservice to Hackley's artistry and her role as a pioneering educator and uplift activist. Moreover, only by evaluating the music Hackley knew and loved does it become possible to understand and appreciate salient aspects of her unique activist philosophy.

Other than the studies by Davenport and Brevard, Hackley has attracted little authorial or scholarly attention, in spite of her onetime prominence. Why have researchers tended to avoid attempts to reclaim her history? I surmise that this seeming lack of interest in Hackley can be attributed, in part, to the type and quantity of surviving source materials about her. Unfortunately, no diaries, journals, or cache of her personal papers have been located. Only scattered sources about her activities remain, and the fragmented nature of these materials makes it impossible to create a tidy, chronological narrative. In addition, surprisingly few reflections about Hackley by persons who knew her well survive. To be sure, information about her public events appeared in every African American newspaper and periodical of her day. Even the white press, generally indifferent or sometimes hostile toward Blacks, respected her musicianship and acknowledged her activist zeal. In the end, newspapers and periodicals constitute the most abundant source materials about her. However, such sources present many challenges to anyone attempting to reconstruct Hackley's life and career. Sadly, and however unintentionally, Hackley herself contributed to the elusive nature of primary sources by and about her. Given the plethora of lectures she gave, especially at historically Black institutions, one would hope to discover a treasure trove of printed programs or her handwritten notes, yet only infrequently did she memorialize her thoughts in writing.

Furthermore, her restless nature and constant traveling interfered with the process of saving items for posterity. With the loss of many issues of historic African American newspapers and periodicals, some publicity about her has, unfortunately, disappeared.

The task of locating and interpreting elusive source materials, especially items from the press, requires considerable investment of patience and time. I liken this reclamation process to that of assembling a complicated jigsaw puzzle, with pieces missing. A final picture gradually comes into view, to be sure, but with significant gaps. In many cases, press accounts yield the only available information about certain individuals and events in African American history, yet, by underestimating or devaluing the importance of these sources, we run the risk of allowing influential persons to linger in perpetual obscurity. This is certainly true for Hackley for, only by mining the Black press can she emerge as one of the most provocative and intriguing figures of her day. Not surprisingly, then, the internet has changed how I think about Hackley. With vast databases of digitized newspapers, periodicals, photographs and archival materials now available online, I have uncovered documentation about Hackley that had previously been unknown, unidentifiable, or impossible to locate. The recent surge in popularity of family genealogy research has also made a myriad of primary sources readily accessible. Although most private correspondence concerning Hackley has been lost, I have become aware of several previously overlooked items and these have been rendered accessible to me via the internet. Many reviews do not offer sufficient information about the music Hackley performed and online resources have made it possible not only to identify the titles and composers of the pieces she programmed most frequently, but also to obtain copies of these scores. A critical evaluation of Hackley's relationship with these pieces, presented here for the first time, offers a lens through which to view her extraordinary musicianship and to identify the ways music provided her with a vehicle for activist endeavors. However, exhaustive searching notwithstanding, it must be admitted that the aggregate of extant sources about Hackley does not yield a coherent, linear narrative.[9] Therefore, I have chosen to organize this book episodically, by addressing themes and philosophical tenets associated with her activist agenda. I devote considerable space to consideration of press reactions to Hackley, thus taking advantage of the focus and interests of journalists in her day. The nature and configuration of such an approach has permitted me to evaluate the ways she harnessed concert and teaching repertoire as interwoven agencies for nurturing both race consciousness and individual self-esteem among her audiences and students. Press accounts also document her abiding appreciation of spirituals, and, by teaching and performing this genre, she promoted the preservation of an invaluable dimension of Black history and culture. Ultimately, then, this book is not a biography, nor is it a reconstructed chronology of a slice of history.

In chapter 1, I present an overview of Hackley's formative years and early career. Hackley (née Smith), known throughout her life as "Azalia," was born in 1867 in Murfreesboro, Tennessee. Her parents and grandparents were of mixed-race ancestry, and Azalia inherited her light skin and wavy hair from her forebears. As a young girl, she demonstrated considerable musical talent, playing piano and singing at a very early age. Around 1870, racist violence forced the Smith family to flee Tennessee, and they relocated to Detroit. After graduating from high school, Azalia completed teacher education at the Detroit Normal Training School. For several years thereafter, she taught in area public schools, gave private music lessons, and performed as a singer and pianist.

Azalia married Edwin Henry Hackley in 1894, and the couple settled in Denver, Colorado. Together, the Hackleys edited and wrote for an African American newspaper, the *Denver Statesman*. They also established a fraternal organization, the Imperial Order of Libyans, which provided Denver's Black residents with a secret society dedicated to social equality and racial justice. Azalia Hackley earned a bachelor's degree in music education from the University of Denver, taught music lessons, performed recitals, and conducted choral concerts. However, the harsh winters and high altitude aggravated her health, so the couple moved to Philadelphia. By the dawn of the twentieth century, Azalia had begun to tour as a soprano soloist, appearing at prestigious venues located in large metropolitan areas. She soon earned national recognition with her renditions of opera arias, art songs, and popular ballads. In addition to touring, she organized community choruses and conducted highly acclaimed concerts in the Philadelphia vicinity. In 1903, she joined the faculty of the newly established Washington Conservatory of Music, located in the nation's capital. But, by 1906, she had come to the realization that, in order to further her career as a solo artist, she needed to supplement her credentials by studying and concertizing in Europe.

Hackley traveled constantly, and I address her experiences as an itinerant activist in chapter 2. She rarely resided in any one locale for an extended period of time, and her ambitious touring schedules took her throughout the United States. In this regard, she envisioned travel as essential to activism as mobility facilitated interaction with the residents of hundreds of Black neighborhoods. As a frequent visitor to the South, she routinely experienced the demeaning and unsafe conditions of Jim Crow travel accommodations. In protest of such treatment, she filed lawsuits against Southern railroads, and her name became associated with efforts to improve rail service for African Americans. She published newspaper articles about her legal complaints against the railroads and lectured about the humiliation of Jim Crow train travel.

Beyond extensive travel throughout the United States, Hackley also sailed overseas between 1906 and 1914, visiting Europe three times and Cuba twice. An effective fundraiser, she financed all her travels through concert ticket sales and by selling photographs and pamphlets. While abroad, she wrote letters to the African American press in which she commented on race relations she encountered in other countries. She sought and discovered empowerment in mobility and the transcendent effect of escaping, if only temporarily, the racism so rampant in the United States. In Europe, Hackley studied singing with arguably the two best-known voice pedagogues of her day: Jean de Reszke (in Paris) and William Shakespeare (in London). That these celebrated teachers accepted her as a private student speaks to her extraordinary talent.

Throughout her career, Hackley explored and appropriated spiritual beliefs associated with the New Thought Movement, especially those that complemented, augmented and extended beyond the Episcopalian tradition in which she participated during her formative years. In chapter 3 I introduce the ways Hackley embraced tenets of New Thought and interwove its principles into her activist agenda. New Thought, an assemblage of ecumenical practices derived from a variety of sources, evolved in the United States during the mid-nineteenth century. Advocates of New Thought do not necessarily abandon more established religions or denominations, but they also tend to avoid strict adherence to prescriptive dogma, ritual, and hierarchy. In addition, they practice mind healing, seek ways to enhance the power of positive thinking, and celebrate the righteousness of bountiful living. Hackley employed New Thought in her pedagogy, noticeable especially in her use of deep-breathing exercises practiced by New Thought adherents, modeled on Yoga traditions. She also emphasized the development of the New Thought concepts of mental concentration and telepathy, both of which contributed, substantially, to the uniqueness of her approach to racial uplift. We can better appreciate the rise in influence of New Thought in Black communities during the 1920s and beyond by illuminating Hackley's promotion of some of the movement's major principles. Her dissemination of New Thought anticipated more recent currency of its ideology among African Americans, beginning with the ascendency of Marcus Garvey in the 1920s and his emphasis on racial self-reliance, and the sanctity of financial wealth and material comforts. That New Thought continues to flourish as a significant dimension of African American spirituality confirms the enduring influence of its life-affirming and liberatory potential.

Hackley also espoused a New Thought approach to reproduction and heredity, and her views correspond with those of other activists of the early twentieth century. Her commitment to what was known as "uplift parenting" included the advocacy of ways African American women could improve their chances of giving birth to healthy babies. Followers of this component of racial uplift endorsed some of the more benign precepts of eugenics, including the preference for procreation among only the "reproductively fittest." Hackley frequently reminded expectant mothers of their racial responsibility to turn to New Thought strategies in order to maintain positive, balanced thoughts during pregnancy. By controlling one's thoughts and emotions throughout pregnancy and childbirth, the general health and intellectual promise of a child could best be nurtured and assured. Such children, Hackley insisted, would ultimately find more opportunities available to them and could, potentially, develop into future race leaders.

New Thought enthusiasts also practiced the reciprocal process of "giving and receiving," commonly articulated and codified as "give to get." In 1907, Hackley inaugurated an ambitious philanthropic initiative—her approach to the New Thought premise of "giving"—when she established the Foreign Scholarship Association, dedicated to funding African American musicians' studies in Europe. Her community events now served yet another purpose: to raise funds for this scholarship program. Through her efforts, she became the first African American philanthropist to sponsor and financially support musicians for overseas study. By offering assistance to promising musicians, Hackley enabled them to receive world-class instruction not usually obtainable in this country as most US conservatories refused admittance to Blacks. Her own success at obtaining and funding instruction in London and Paris provided her with an incentive and model for these philanthropic efforts.

In chapter 4, I discuss Hackley's philosophy of, and approaches to, music teaching and learning. She developed a unique method of instruction that combined the methodology of what was then known as "voice culture" with principles she learned at the University of Denver and in her European studies. For Hackley, music education also served as a spiritual endeavor, and accordingly, she infused her pedagogy with New Thought ideology, particularly recognizable in her promotion of the Yogic breathing techniques she considered essential for singers. Throughout her career, she offered advice on ways to increase opportunities for music instruction in Black communities, especially for children, and she demonstrated the teaching methods she deemed most appropriate for the general population. She perceived music performance and education as vehicles for, and texts of, activism, and, through song, she communicated provocative messages of social and racial justice and race pride. Furthermore, she strove to legitimize the community at large as her student body and auditoria and churches as teaching classrooms. Her efforts on behalf of Black communities won praise throughout the nation, and her accomplishments add an important chapter to the early twentieth-century history of US music education. Through her devotion to audience education and her promotion of Black music talent, she earned the press sobriquet "vocal teacher of ten thousand."[10]

When World War I erupted in July 1914 in Europe, Hackley resided in Paris and she witnessed the confusion and fear of a country swept up in preparation for armed conflict. In chapter 5, I focus on the changes in Hackley's career after she returned to the United States in September 1914. As European hostilities escalated, Black newspapers and activists debated whether or not the United States should enter the war and what effect US participation in the conflict might have on race relations. Some African American leaders condemned, as race betrayal, any support for a government that sanctioned or turned a blind eye to racism and segregation. Others, most notably W. E. B. Du Bois, envisioned the war as a unique opportunity for Blacks to demonstrate patriotism and loyalty and to participate in the struggle, as US President Woodrow Wilson famously declared, "to make the world safe for democracy." Yet, rather than participate in political agitation or in the war debate, Hackley navigated clear of confrontation. Instead, she pursued a pragmatic and conciliatory agenda and earned renown as a producer of extravagant patriotic events in African American communities. These initiatives came in response to parallel efforts among whites who generally refused admittance to, or participation by, Blacks at their patriotic rallies. Hackley produced patriotic events throughout the United States and engaged thousands of participants in communal singing, parades, and elaborate costumed pageants—all of which offered Blacks the opportunity to express and experience, publicly, their patriotic fervor.

In 1915, Hackley contemplated whether or not she could reconfigure her activist mission by concentrating more on writing and publishing, and less on touring. Toward this end, she corresponded with musician and author James Weldon Johnson and sought his assistance regarding some writing projects on which she had been working. Several of their letters survive, and I assemble chapter 6 using this correspondence as a framework for discussion of Hackley as an aspiring author. In her letters, she revealed her hopes of publishing at least a few of her manuscripts, and Johnson offered his support, along with sage advice. Much of the correspondence between Hackley and Johnson concerned her most extensive manuscript, eventually published as the advice manual *Colored Girl Beautiful*. Hackley based this book on lectures she gave at historically Black institutions and at innumerable public events. Yet the content of lectures she selected to include in her book did not reflect her customary emphasis on music making and instead dealt with matters of interest to African American girls and women, such as grooming, deportment, attire, courting, marriage, and motherhood. The book received disappointingly little press attention, and only a few reviews were published. Quite possibly, Hackley's followers were not ready for a publication from her that hardly mentioned music. Nonetheless, the book provides a rich repository of her viewpoints, especially noteworthy for details of her approach to New Thought and to issues of racial identity.

Even as Hackley traveled constantly, she also experienced periodic episodes of ill health that sometimes forced her to cancel public appearances and alter her touring schedules. I devote chapter 7 to a discussion of her struggle with illness and the relationship of her health to her appropriation of New Thought, generally, and mental healing, in particular. While she resided in Denver, she experienced respiratory problems that recurred at increasingly shorter intervals and with more intensity as her career unfolded. By 1905, she admitted to suffering from substantial hearing loss and other complications. As was true of women activists of her day, she went to considerable lengths to maintain, before the public, an image of robust health. Yet, she endured hospitalizations, surgery, considerable pain, compromised mobility, and impaired hearing—all of which required her to alter her repertoire, abandon projects, and reschedule concert events. That she continued to tour and pursue an activist agenda can be attributed, at least in part, to the solace she must have experienced from the New Thought strategies she practiced. But, more importantly, her perseverance attests to her indefatigable commitment to musical social uplift and to her stoicism and extraordinary resolve.

In the coda, I summarize and critique Hackley's multilayered agenda of musical social uplift and its various components. As a pedagogue, she employed music making as a vehicle for the celebration of Blacks' innate vocal gifts and cultural expressivity. The addition of New Thought ideology to her activist agenda enabled her audiences to experience, through her guidance, transcendent spirituality and an abiding sense of optimism. However, Hackley's activist approach manifests contradictions and inconsistencies, many reflective of the tension and conflict so prevalent during the postbellum-pre-Harlem era. For example, even as racists resorted to violence and dogged enforcement of segregation, she did not agitate for an end to Jim Crowism. Instead, she crafted and carefully maintained a mediatory cultural space, particularly evident in her refusal to wholeheartedly endorse either Booker T. Washington's or W. E. B. Du Bois's philosophies. The shifting political climate of her day required her to realign her views and activist strategies, periodically, so that her message remained relevant. At no time did this tendency become more apparent than during World War I, when she altered her repertoire and introduced an innovative style of activist pageantry to Black communities. However frustrating her conciliatory posture may seem when viewed in a contemporary light, we should remember that she directed her energy toward the realization of goals she felt best served the needs of the African American population of her day and would prove most effective in deflecting the ravages of racism.

Hackley's unique racial uplift initiatives warrant inclusion in the historiography of African American activism, and American music, more generally. Her accomplishments as a concert artist and facilitator of community music making helped lay a solid foundation upon which the Harlem Renaissance could unfold and flourish. Certainly, the success of celebrated African American concert singers who followed her, especially contralto Marian Anderson, tenor Roland Hayes, and bass Paul Robeson, can be attributed to Hackley's groundbreaking career and her support of Black musicians, their compositions, and their stellar performances. Beginning in the 1920s, white US audiences gradually became more receptive to African American artists who programmed both spirituals and classical European-derived repertoire because so many had been introduced to this innovative mingling of style and genre at Hackley's concerts, through her lectures, and by reading press items about her.

It is my hope that this book will inspire cultural, authorial and scholarly dialogue about Hackley. This complex and gifted woman, her philosophies, and her contributions to racial uplift offer opportunities to reconsider the contours of postbellum-pre-Harlem activism. The dynamics of her career invite us to contemplate the extraordinary value and courage of mediatory activists of the early twentieth century who refused to align themselves with any particular philosophy or methodology. Furthermore, my study cannot be considered comprehensive as, surely, someone will locate additional primary sources by and about Hackley, thereby offering tidbits of information waiting to be carefully evaluated and added to our knowledge of her life and times. However much Hackley's inconsistent and contradictory viewpoints might frustrate contemporary readers and researchers, we can do no less than acknowledge her enormous popularity, influence, and artistry. To do otherwise is to let a compelling figure of the postbellum-pre-Harlem era continue to drift in obscurity.

CHAPTER ONE

Formative Years and Early Career

A young Azalia Smith drew initial inspiration for her unique approach to racial uplift from her mother, Corilla Smith, who ran a school for freed enslaved people. Azalia also inherited, from her mother, an abiding appreciation for the empowering and activist potential of teaching and music making. Even as a small child, she manifested considerable suitability and requisite talent for a career as a concert artist and music educator. She soon came to envision music as an agency through which she could assist the Black population in the struggle to cultivate race pride and achieve personal fulfillment amid relentless racism. Yet her youthful musical exuberance and nascent activist zeal belied the troubled relationship she experienced with her emotionally distant parents. She learned that by performing in public she not only attracted an enthusiastic following, but she also formed alliances with persons who admired her prodigious gifts and irrepressible spirit. Music making, then, not only provided solace as she coped with an unsettling home environment, but it also yielded a compelling incentive and model for her subsequent uplift initiatives and unprecedented worldview.

Murfreesboro and Detroit

Azalia Smith was born on 29 June 1867 in Murfreesboro, Tennessee. Only two years prior to her birth, the Ku Klux Klan had organized its inaugural branch in central Tennessee—the first in the nation. Klan members and other supporters of white supremacy rapidly expanded their campaign throughout the state. They directed much of their intimidation and hostility toward Black organizations and institutions, especially schools and churches.[1] As Azalia's mother operated a school for former enslaved people in a small, local Black church, she and her students were likely targets for Klan marauders. Not surprisingly, Smith family members lived in constant fear for their safety as did Murfreesboro's African American residents.[2] In 1870, a white mob attacked Corilla Smith's school and terrorized Blacks living in the area. This display of violence and the resultant damage to the church forced the closing of her school. Azalia's parents decided to flee Murfreesboro, and they settled in Detroit, where other family members resided. The move must have been arduous as the family not only included three-year-old Azalia, but also her infant sister, Marietta, born in 1869.[3]

Once in Detroit, the Smith family lived, temporarily, with relatives. They soon acquired permanent housing in a racially mixed, relatively affluent, neighborhood. Although the Smiths maintained ties to the Baptist denomination while they resided in Murfreesboro, they eventually attended services at Detroit's St. Matthew's Episcopal Church, an African American parish noted for its commitment to racial uplift. Founded in 1846 by organizers of the Underground Railroad and the Abolitionist Movement, the church maintained a tradition of service and activism of considerable significance and appeal to the Smith family, only recently uprooted by racist violence.[4] Azalia's father, Henry B. Smith, found work in a nearby museum, and he also maintained a curio shop.[5] Azalia's mother, Corilla Smith, an accomplished singer and pianist, taught private music lessons. Under the guidance of her mother, Azalia became a proficient pianist and learned to read music before she entered school. She began to entertain house guests at an early age, singing the songs and playing the piano pieces she learned from her mother. When she enrolled at the elementary school located near the family's residence, she was the only Black student.[6] She took full advantage of music opportunities available at the schools she attended, such as choral activities and lessons in singing, piano, and violin.[7]

Although music making held forth the potential to forge a lasting and affectionate bond between Azalia and her mother, such a relationship proved elusive. Instead, the elder Smith daughter was frequently at the mercy of her mother's authoritarian parenting style. As Azalia approached adulthood, her interaction with her parents became increasingly strained and remote. Her sister, Marietta, recalled Corilla Smith's autocratic propensities, inordinately directed toward Azalia: "Mama exercised extreme authority over us even after we reached the ripe age of one and twenty. Azalia assumed the family responsibilities early, but Mama's peculiar and dominating tendencies continued such a restraint that Azalia's young masculine admirers were never very sure of their reception when calling."[8] Nevertheless, Corilla Smith laudably instilled in her daughters a strong sense of African American identity and race pride. According to a long-time friend, Marie A. D. Madre, Azalia "was not only inspired [by her mother] with the thought that she could do anything that anybody could do, but she was [also] cautioned that if she failed to excel where other races were concerned that no excuse could prevent a speedy home accounting. . . . The talented and severe mother never wearied in preaching that the gray matter—the brain—was the same color and texture in every head."[9] Another friend, Kate Johnson, remembered that Corilla Smith "not only bequeathed [to] her [the] gift of teaching, the love of music and faith in the power of the Negro's voice as a medium and power of good, but she also bestowed upon her the love of duty, the love of service as well as indomitable will power, tremendous courage and boundless energy."[10] Years later, Azalia reminisced: "I thought of my own mother, a pioneer[ing] musician who did so much musical work among our people, especially in the South, where she went to live after her marriage, just after the [Civil] war." She valued, and was influenced by, the stories of her mother's "thrilling experiences of teaching the freedmen how to sing by note [i.e., taught to read music], while an opposed white community entered into protest by throwing stones in the windows of the church" where she taught.[11] Still, her parents' lack of warmth profoundly affected her throughout her life. She later confirmed: "I have never had any affection bestowed upon me by any of my family [i.e., parents], for there was no affection in them."[12] In fact, she claimed she had never been kissed by her mother.[13] Her close relationship with her sister provided the only relief to an impassive childhood and one substantially lacking in essential emotional support from her parents.

Nonetheless, the Smith family attained a level of material and financial comfort associated with what historian Willard B. Gatewood identifies as "aristocrats of color." The Detroit press counted the Smiths as members of the city's "cultured colored 40," an elite coterie of African American families who enjoyed relatively privileged status.[14] Henry Smith's entrepreneurial initiatives apparently thrived, and, according to the Detroit city directory, Corilla Smith continued to teach music. However, the Smiths' marriage began to falter, and, around 1883, the couple separated and eventually divorced. It seems likely that Azalia's father did not contribute sufficient financial support to his wife and daughters after the breakup of their household. Subsequent recurring illness sometimes prevented Azalia's mother from giving music lessons, and her sister, Marietta, experienced serious vision problems and occasional health crises that required costly medical treatment. As the only member of the family able to work regularly, Azalia assumed substantial financial obligations when only in her teens. To help her family meet ends, she performed regionally as a pianist and singer and also taught music lessons throughout her high school years.[15] After graduation, Azalia attended Detroit Normal Training School to prepare for a teaching career and was that institution's only Black student at

Fig. 1.1. E. Azalia Smith, ca. 1885. J. Wesley Hughes, photographer. Courtesy, E. Azalia Hackley Collection of African Americans in the Performing Arts, Detroit Public Library, Detroit, Michigan.

the time of her enrollment. Beginning in 1886, she taught at Detroit's Clinton Elementary School for several years, at some point also serving as assistant principal. She was the school's second African American teacher and the fourth Black public-school teacher in the entire state of Michigan.[16] Teaching rapidly assumed activist significance for Azalia, and her salary also allowed her family to maintain their status as members of Black Detroit's elite.

Some of the earliest surviving photographs of Azalia Smith date from the 1880s. These images show her with wavy hair and light skin. Her racial ambiguity reflected that of her parents and grandparents as censuses and city directory entries identified Smith family members as "mulatto."[17] One early photograph, produced in the popular cabinet card format, commemorated her graduation from high school (figure 1.1). For this studio session, she wore a variant of the fashionable Gibson Girl hair style with luxurious waves falling over her forehead. Her downward gaze, heavy eyebrows, and pince-nez reinforce a serious countenance. Other photographs from this time period allow us to appreciate Smith in a more light-hearted moment. Smith posed with a friend, Elizabeth C. Carter, with whom she clearly enjoyed a close relationship, for a series of five images, (figure 1.2). It is not certain when Smith and Carter may have met. They had much in common, including dedication to racial uplift and women's issues and a commitment to pursuing careers in education.[18]

Azalia Smith also became involved in some of Black Detroit's social, charitable, and musical organizations. One of these, the Chandler Odd Fellows Lodge (of the Ancient Order of United Workmen), produced many fundraising events for philanthropic causes.[19] Smith often furnished music for the more

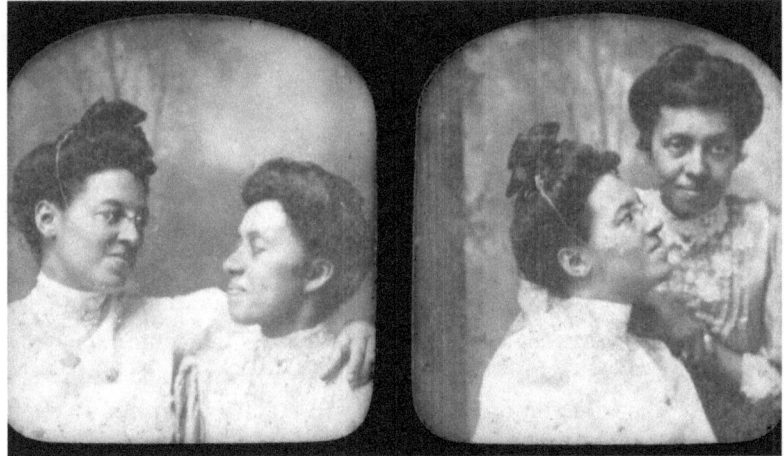

Fig. 1.2. E. Azalia Smith and Elizabeth C. Carter, ca. 1885. Courtesy, Library of Congress, Washington, D.C.

lavish of these events. Of one such occasion, she recalled the presence of a large, appreciative gathering: "Talk about a crowd! Everybody was there. I don't mean the rough element, but everyone else."[20] In addition, she performed as pianist for the Detroit City Band and also played and sang with the Detroit Musical Society.[21] Among her musical associates were soprano Maggie Porter (later Cole, 1853–1942), one of the original Fisk Jubilee Singers, and Mabel A. Hill (later Battles, 1868–1916), a violinist and piano accompanist.[22] Smith gave several voice recitals in collaboration with Hill. As the *Detroit Plaindealer* noted of one of their performances, "the song recital under the direction of Misses E. Azalia Smith and Mabel Hill took place at the Second Baptist Church . . . before a fair audience. The participants were all cordially greeted and rendered a program of twelve excellent numbers."[23] Months later, the *Plaindealer* announced, "Miss E. Azalia Smith and Miss Mabel Hill will give a musical and literary entertainment for Bethel Church Friday Dec. 12 [1890]. The young ladies have prepared an excellent program and promise a pleasant evening to all those who attend."[24] Smith and Hill eventually traveled to Ohio and performed their program in various locations in that state as well. A Cleveland journalist offered this comment: "Notwithstanding the intensely warm weather during the last few weeks, society has been extremely gay. Picnics, dinners, teas, receptions and musicales have followed each other as rapidly and regularly as in mid-winter. Much attention had been shown . . . Misses Mabel Hill and Azalia Smith of Detroit."[25]

Smith also starred in some of Detroit's music theater productions. For her performance of the title role in a staged "burlesque imitation of Cinderella," the press quipped, "Miss Azalia Smith hardly makes the petite Cinderella of childhood imagination, but she sang as sweetly as ever."[26] She also sang the title role in a staged rendition of William B. Bradbury's enormously popular choral work, *Esther, the Beautiful Queen* (1856). Community organizations, especially churches, libraries, and schools, often produced *Esther* for fundraising purposes.[27] A review of Black Detroit's performance of *Esther*, printed in the *Plaindealer*, noted: "The delightful cantata of 'Queen Esther' was given under the auspices of St. Matthews [Episcopal Church] Lyceum at Fraternity Hall on Christmas night [1890]. The attendance was large and hence the Lyceum must have netted a neat sum as the result of their efforts. . . . Miss E. Azalia Smith made a very pretty queen and sang as sweetly as she always does."[28]

In 1893, an item from a Detroit newspaper correspondent, printed on the front page of the *Indianapolis Freeman*, stated that Smith had recently become engaged: "Marriages to come off—Madame Rumor says Edwin Hackley of Denver, Col., to Miss Azalia Smith, the sweet warbler of song in our city."[29] However, less than a month later, a retraction of this announcement appeared and quickly squelched such speculation: "The bubble burst—Miss Azalia Smith

Fig. 1.3. Edwin Henry Hackley. Courtesy, Paul Stewart Collection, Black American West Museum, Denver, Colorado.

returned to her post as teacher in one of the Detroit schools—not yet married."[30] Still, the press rumors contained an element of truth as Smith had been maintaining a clandestine relationship, for an undetermined length of time, with Edwin Henry Hackley (1859–1940) (figure 1.3). It is not known how or when Hackley and Smith became acquainted. Edwin Hackley, a native of the greater Detroit area, graduated from the University of Michigan's law school and moved to Denver in 1885.[31] After relocating, he made regular trips to the Detroit area, where his mother and members of his extended family resided. During these visits, he and Smith spent time together.

After meeting, the couple sustained their long-distance relationship through frequent correspondence. Anticipating and fearing the disapproval of her mother, Smith routed their letters through the hands of a sympathetic relative, James Frank Rickards, affectionately referred to by her as "Uncle Frank."[32] At some point after becoming engaged, Smith entertained the idea of a formal wedding ceremony. She acquired a gown with a train, most likely for the occasion (figure 1.4). However, certain her mother would not consent to the marriage, Smith abandoned her original wedding plans.[33] Yet, members of Smith's family, including her mother, would have known of the couple's intention to marry as the Black press had published notices about their engagement in 1893. Furthermore, there seems to have been at least some advanced planning for the event, as Smith sent out a few invitations. In response, for example, the *Cleveland Gazette* published this notice: "The editor of the *Gazette* acknowledges the receipt of an invitation to be present at the marriage of Mr. Edwin H. Hackley

Fig. 1.4. E. Azalia Smith. Alfred G. McMichael, photographer, Detroit, Michigan, 1893. Courtesy, E. Azalia Hackley Collection of African Americans in the Performing Arts, Detroit Public Library, Detroit, Michigan.

to Miss E. Azalia Smith, which occurred in Detroit, Mich., Monday January 29th [1894]."[34] Ultimately, Smith and Hackley elected to elope, and they were married in a private ceremony. The Rev. Joshua Bowden Massiah, the newly appointed pastor at St. Matthew's Episcopal Church and a respected uplift activist, officiated. Only two friends of the couple attended and no one from either the Smith or Hackley families witnessed the ceremony. The newlyweds honeymooned briefly in Chicago.[35]

Azalia Hackley's teaching position must have been a factor as the couple contemplated where they would eventually reside. However, the Detroit public-school administration adhered to the dictates of the "Marriage Bar," a rule that required female teachers in many states to relinquish their positions when they married.[36] Thus, as a married woman, Azalia Hackley would have been compelled to tender her resignation. Accordingly, she gave notice to the board of education, but only did so on the day before her marriage. Members of the Clinton School community reacted with surprise to her decision, and much weeping among the students followed her announcement. The Clinton School's white principal, James M. Manderville (1851–1938), expressed disappointment after hearing of Hackley's plans to leave. He lauded her as "an excellent teacher" and added that the students were quite attached to her.[37]

Denver

Ultimately, the newlywed Hackleys decided to settle in Denver. African Americans had established a small but vibrant community there in the early 1880s, the area often referred to as the "Harlem of the West." The Hackleys resided in the city's "Five Points" neighborhood, the only location where Blacks were permitted to purchase homes.[38] Black Denver acquaintances of the Hackleys included poet Paul Laurence Dunbar (1872–1906) and cosmetics entrepreneur Madame C. J. Walker (1868–1919). Edwin Hackley also struck up an enduring friendship with activist Ida B. Wells during her visit to Colorado in 1886.[39]

Among his sources of income, Edwin Hackley practiced law and held a position as Denver's county clerk. In addition, he assisted with the management responsibilities of the Iron Duke Mining Company and provided legal advice for the firm. A highly speculative entrepreneurial venture, to be sure, the company proclaimed itself "the only incorporated gold and silver mining company ever organized by colored men. . . . It owns and is working four splendid gold and silver lodes."[40] Hackley also edited an African American newspaper, the *Denver Statesman*, founded by him around 1888. As a journalist, he sustained a reputation as an outspoken leader in racial matters.[41] Owing to his prominence, journalists elected him president of the Northwestern Negro Press Association, a position he fortuitously used to disseminate his views on racial uplift and political activism.[42] Ohio newspaper correspondent David Wilborn recorded this impression of Hackley as an editor and journalist:

> Mr. E. H. Hackley, editor of the *Statesman*, an old Michigan boy, is a young man of push, and is doing wonderful work for the race. He is much loved by the best citizens here, who are willing to follow where he leads. . . . Mr. Hackley is trying to build the people up and [inspire them to] demand their rights, which are due them as citizens. The paper [*Denver Statesman*], indeed, is an able exponent of the race, and is also subscribed for by the best white citizens here.[43]

In 1900, Edwin Hackley became involved with nationally prominent uplift and political organizations. He served as a founding member and officer of the National Afro-American League, a cohort of activists dedicated to the promotion of racial solidarity and self-help.[44] The following year, he abandoned the league over philosophical differences and inaugurated the more militant Constitutional Union, an effort praised by Ida B. Wells.[45] He proposed the establishment of local and regional branches of the union to pursue its goals: "It shall be the object of this organization," he announced, "to secure for ourselves and for those citizens whose legal and natural rights and opportunities are abridged in the exercise of citizenship, by prejudice, oppression or the nullification of the laws, a more just, equal and untrammeled opportunity as citizens of this community, commonwealth and republic."[46]

Azalia Hackley rapidly assumed prominence in Black Denver's civic organizations and uplift initiatives. She joined the Denver affiliate of the Republican Women's Club in 1894 and served as the organization's vice president.[47] With her husband, she helped inaugurate a secret fraternal society, the Imperial Order of Libyans. As its mission, this organization pledged to combat racism and promote patriotism.[48] She also assisted with the establishment of the Denver branch of the National League of Colored Women and held the office of secretary. League members announced their intention to promote "the moral, intellectual, industrial and social growth of the colored people; to foster unity of purpose" and to "consider and determine the best interests of Denver's black community." Beyond these general aspirations, the league also promised to address the needs of Black females by encouraging "a pure girlhood" and "a noble, intelligent motherhood."[49] In July 1896, delegates of the National League of Colored Women and the National Federation of Afro-American Women met for the first time, in Washington, DC. Hackley most likely represented Denver's African American women at this meeting. Attendees voted to merge the league with the federation, and the combined membership of these two organizations formed the National Association of Colored Women (NACW). This merger came about, in part, as an impassioned and vigorous response to a widely circulated racist letter, written by journalist John W. Jacks. African American women activists distributed copies of Jacks's letter to race leaders throughout the United States. In his letter, Jacks attacked persons of African heritage and debased Black Americans as "wholly devoid of morality." However, he reserved most of his vitriol for Black women whom he labeled "prostitutes, natural liars and thieves."[50] Readers of the nationally circulating *Indianapolis Freeman* knew these remarks all too well as the paper printed Jacks's letter in its entirety.[51] The letter so incensed members of the fledging NACW that they deemed it "too indecent" to be reprinted in the inaugural literature published by the organization. However, NACW officials urged recipients of one of their early promotional pamphlets "to read this document carefully and use discriminately and decide if it be not time for us to stand before the world and declare ourselves and our principles. . . . The letter of Mr. Jacks which is also enclosed is only used to show how pressing the need of our banding together if only for our protection."[52] With their motto of "Lifting as We Climb," the NACW promoted self-help among Black women and raised awareness about such pressing issues as lynching and the struggle for universal suffrage. The organization's philosophy generally coincided with that of Booker T. Washington, especially in its allegiance to pragmatic economic approaches to racial uplift and an avoidance of radical militancy. Through her association with the NACW, Hackley made the acquaintance of several prominent uplift leaders, such as the following: Mary Church Terrell, first president of the NACW; journalist Victoria Earle Matthews (1861–1907); activist, educator and author Anna Julia Cooper (1858–1964); and Fanny Barrier Williams, co-founder of the National League of Colored Women.[53]

Work with the *Denver Statesman* also occupied Azalia Hackley. According to one account, she "set the [paper's] type, read the proof, wrote articles and editorials for it, made up the paper [i.e., finalized its layout], and so on."[54] In one of her earliest articles, she established herself as a spokesperson for women's issues with these comments: "We have borne in mind the great need for thought and talk on the practical as well as the cultural side of woman's life. Our first work will be toward the education and improvement of our Colored women and the promotion of their interests."[55] With the assistance of several of Denver's prominent Black women leaders, she edited a special women's section of the *Statesman* entitled *Statesman-Exponent*. The press lauded Hackley's choice of subject matter and viewpoints, as her editorial skills and selection of assistants demonstrated "conclusively that our ladies, whenever they take an interest in anything, not only equal but surpass the men. After all, the great reserve force which ultimately must make a race of our people lies almost wholly within the influence of our ladies. It is to them, and upon them, that the future prospect of the race depends."[56] Hackley published one of her earliest articles about African American music in the *Exponent* section of the *Statesman*, entitled, "Women Musicians." In this article she expressed admiration for several rising Black performers, including violinist Carrie Melvin Lucas and pianist Maude Cuney.[57] She praised the accomplishments and determination of these women, both of whom advocated and pursued formal conservatory training. Hackley urged aspiring Black women musicians to follow their lead rather than remaining complacent with what she admitted had become a common practice of depending "on natural talent alone."[58]

Azalia Hackley also earned acclaim in Denver's musical circles as both a singer and a conductor. She organized what the press described as "the largest chorus ever brought together in Denver," the founding of which impressed upon residents "a new idea of the musical capabilities of the race and lifted the tone

Fig. 1.5. E. Azalia Hackley. Jones and Lehman, photographers, Denver, Colorado, August 1897. Courtesy, E. Azalia Hackley Collection of African Americans in the Performing Arts, Detroit Public Library, Detroit, Michigan.

of music to a plane hitherto unattempted [sic] by them"[59] Her well-received concert of oratorio selections, performed in 1898, included a chorus of some seventy voices trained by her.[60] She also produced a staged rendition of Bradbury's *Esther, the Beautiful Queen*, reprising the title role she had previously performed in Detroit.[61] Edwin Hackley, an accomplished musician in his own right, sometimes collaborated with his wife. In 1899, the couple produced and performed in the "bright, witty" and "sparkling" musical comedy *Honeymoon in Soudan*, written by Edwin Hackley. The production featured solos and choruses with instrumental accompaniment. Highly successful in greater Denver, the Hackleys and their cast toured and gave several performances in the region, earning positive reviews.[62]

Azalia Hackley also sought ways to bolster her training and credentials. In 1894, she became the first African American applicant to pass Colorado's civil service examination.[63] She also enrolled in classes at the University of Denver to work toward a bachelor's degree with concentrations in music education and performance.[64] While a student at the university, she taught music and made solo appearances. She expanded her choral activities and assumed the directorships of the Denver Choral Society and the choir of the local Zion Baptist Church.[65] Her graduation from the university in 1900 marked the first time an African American had earned a degree from that institution.[66] A photograph of Hackley, taken during this time period, reveals her taste for elite high fashion. In this sitting, she wears a gown with a flattering, gathered neckline, accessorized with elaborate, layered lace. She arranged her hair into a rather severe bun perched atop her head, with curls falling to her forehead (figure 1.5).

In 1901 Hackley gave what she considered to be her debut solo voice recital. A glowing review of this performance included these remarks:

> After a brief but interesting talk on music, Mrs. E. Azalia Hackley sang [Félicien-César David's] "Thou Brilliant Bird." . . . The audience sat enrapt during Mrs. Hackley's rendition of this beautiful piece. Her vocalization was perfect and her manner charming and without affectation. . . . Mrs. Hackley's voice is rich and mellow and has a range of three octaves; her singing is highly artistic and effective, [and] seems equally charming to the trained and untrained ear. Mrs. Hackley is accomplished, cultured, energetic and ambitious, and excels in all she undertakes.[67]

Following the success of this debut recital, she embarked on her first concert tour with performances in the Midwest, on the East Coast, and in Washington, DC. Her repertoire at this early point in her solo career consisted of spirituals, popular ballads, art songs, and virtuosic showstoppers. The program mentioned in the review quoted above also included the art song "Spring" (1893) by Sir George Henschel, "La Villanelle" by Hector Berlioz, and "Dolce Amor: Valse per Canto" by Emilio Pizzi (1861–1940). The selections "Spring" (excerpt 1.1) and "La Villanelle" (excerpt 1.2) illustrate two distinct styles in which she excelled: the former featuring virtuosic trills, grace notes, and vocal imitations of bird calls; the latter, a nineteenth-century *mélodie* or French art song, requiring considerable lyrical control and expressivity.[68] She also began to give lectures as part of her recital programs, on both musical and nonmusical subjects—a practice she continued throughout her career.

During her inaugural tour, Hackley attracted considerable publicity and enthusiasm among the Black press. The headline of an article in the *Indianapolis Freeman* succinctly described her reputation at this point in her career: "Winning Laurels for Herself and Race: Madam E. Azalia Hackley Now Touring the Country."[69] Not only did the press now refer to her by the honorific title "Madam," but newspapers had also begun to print photographs of her. One of the early portraits Hackley commissioned for the purposes of publicity and advertising was taken in Denver. For this studio session, Hackley wore a corsage and an elaborate lace gown of the sort befitting a rising concert artist.[70] The most striking feature of this image, her head attire, consisted of an assemblage of feathers, ribbons and curls that seems to extend nearly a foot above her head. Beyond its utility for advertising, this photograph conveys a

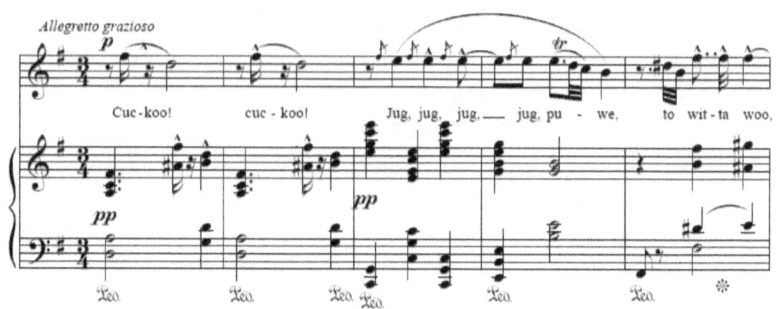

Ex. 1.1. George Henschel, "Spring" (London: Boosey and Hawkes, 1893), mm. 63–79.

subtle activist purpose as well, as through her choice of *haute couture* attire, especially her hat, Hackley insisted that African American women, too, could assume a regal, fashionable appearance (figure 1.6).

A review from Hackley's inaugural tour, of a concert that took place in Indianapolis, reflects the adulation and detail her recitals inspired among journalists:

> Mrs. E. Azalia Hackley, who has appeared several times before Indianapolis audiences as a singer in the recent past, has made a decided impression in her favor as to her ability. She is a soprano of very high register, reaching high C with ease and

Ex. 1.2. Hector Berlioz, "La Villanelle" (1841), mm. 1–15.

Fig. 1.6. E. Azalia Hackley. *Times* (Philadelphia) 24 April 1901, 5.

evident pleasure. Mrs. Hackley's voice shows the utmost cultivation so far as execution goes. This is shown by her vocal agility. This agility, coupled with a voice remarkable for what might be called "tallishness" [high tessitura] rather than breadth, produced a brilliancy that causes admiration. Her voice shows considerable native sweetness in its tone, but not as much as might be expected. This is not apparent at once, owing to the transfixion caused by the skill displayed in the use of her voice—vocal agility. . . . To elucidate, it will be remembered that the song,

Ex. 1.3. Luigi Caracciolla, "Unless" (Chicago: National Music, 1893), mm. 35–39, illustrating the octave leap, in m. 35, referred to in the review quoted below.

Ex. 1.4. "Comin' Thro' the Rye," E. Azalia Hackley, arr., *Guide in Voice Culture*, 9, showing the crowd-pleasing ornamentation Hackley performed on the word "when."

[Luigi Caraciolla's] "Unless," her last encore, was the most soulful of all that she sang, yet it was the simplest song.... Then, too, the song is one where the octave plays such an important part [excerpt 1.3].... The audience, it may be believed, carried away the tones of that song with them not because they heard the song last, but because it was most sweetly sung. Mrs. Hackley's [choice of] music is of the highest order. Her "La Villanelle" was brilliantly rendered. Her encore, "Comin' Thro' the Rye," a song sweet and effective, even when tolerably, fairly, rendered, was a little too elaborate at the finale for such a simple song. The finish [of "Comin' Thro' the Rye"] was her own version; it was brilliant. To hang on the word "when" in that song sets it off sufficiently [excerpt 1.4].... Mrs. Hackley's rendition of "Spring" by Henschel, was an amazing performance.... Her quips [grace notes] and trills were strictly professional. Her facial expressions were pleasing, her words distinctly uttered.... Given evidence of her very high artistic ability, we have no doubt but what she is a thorough all around musician. She is easily the leading singer of the Negro race today.[71]

The final sentence of the review quoted above, in which the writer lauds Hackley as the "leading" African American singer of her day, merits further contextualization. When she commenced her first tour in 1901, a void, of sorts, existed in the world of concert music as the most celebrated African American female singers of the late nineteenth century were already in the declining years of their careers. For over two decades, beginning in the 1870s, the concert-going public and the (mostly) Black press enthusiastically followed the careers of, in particular, sopranos Marie Selika (ca. 1849–1937) and Sissieretta Jones (1869–1933). At times, Jones and Selika competed vigorously with one another for press acclaim and favored status. When Hackley emerged as a recitalist, she did not encounter this level of rigorous competition and press comparison as Selika had already largely retired from the solo stage and Jones had shifted her focus to musical comedy. Hackley faced a very different concert world than that encountered by Selika and Jones—one that left her more flexibility as to programming choices, concert venues, and whether or not teaching and activism could become viable and appropriate options for a prima donna.[72]

Philadelphia

While residing in Denver, Hackley experienced respiratory problems she blamed on the city's climate and altitude. Not surprisingly, these occasional illnesses interfered with her pursuit of a solo career. In addition, the Iron Duke Mining Company apparently did not thrive, and Edwin Hackley probably lost considerable money in the venture. Of even more significance, however, race relations in Denver had deteriorated. As reported by journalist David Wilborn when he visited the city:

> I did not find it [Denver] at all what it is cracked up to be and of which I had heard so much. Since I have been here, I have taken a great deal of pains to inquire about the condition of the Afro-American in this city, generally, and, because of its reputation, I am surprised to find so much prejudice. The hotels are largely against us. If you wish to go to the opera houses, you are compelled to sit in certain places [in segregated seating] and many other places [businesses and restaurants] are closed to the race that ought not to be in a city like Denver. . . . I am forced to say that Denver is the wickedest city I have ever been in.[73]

With Azalia Hackley's health a serious consideration and, in an effort to escape escalating racist tension in Denver, the couple moved to Philadelphia around 1902. The reason for their selection of Philadelphia remains unclear, but they may have been attracted to the city owing to the possibility of working for the *Philadelphia Tribune* (founded in 1884), the widely circulating African American newspaper. So, too, Hackley intended to organize recitals on the East Coast, and Philadelphia provided her with a convenient location from which to launch concert tours. Shortly after their arrival, the Hackleys joined the Episcopal Church of the Crucifixion, an African American congregation established in 1846.⁷⁴ Like W. E. B. Du Bois, a one-time member of this church, the Hackleys found the congregation's commitment to community service and its support of music appealing. The church helped sustain cultural life for Black Philadelphians and provided a home for the significant and influential American Negro Historical Society, founded in 1897. Du Bois held the Church of the Crucifixion in high regard as

> the most effective church organization in the city [of Philadelphia] for benevolence and rescue work. . . . Probably no church in the city . . . is doing so much for the social betterment of the Negro. . . . This church especially reaches after a class of neglected poor whom the other colored churches shun or forget. . . . It has been built up virtually by one Negro, a man of sincerity and culture, and of peculiar energy. . . . It makes an especial feature of good music with its vested choir.⁷⁵

The man of "sincerity and culture" and "peculiar energy" to whom Du Bois referred was the church's pastor, Jamaican native Rev. Henry Laird Phillips (1847–1947). Highly respected for, among other things, the cultivation of musical excellence in his church, Phillips engaged Hackley as organist and choir director. Her experience at the Church of the Crucifixion proved enormously instructive and inspirational, especially regarding how music could be combined with community outreach for the purposes of racial uplift. With Phillips's support, Hackley founded an influential community ensemble she named the "People's Chorus." To maintain the ensemble's optimal membership of around 100 voices, she invited experienced amateur singers from the greater Philadelphia region to join.⁷⁶ Her recruits did not routinely include less mature vocalists, yet she sought out a young Marian Anderson (1897–1993) to sing occasional solos with the People's Chorus. Hackley was the first concert artist to recognize the extraordinary potential, beauty, and power of Anderson's now legendary contralto voice.⁷⁷ With Anderson's participation, Hackley hoped to "inspire the other members" of her choir "to higher things."⁷⁸ One of the advertisements for a solo appearance by Anderson enticed potential audience members to "come hear the baby contralto." Hackley perched the diminutive Anderson on a chair for these performances: "I want her to feel elevated. . . . I want no one in the back of the hall to have the slightest difficulty in seeing her."⁷⁹

Conservatory of Music

Hackley maintained a hectic schedule in greater Philadelphia, performing recitals, conducting choruses, and teaching voice lessons. In 1903, she received an invitation to join the faculty of the newly established Washington Conservatory of Music and School of Expression, as the institution's instructor of singing.[80] The conservatory's founder, Harriet A. Gibbs (later Marshall, 1868–1941), an Oberlin College Conservatory of Music graduate, explained that she intended "to give the [nation's] capital city a broader field to do good. . . . We must not only train the hand but also the mind, not only the mind, but also the feelings; hence the necessity of our youth being trained musically as well as otherwise is duly receiving more and more attention. . . . If we desire racial progress, we must encourage all worthy movements that tend to uplift a community."[81] This philosophy was one Hackley could wholeheartedly embrace, and she responded with evident appreciation for Gibbs's invitation:

> Your letter containing the proposition for a Conservatory of Music position reached me yesterday [14 September 1903]. The idea is splendid, and your enthusiasm is "catching." I would enjoy very much the association with you and the other persons mentioned as [being on] the faculty. In a kind of faint, far off way, we have nursed a somewhat similar idea here [in Philadelphia], but we are not so blessed with talent as is Washington. So I will be happy to consent to your proposition if in some way I can be made financially whole. Everybody else [on the conservatory's faculty], possibly, will be at home [i.e., lives in greater Washington, DC], but my weekly excursions [from Philadelphia] will [possibly] cost all or more of what I will earn. . . . Please write me fully the particulars, . . . possible compensation, and other business arrangements.[82]

In selecting Hackley for her faculty, Gibbs chose wisely as Washington, DC, audiences and the Black press had already showered her with accolades. Although she intended to remain a resident of Philadelphia, she would not have refused a lucrative opportunity to return to the nation's capital on a regular basis. Her enthusiasm for a position at the conservatory notwithstanding, she expressed concern about the financial aspect of such a commitment. She wrote a subsequent letter to Gibbs informing her of the fees she expected for teaching: "In regard to the price of lessons, I receive one dollar a lesson, and think it a fair price for our people to pay." She proposed to teach several students in private lessons at this price, "one-half hour each, in true conservatory fashion."[83] She also agreed to teach one or two classes in singing techniques over the course of a weekend. Accordingly, the conservatory drew up a contract specifying Hackley's remuneration. However, by 1904, her relationship with Gibbs had soured owing to the alleged inability of the conservatory's administration to honor its financial agreement.[84] Hackley remained on the conservatory faculty through 1904, but it is unclear how much longer she continued her affiliation.

Her contractual dispute smoldered for some two years, and Edwin Hackley, acting as his wife's lawyer, wrote letters to Gibbs and threatened the conservatory with legal action. No record of any legal settlement has been located, nor has any additional information about Azalia Hackley's work at the conservatory surfaced.[85]

Retirement from the Solo Stage

Hackley continued to travel constantly during the early years of the twentieth century, concertizing, teaching, lecturing, and conducting. Her frequent absences from Philadelphia imposed serious stress on her marriage. For this reason and probably others as well, the Hackleys separated around 1909. The childless couple never lived together again for any extended period of time, but their relationship remained amicable. No documentation survives to indicate they ever pursued divorce proceedings.[86]

In 1910, Hackley began to reduce the number of solo performances she gave and to concentrate more on teaching and choral conducting. She announced her intention to retire from the solo stage and embarked on what she advertised as a "retirement tour." In these recitals, she replaced some of her solo singing with lectures and ensemble and choral performances.[87] Not only did such large-scale events mark the close of a highly acclaimed solo career, but they also enabled Hackley to reconfigure her public appearances to meet the goals of a more specialized approach to activism she called "musical social uplift."[88] Her retirement recitals drew considerable press attention, and many took place at prestigious venues. For example, she performed a particularly well-received program on 19 October 1911 in Chicago's famous Orchestra Hall and attracted a capacity crowd of 1,500. The *Broad Ax* noted: "This will be positively the last appearance of Madame Hackley upon the concert platform [stage] in the city of Chicago. After her retirement, she will devote her time to teaching." In addition, the *Broad Ax* announced that "a limited number of beautiful panel souvenir photographs of Madame Hackley, made [taken] by [Addison] Scurlock, the famous Colored photographer of Washington, D.C." would be given to those who purchased tickets in advance (figure 1.7).[89] The varied program Hackley presented at this event included not only acclaimed renditions of solo repertoire, but also talks on the techniques of singing, referred to by her as "vocal demonstrations." Critic Minnie Adams wrote of Hackley's lessons in singing that "her voice demonstrations were marvels of art as she has acuteness enough to sing them, and her power of elucidating is exceedingly interesting. Very useful were the demonstrations of the fundamental principles of vocalization, . . . illustrated

Fig. 1.7. E. Azalia Hackley. Addison Scurlock, photographer, Washington, DC, ca. 1911. Courtesy, E. Azalia Hackley Collection of African Americans in the Performing Arts, Detroit Public Library, Detroit, Michigan.

in the most unique, clear and pleasing manner." Journalist Sylvester Russell also weighed in with glowing comments about Hackley's lectures, referring to her, in a string of lofty superlatives, as "the prothonotary administrator of musical science and the queen of extemporaneous bewitchery."[90]

Hackley's decision to use the portrait by Addison Scurlock for advertising purposes proved ingenious and highly effective for attracting sizeable audiences. She employed the same strategy for a concert in Carnegie Music Hall, Pittsburgh, Pennsylvania, scheduled for 1 July 1912. To promote this event, she turned to another respected African American photographer, Chicago resident Peter P. Jones.[91] For a session at Jones's studio, she wore a gown designed and assembled by her friend and favorite *modiste*, Denver resident Anna M. Skillern.[92] Newspapers promised a copy of Jones's photograph to anyone who purchased tickets to attend Hackley's upcoming performance. This advertising scheme paid off, and a capacity audience of 1,900 greeted Hackley for this event. Her varied program included a few solos and several talks, all of which

Ex. 1.5a. Félicien-César David, "Thou Brilliant Bird" (New York: G. Schirmer, 1883), mm. 12–19.

earned her complimentary reviews.[93] At many of her retirement appearances, Hackley continued to delight audiences with her skill as a pianist. She usually accompanied herself "without apparent effort, or detraction from her art as a vocal soloist," journalist A. R. Taylor remarked. Her performances of the challenging obbligati sections of the piano part in David's "Thou Brilliant Bird" (excerpts 1.5a and 1.5b) particularly impressed Taylor, as did her overall "splendid interpretation" of this piece.[94]

Hackley did not limit her travels to the United States. She also visited Europe and Cuba. While in Europe, she pursued private instruction in singing with two of the most celebrated voice pedagogues in the world: Jean de Reszke, in Paris, and William Shakespeare, in London. Hackley's writings about her travels reveal the extent to which she observed and analyzed differences in race relations at

Ex. 1.5b. Félicien-César David, "Thou Brilliant Bird" (New York: G. Schirmer, 1883), mm. 20–28.

home and abroad. The racial discrimination rampant in the Jim Crow South motivated her to file lawsuits against southern railroads and to write articles and lecture to audiences about her experiences. Because travel constitutes a major theme in Hackley's career, I devote the next chapter to a more detailed appraisal of the ways travel reinforced her commitment to racial uplift and enriched her own identity as an African American.

CHAPTER TWO

Travel, Domestic and Abroad

Itinerancy and frequent travel proved empowering and transcendent for Hackley. Traveling also enabled her to earn a living through concert tours and from sales of photographs and pamphlets to audiences. As a domestic traveler, she established herself as a nationally renowned ambassador of music education. Innumerable Black communities from coast to coast also engaged Hackley as a lecturer, and she addressed a variety of topics on both musical and nonmusical matters. By interacting with African Americans in countless locations, she deepened her knowledge of, and appreciation for, their lived and daily experiences, especially those quite removed from the comfortable status of Detroit's "cultured colored 40" she knew during her formative years. The nascence of Hackley's love of travel can be traced to the 1880s, when she began to perform concerts beyond the greater Detroit area. The destinations for most of these early trips were located in the Midwest and New York state. As discussed in the previous chapter, her first extensive concert tour as a soloist commenced shortly after she graduated from the University of Denver in 1900. Press notices confirm the long distances she traveled for this inaugural tour, during which she performed in Delaware, Indiana, Kansas, Maryland, Massachusetts, Ohio, Pennsylvania, South Carolina, and Washington, DC. Ambitious itineraries, such as that of her first tour, were commonplace for much of her career.

Hackley also traveled overseas. Between 1906 and 1914, she sailed to Europe three times and to Cuba twice. In Europe, she intended to pursue vocal studies as opportunities for the level of instruction she sought were routinely denied to Blacks in the United States. While abroad, she also became cognizant of the fact that by visiting foreign destinations, she could escape, however temporarily, the enervating affects and humiliation of US racism and Jim Crow segregation. From a more distant perspective, she was able to compare differences in the race relations prevalent in the United States with those she experienced in other countries. The observations she made in this context comprised lectures she delivered to audiences and articles she submitted to newspapers. They also contribute another significant viewpoint to discussions of race and identity in circulation during the postbellum–pre-Harlem era.

Domestic Travel

As would be expected, Hackley traveled extensively by rail. Touring often took her into the Deep South, such as, for example, during the early months of 1910, when newspapers announced her itinerary, which included performances in Nashville and Memphis, Tennessee; Vicksburg, Mississippi; New Orleans, Louisiana; Mobile, Alabama; Atlanta, Augusta, and Savannah, Georgia; and Jacksonville and Tallahassee, Florida.[1] The degradation associated with southern rail regulations motivated her to lecture and write about the unsafe and deleterious conditions of segregated trains. From the perspective of a frequent railroad traveler, Hackley unflinchingly and courageously expounded upon what the press assured readers were "the true conditions" of Jim Crow cars "as they really exist."[2] She directed some of her most vociferous comments at those responsible for maintaining the cleanliness and sanitary conditions of Jim Crow cars and depot facilities:

> Cleanliness in the coaches set apart for those of our race is an unknown quantity; the garbage that accumulates . . . is left on the floor of the waiting rooms until it has almost rotted, and from the look of the cuspidors and ash boxes around the depots that are filled with sputum, which is the greatest of germ producers, makes one's head swim trying to calculate the length of time that elapses between their thorough cleanings. . . . And the coaches in which one must ride for hours at a time, and perhaps all night, are nauseating to look into, much less be an occupant of. I doubt it if some of these compartments do not go for six months without being touched by a broom or duster. In many instances the windowpanes and casings were so bedaubed with soot, grease and cinders that nothing less than a good scraping would improve them. Going from San Antonio to Austin over the International and Great Northern railroad, the coach was so unbearably filthy I was compelled to ask the conductor to have it cleaned and he straightaway informed me that I would have to stand it as they had no time to waste cleaning our coach. At that moment the car-cleaner was passing through carrying a broom and duster, which articles I seized, and swept and dusted the car, while another

traveler opened the windows and let into the stench-ladened [*sic*] car the pure air of the sunny southland.³

During the trip described above, Hackley claimed she occupied only one train coach she considered to be reasonably clean.⁴

The regulations regarding the consumption of tobacco constituted another contested terrain for train travel and one Hackley knew all too well. White passengers who used tobacco could count on a space designated expressly for this purpose. However, southern railroad officials did not require whites to sit for an entire trip in a smoking car. In contrast, Black travelers, often forced to occupy smoking areas, seldom rode on a tobacco-free coach, nor were they assured of any accommodations devoid of the sight, noise, and smell of persons expectorating tobacco. Moreover, railroads often positioned Jim Crow cars (which usually doubled as smoking cars) directly behind a train's coal-burning locomotive, and passengers in this location could count on engine-generated airborne soot, smoke, and debris invading their car. If white tobacco consumers found a smoking car to be full of passengers, they smoked in Jim Crow cars. Railroad employees, too, openly smoked in Jim Crow cars but refrained from doing so in cars reserved for whites. On one of Hackley's trips, an employee (presumably white) thought nothing of smoking in the compartment she occupied. As she explained the situation: "The auditor [fare collector] of the train from Clarksville [Tennessee] to Texarkana [Texas], over the Texas and Pacific Railroad, did his smoking in the coach reserved for the race; then he left his cigar in our compartment until he finished collecting fares in the other coaches; then [he] returned and resumed his smoke."⁵ Hackley's trip from Clarksville to Texarkana spanned some 500 miles. At an average speed, typical of passenger train travel in this era and location, of somewhere in the vicinity of twenty miles per hour (accounting for many station stops en route), it would have taken Hackley a full day to reach her destination. Her mention of riding in a "compartment" suggests that she had procured some sort of sleeping accommodation. The ticket collector for the coach on which she rode thought it quite acceptable to consume a cigar in a Jim Crow car rather than postpone his smoking until he could go to the coach set aside for this purpose. That he left a lit cigar in a woman's sleeping compartment underscores both the racist and sexist motivations for his callous actions.⁶

Hackley also accused whites of ignoring the potential role of unsanitary Jim Crow railroad services in the spread of infectious diseases. After a lengthy tour through Texas, she admonished railroad officials: "The mistaken idea that anything is good enough for the Negro may cost Texas the lives of many of its valued citizens. Neglect the health of the Negro and the health of the whole state is neglected." The Texas public had considerable reason for concern about the implications of unclean travel accommodations in the proliferation of serious diseases as a widespread and deadly outbreak of meningitis had ravaged the state from 1911 through 1913.[7] Hackley castigated the railroad industry accordingly: "The recent meningitis epidemic should prove a valuable lesson to everyone in Texas. The Railroads may be the cause of the spread of this disease. The germs have been carried from Dallas and Fort Worth to Austin, Houston and Galveston.... [I]n some [Jim Crow] trains and waiting rooms there must still be lurking the germs of this dreaded scourge." Citing also a "special interest" in the prevalence of tuberculosis, Hackley lashed out at the railroads for their failure to clean out cuspidors used by tobacco chewers: "Sputum in any form is nauseating. A cuspidor nowadays literally turns one's stomach because one knows how much disease it carries.... No one can know how many people have carried diseases from this source to spread in different locales."[8]

Beyond her censure of Jim Crow travel conditions, generally, Hackley also added to the growing protests against the targeted maltreatment of Black women as train passengers. She condemned the perpetrators of verbal and physical abuse African American women endured on trains and leveled caustic criticism at the railroad industry for its failure to safeguard them. Of these egregious circumstances, she wrote of the "humiliations" continually foisted upon Black female travelers, adding, "Our women are subject to every indignity, most insulting remarks and [lascivious] offers given them, and on resenting same you run a risk of being assaulted and perhaps fatally injured."[9] Hackley remained vigilant regarding the threat of sexually motivated harassment and violence, especially when she traveled in the South. She laid blame for such demeaning and mendacious behavior on the system of segregation that failed to extend to Black females the same respect, protection, and courtesies routinely granted to white women. As a frequent traveler, she knew from personal experience what she described as the "immoral designs which are forever in the minds of southern white men regarding our women."[10] To Hackley, these were not occasional or idle threats, rather, the perpetrators of these commonplace degradations singled out, specifically, Black girls and women.

Hackley's observations about the threats to a Black woman's very personhood while traveling by train recall the provocative and groundbreaking views of other Black woman activists. For these activists, as well as for Hackley, Jim Crow train cars existed as shameful sites of abuse, while they also inspired courageous revelations by African American women, of intolerable and humiliating travel experiences. In the 1890s, Anna Julia Cooper acknowledged the double burden of racism and sexual discrimination confronting Black women travelers: "I purposely forbear to mention instances of personal violence to colored women traveling in less civilized sections of our country, where women have been forcibly ejected from cars, thrown out of seats, their garments rudely torn, their person wantonly and cruelly injured."[11] Hackley's friend Mary Church Terrell felt similarly—that as a Black woman traveling on a train, she constantly placed herself "at the mercy of the conductor or any man who entered" the car on which she rode.[12] As Terrell confirmed, "there are few experiences more embarrassing and painful than those through which a colored woman passes while traveling in the South."[13] Another influential writer from this time period, Carrie Williams Clifford, also insisted that Black women rode on Jim Crow cars at their peril, without the protection of Black men. She commented: "I make an appeal to the colored men of America to protect colored women from the horrible 'Jim Crow' cars. Of all the infamous schemes which the white South has devised for the humiliation of self-respecting Negroes, the 'Jim Crow' car is the most infamous. Naturally, the worst sufferers from them [Jim Crow train regulations] are colored women, whom white Southerners have studiously and systematically degraded and insulted for nearly three centuries."[14]

Hackley conflated gender bias and racism, particularly evident in her criticism of segregated train travel. Among the most influential references to this nexus of discriminations faced by African American females, Anna Julia Cooper's insights laid the foundation for Black women's more recent feminist discourse. Hackley's comments about her maltreatment as a Black woman traveling by train clearly owe a debt to Cooper, who, in her now classic statement of 1892, argued: "The colored woman of to-day occupies a unique position in this country.... She is confronted by both a woman question and a race problem, and is yet an unknown or an unacknowledged factor in both."[15] Eventually, Hackley and Terrell subsumed Cooper's words for their own agenda and that of the NACW. The two women occasionally shared the stage, and together they delivered unstinting criticism of Black women's status as a multi-burdened and underappreciated member of African American society. The *New York Tribune* offered this summary of their message: "While the colored man or the colored race as a whole has been the object of considerable public attention, the development of the colored woman since the abolition of slavery has been almost unnoted."[16] Nonetheless, Hackley viewed train travel as an avenue toward self-fulfillment and sustained activist purpose. Travel enabled her to embark on a crusade of sorts, as she toured incessantly in order to disseminate her viewpoints and agenda of musical social uplift. I surmise that during prolonged train excursions, she also pursued another component of her uplift activities—her writings. Surely, she passed the time, while onboard a train, by writing—both personal communication and articles that eventually appeared in the press. The epigrammatic nature of her published writings reflects the very essence of railroads, as her succinct statements and rather fragmented style resonate with the noises, unanticipated delays, stops, and interruptions of train travel in the era of Jim Crow.

Hackley sued the southern railroads an undetermined number of times from 1911 through 1914. In her earliest complaints, she cited safety concerns on Jim Crow cars and their generally filthy and unsanitary condition as the premises of her lawsuits. The *Philadelphia Tribune* proudly announced: "Mme. Hackley goes right into the thickest of the battle and tells those who are responsible for the barbarous treatment [on trains] accorded our people. She practices what she preaches." Hackley also distributed a "circular letter" in which she summarized her grievances with the railroads. Recipients of the letter included "leading politicians, lawyers, newspapers, the Governor [of unspecified southern states] and members of the State Legislature."[17] She also sought legal recourse for the railroad's refusal to seat her in a "ladies" car after the purchase of a first-class ticket. In this suit, she challenged the contours, limits, and implications of the term "lady" as an honorific appellation reserved exclusively for white women. She argued that as a "woman," she was entitled to ride in a "ladies" car regardless of her race, especially as she had paid the highest fare to do so.[18] Hackley's stance brings to mind Anna Julia Cooper's critique of the stultifying and racist notions of Black womanhood that perpetuated an "all-leveling prejudice . . . which cynically assumes 'a Negro woman cannot be a lady.'"[19]

In another legal procedure, Hackley sued a Texas railroad over a humiliating incident and its resultant illness she blamed on the racist behaviors of railroad personnel. The incident occurred as she boarded a train and, her hands occupied with maneuvering her baggage, she asked the conductor to hold a smoker car door open for her. The conductor refused to grant her request as any such courtesy would not have been extended to an African American woman. That she asked for and expected this courtesy represented, in and of itself, an act of courageous defiance. Eventually, the conductor relented and begrudgingly held the car door open for her. As tobacco smoke drifted toward her from inside the car, she experienced an incapacitating episode of severe coughing and respiratory distress. The insolent conductor verbally insulted her and told her to "cough, cough until she choked herself to death." According to the *Chicago Defender*, Black citizens of Texas "asked her to . . . start the ball rolling" with a legal complaint, in order to serve "as an example to others." She "good naturedly consented to be the first martyr in the Jim Crow car agitation" as legal action against the railroads was still in its infancy in the region. Her estranged husband, Edwin Hackley, provided her with legal assistance and representation. Realizing that she faced protracted legal wrangling, she promised to remain in Dallas and "stay as long as necessary" to see the process to completion.[20] As a result of her Dallas actions, Hackley's name became associated with the struggle to establish clean and safe train accommodations for Black travelers, especially girls and women. However, her legal battles with southern railroad authorities apparently lost traction at some point, and they remained unresolved.

First Trip to Paris

The history of Hackley's overseas travels adds considerably to our knowledge of African Americans' experiences in foreign countries at the beginning of the twentieth century.[21] Furthermore, she was, arguably, the first African American singer to pursue instruction with celebrated white teachers who resided in Europe.[22] That she successfully obtained places in the studios of the respected European teachers Jean de Reszke and William Shakespeare represents an extraordinary accomplishment. As a de Reszke protégée, she shared, equally, with her fellow students, all the sumptuous surroundings of his Paris mansion and the inimitable instruction he offered, without regard for her racial heritage. Studies with de Reszke and Shakespeare yielded desirable results as music impresarios, enticed by Hackley's credentials, invited her to perform in prestigious events, held at renowned Parisian and London venues.

In a letter to music comedy stars Bert Williams and George Walker, Hackley stated that it had long been her "heart's desire" to study overseas.[23] She undertook preparations, in 1905, for a lengthy stay in Europe. To finance her travels, she organized a series of "farewell" concerts in large metropolitan venues. These performances yielded her a sum of money, principally through ticket sales, of an amount sufficient to sustain her in Europe. With Paris as her destination, she left the United States in early 1906. On board ship, she met and passed the time with Edwin J. Chesnutt, son of her friend Charles W. Chesnutt. The elder Chesnutt introduced Hackley to his son in a letter and recommended her as an ideal travel companion: "She is a cheerful soul, will doubtless prove a congenial spirit, and tide you over any little period of loneliness or depression."[24]

Hackley chose a most appropriate destination for her first overseas trip, for Europe had acquired a reputation of welcoming African American travelers and expatriates. As Black journalist Charles H. Brooks observed, "Negrophobia is not popular in Europe and the people are taught to judge character more than color, to esteem worth above conditions of birth.... Go where you please across the Atlantic ... without regard to color."[25] Another African American journalist, Roscoe Conkling Simmons, concurred with this viewpoint and wrote, "the reception recently tendered Negro talent across the waters was unusually warm, personally sincere, yet well deserved, and argues that the American Negro has little to fear in the . . . important foreign capitals."[26]

Hackley formed friendships with several respected Black expatriates who resided in Paris during her time there. Her best-known Parisian associates included painter Henry O. Tanner, author Jessie Redmon Fauset, and sculptor Meta Vaux Warrick. Tanner had already acquired an international reputation by the time Hackley visited Paris, while Fauset and Warrick are best remembered as flourishing members of the Harlem Renaissance intelligentsia.[27] One of Hackley's Denver acquaintances, Rev. John Elijah Ford, fondly remembered attending social gatherings with his African American friends while he vacationed in the French capital: "In Paris, a visit to the colony of American Negroes composed of Mme. Hackley, Henry O. Tanner, Dr. and Mrs. Furniss, et. al., will show you what aristocratic, intelligent and deserving people of color can do."[28] The ability to travel overseas and associate with other aristocrats of color, as mentioned by Rev. Ford, symbolized and confirmed sought-after upper-class gentility for well-heeled African Americans. Association with the likes of the highly acclaimed Tanner, along with the Furnisses, who were respected and privileged citizens of Black Indianapolis, granted Hackley membership in this status-conscious group.

Several of Hackley's contemporaries expressed considerable enthusiasm for the way Parisians treated African Americans. Tanner detailed the positive reception he enjoyed among the celebrated Parisian artistic community: "In Paris no one regards me curiously. I am simply Mr. Tanner, an American artist. Nobody knows or cares what was the complexion of my forebears. I live and work there on terms of absolute social equality. Questions of race or color are not considered—a man's professional skill and social qualities are fairly and ungrudgingly recognized. . . . In this European art world there is a perfect race democracy."[29] Mary Church Terrell felt similarly welcomed when she traveled throughout Europe in 1904. Terrell spent considerable time in France and, later on, in Berlin, where she addressed the International Congress of Women. In an article about her travels, she remarked: "In France there is absolutely no prejudice against a man or woman on account of the color of his skin. . . . It is impossible for the average foreigner to comprehend the race problem, as it presents itself in the United States."[30]

While in Europe, Hackley hoped to study with an esteemed European singer and to take advantage of the benefits of such an association. Her activities for many months prior to her departure from the United States demonstrated her determination to realize this goal. That she was motivated to endure an ocean crossing in order to pursue the instruction she knew she deserved confirms her awareness that Blacks, even those of considerable talent, were usually denied access to the highest level of musical training in the United States. Furthermore, as an African American in Paris, she anticipated better treatment from whites.

In order to secure a place in a respected European voice studio, Hackley needed to audition. She knew she would be competing with other experienced singers for a sought-after studio opening, yet she obviously had confidence in her ability to impress a famous teacher. It is important to remember that, even in more racially tolerant Paris, she was still entering into the highest echelon of music study and performance—one historically reserved by and for whites. After much consideration, she decided to pursue studies with Jean de Reszke, a voice pedagogue and opera performer without peer in the classical music world of his day. This was an audacious choice on Hackley's part, yet it was quite in keeping with an imperturbable singer of extraordinary assuredness.

As a performer, de Reszke enjoyed a reputation as the most celebrated tenor among the US music-loving public. After achieving unprecedented success in Europe, he moved to New York City and sang to rave reviews at the Metropolitan Opera from 1893 to 1900. De Reszke's interpretations of romantic-era tenor roles, especially in the operas of Richard Wagner, thrilled glittery audiences and high-brow critics. Newspapers and magazines frequently printed photographs of the handsome de Reszke in lavish costumes, and they promulgated his image as a dashing, flamboyant star. During a remarkable stage career that spanned some twenty-five years, de Reszke became the world's highest-paid singer. In 1901, he sagaciously decided to retire from the operatic stage before his voice aged and he returned to Europe to teach. Although he seldom sang in public after retirement, the press remained fascinated by his every move. In the spring of 1904, newspapers gleefully announced the opening of his voice studio, located in his Parisian estate.[31]

According to Henry Theophilus Finck and other music critics, successful study with de Reszke offered singers the ultimate credential with which to further their careers.[32] Hackley certainly hoped to establish a connection with de Reszke for just this reason. So, too, she would have been aware that several former de Reszke students and associates could be counted among the *crème-de-la-crème* of internationally respected singers—a status Hackley would have welcomed.[33] Moreover, it seems probable that she contemplated, at this point in her career, a permanent move to Europe with the intention of finding more professionally fulfilling performance and teaching engagements; studies with de Reszke could only enhance her chances of achieving such a goal.

We can only speculate about Hackley's initial encounter with de Reszke. To be sure, an audition before a musician of de Reszke's fame is a stressful event, no matter how well an applicant prepares their repertoire or manages to maintain composure. Furthermore, de Reszke usually held his studio enrollment to only around twenty students, so the audition process presented considerable competition.³⁴ As *London Daily News* writer John MacDonald observed of de Reszke's auditions, "In his testing of would-be pupils," he remained "as patient and sympathetic as he was inexorable."³⁵ English singer and opera performer Walter Johnstone Douglas anticipated his audition for de Reszke as "rather an alarming prospect, it is true, but the great man was so much less alarming than great men often are, in fact, he was so friendly and cheerful that it was impossible not to feel at one's ease." Douglas's audition assumed the configuration of a voice lesson as de Reszke gently coached him through the pieces he had selected to sing. Using this method—one not atypical for voice auditions—de Reszke could evaluate both the quality of an applicant's voice and their receptivity to instruction and constructive criticism. Undoubtedly, Hackley's audition also segued into a teaching and learning opportunity.³⁶

Hackley must have been well prepared for an audition, and her performance convinced de Reszke to accept her into his studio. That de Reszke welcomed her as a student speaks to her unassailable vocal technique and musical talent. Furthermore, as de Reszke maintained a relatively small studio, he upheld exacting standards for selecting new students. For, as he stated, "I accept no one who has not talent," and he added, "I take only pupils as interest me."³⁷ As veteran arts critic Henry Taylor Parker confirmed, de Reszke taught only those singers he believed "to be of exceptional powers and promise."³⁸ In an interview, de Reszke elaborated on the type of student he sought: "The accepted candidates [I select to teach] must have something more than pleasing voices. There must be something in the voice besides sound—something of the mind, the feeling, the passion."³⁹ Hackley, already a seasoned concert artist when she auditioned for de Reszke, clearly possessed the unequivocal vocal qualities, expressivity, and compelling dramatic persona he considered essential in a cultivated singer and prospective student. Quite possibly, too, de Reszke may have been intrigued by the idea of having an African American singer in his studio, and Hackley was, most likely, the first Black student to study with him. As he usually spent instructional time on opera arias and stage dramatization, the opportunity to coach a Black female singer in the role of an African queen or princess surely must have entered de Reszke's mind. He would have been quite familiar with the most celebrated examples of such roles, especially the African queen Sélika in Giacomo Meyerbeer's opera *L'Africaine* (1865); Giuseppe Verdi's *Aida* (1871), the title role a depiction of the beautiful daughter of the King of Ethiopia; the title role of the Black *Queen of Sheba* (1875) by Karl Goldmark; and Charles Gounod's *La Reine de Shaba* (*Queen of Sheba*, 1862).⁴⁰

Lessons with a world-renowned artist usually came with a hefty price tag, and de Reszke reputedly charged exorbitant fees for instruction. Although

Hackley had raised substantial funds for her trip to Paris, only the wealthiest of students could afford de Reszle's fees, which ranged between $5 and $10 per lesson.[41] However, as one of his students remarked, "to be a pupil of de Reszke's, even to be near him, is, as you may imagine, worth almost anything."[42] Yet the potential impediment of accumulated debt incurred by studies with de Reszke in no way discouraged Hackley for she stated she had read "in the daily papers" prior to her trip that he sometimes reduced or waived his fees. She must have been confident he would extend such magnanimity in her direction.[43] In fact, Walter Johnstone Douglas recalled de Reszke's "generosity to those pupils who had real financial difficulties was quite unbounded."[44] Another student of de Reszke also observed and lauded his spirit of goodwill: "Many and many a time he has not only taught a girl for nothing, but I know for a fact that both he and his friend and secretary, Monsieur [Maurice] de Noufflard . . . have defrayed from their own pockets the board [housing and food] bills of likely singers in order that they could hang on to their musical education until the end."[45] As de Reszke explained, "there will be two [fee] scales in my school. As a general principle, the rich will pay for the poor. If a poor student comes to me with a magnificent voice and talent, I shall never refuse him."[46]

De Reszke's students also became immersed in his extravagant lifestyle. According to press accounts, most opera stars' retirement residences paled in comparison "to the costly refinements of existence" with which de Reszke surrounded himself.[47] His morning routine, if eccentric, was nonetheless intended to help students feel welcome and at ease. All students scheduled for a particular day's instruction observed each other's lessons, and hence they met together in the late morning, in a sumptuous foyer, awaiting de Reszke's arrival. Students first caught a glimpse of the aristocratic and ever-dramatic de Reszke and his retinue as they descended an expansive circular staircase leading to a front parlor. De Reszke's *valet du chamber* led the procession carrying, of all things, a large birdcage. De Reszke followed close behind, his green parrot, Coco, perched on his shoulder. In the penultimate position, his wife, Countess Marie de Goulaine, a respected soprano, then appeared. And finally, de Reszke's personal valet approached the students, cradling the tenor's beloved dachshund. Following European custom, de Reszke formally greeted everyone present by name and planted a kiss on the cheek of each female student.[48]

De Reszke not only resided in a palatial and ostentatious mansion, but he also added a custom-designed theater to the original structure. As he confirmed, "I have had this theater specially built. It forms a part of my house." With seating for only around 100, de Reszke's private theater provided an ideal instructional space for coaching singers in arias and opera scenes.[49] These coaching sessions covered the gamut of theatrical training, including stage deportment and

Fig. 2.1. E. Azalia Hackley in opera costume, ca. 1907. Courtesy, E. Azalia Hackley Collection of African Americans in the Performing Arts, Detroit Public Library, Detroit, Michigan.

dramatic characterization. With an audience comprised of invited guests, his theater offered students a unique opportunity to perform in a congenial environment, attired in costumes provided by him. A photograph of Hackley from this time period, most likely taken in de Reszke's theater, shows her wearing an elaborate opera costume (figure 2.1). The press printed this photograph on several occasions and therefore the US public knew it quite well.[50]

While in Paris, Hackley resided at 9 Rue de la Grande Chaumière, a building dedicated to housing visiting musicians, writers, and artists, located in the heart of the famous and picturesque Montparnasse district. Inexpensive living quarters and a vibrant creative and intellectual milieu attracted aspiring artists, performers, and intellectuals to this area. Situated on the Left Bank of the Seine,

Montparnasse's cafes provided meeting places for exchange of ideas and the cultivation of significant relationships with like-minded residents. To pay for food and rent for her modest accommodations, Hackley taught private music lessons to Montparnasse residents, charging students what she referred to as "advanced prices." Among her students were visitors from Australia, Canada, England, and Germany. She also found time to explore the district's charming streets and often strolled through the nearby Jardins du Luxembourg.[51]

Hackley took advantage of her association with de Reszke to solicit interest in her performance ability among Paris's musical elite. The US press kept readers informed about her appearances, and the *Indianapolis Freeman* boasted, "Mme. E. Azalia Hackley . . . is captivating all Paris with her beautiful voice."[52] One journalist in particular, Maurice Rosseau, indicated that she had assumed an influential role among de Reszke's students:

> Of the many foreign students who have come here to study, perhaps none of these has ever accomplished more than Mme. E. Azalia Hackley of Philadelphia, formerly of Detroit and Denver, who came here a little over a year ago, a perfect stranger. . . . She had been here but a very short time when she had won the admiration and esteem of the entire class [of de Reszke students], and her unusual sweet and flexible voice, quick conceptions of music and amiable disposition soon placed her in a position where all students looked to her as an authority to solve difficult musical problems.[53]

Hackley also made many acquaintances among boarders at the Holy Trinity Lodge, a small but influential institution that offered amenities for female English-speaking visitors to Paris. Of the lodge, travel writer Arthur Guthrie noted: "It's a woman's club, a school of art, a school of music, a salon, a small hospital, and something more than all these, hard to define."[54] Maintained by the Episcopalian church, the lodge provided studio spaces for artists and a lending library and served as an indispensable "focus of helpfulness, both moral and physical."[55] The administration of the lodge appointed Hackley to oversee music activities and provided her with performance, teaching, and conducting opportunities. She played keyboard accompaniments for recitals, church services, and musicales at the lodge. In her capacity as the director of choral activities and music instruction, she taught singing classes and assembled what the press called "a most enthusiastic" choral group, its members representative of many countries. Of this ensemble's performances, one in particular, on 3 March 1907, attracted glowing press attention. For this event, Hackley organized a chorus of lodge residents and other regional singers and prepared Charles Gounod's oratorio, *Gallia*. Scored for soprano solo, chorus, and orchestra or keyboard accompaniment, *Gallia* has proven an accessible work for less experienced vocalists and hence was a most appropriate choice for Hackley's singers. Quite possibly, Hackley may have sung the solo vocal part as she also served as the lodge's featured soprano soloist for public events and worship services. Maurice Rosseau reported that she "received many congratulations" for her fine interpretation of Gounod's work, which reflected well on her "most excellent teaching" of chorus members.[56]

Under Hackley's direction, the Holy Trinity Lodge sponsored a particularly noteworthy event on 19 April 1907 that featured a concert and gala reception given in honor of Henry White, the newly appointed US ambassador to France. Hackley selected all the musicians, arranged the programing, provided piano accompaniments, and sang solos. An audience of around 1,000 greeted and enthusiastically applauded Hackley and the other musicians. The widely read weekly *Musical Courier* attributed the ultimate success of the whole affair to the musical portion of the festivities. For her solo offerings, Hackley sang Henschel's "Spring" and Ambroise Thomas' "Je suis Titania" from his opera *Mignon* (1866)—by this time two reliable and popular staples of her repertoire.[57] Commenting on this performance, the *American Register* lauded Hackley as an "attractive singer" whose technique exhibited "much finesse."[58] Still another event at the lodge, with music coordinated by Hackley, took place on 4 July 1907, as a celebration of Independence Day for Americans in Paris. Billed as a "*fête champêtre*," this outdoor extravaganza allowed guests to enjoy the lodge's recently opened gardens.[59]

Hackley also performed in other Parisian venues. As announced by the popular magazine *L'Aurore*, on 21 October 1906, she sang at an international meeting of the Society for the Propagation of Foreign Languages. The event took place at the L'Hôtel des Sociétés Savantes (Hotel for Learned Societies), an institution dedicated to large intellectual, artistic and cultural gatherings that also provided overnight accommodations for participants and audience members. Following an afternoon of musical and literary presentations, all those present could look forward to an evening reception and festivities.[60] The *French Bulletin* reported: "It was our pleasure to hear and applaud Mme. Hackley, an American cantatrice, whose powerful and melodious voice poured out in perfect tones a selection of songs popular in the United States, [including] 'Staccato Polka' by R[ichard] Mulder, and the captivating simplicity of the old Negro slave songs."[61] Hackley frequently sang Mulder's "Staccato Polka," a virtuosic show-stopper requiring extreme vocal flexibility and stamina (excerpt 2.1a and excerpt 2.1b).[62] Hackley also sang at several formal evening events, or "grand soirées," to appreciative audiences. For example, in April 1907, at "Salle Eylau, . . . she was the star of the evening, the large audience persisted in its

Ex. 2.1a. Richard Mulder, "Staccato Polka: A Bravura Piece for Soprano," Op. 45 (New York: Gordon, 1875), mm. 51–64.

cries of 'bis' (again), until she was compelled to repeat Henschel's 'Spring' before permitted to sing the second number of a group."[63]

Hackley offered an assessment of Parisian race relations that differed from opinions expressed by her African American compatriots. Writing for the *A. M. E. Church Review*, she opened her essay with an acknowledgment of the reputedly more cordial reception of Blacks in France: "In America we hear some wonderful stories of the liberal treatment accorded the black man by the French." Yet while in Paris, she observed a disturbing lack of racial pride among Blacks: "It seems that everyone has been trying to forget his color.... There seems to be a perfect mania for getting away from anything suggestive of the negroid." We can assume this statement also reflected Hackley's distain for the vogue of passing for white while residing in Paris. Apparently, she encountered fewer Blacks than she anticipated, and she commented that "there

Ex. 2.1b. Mulder, "Staccato Polka," mm. 114–43.

are still so few Negroes in France that they are still objects of curiosity to the [white] masses; for some reason they seem to think a black person infinitely amusing." For Hackley, white reactions to Blacks as "amusing" or as "objects of curiosity" did not convey racial tolerance or enlightenment. Although she failed to describe any specific incidences of racism she, herself, experienced while in Paris, she nonetheless insisted: "The French delight in saying that it does not make any difference what the color of the skin is in France, and yet these same people will laugh in the faces of Negroes on the street.... There is sufficient [evidence] to remind me that black and white are distinctly different, even in France." Ultimately, she concluded, "I believe that 'down in their hearts' the French despise black people."[64]

Hackley's opinion of Parisian race relations aside, she evidently found her lessons with de Reszke to be quite satisfactory, so much so that she contemplated a future trip to Paris to resume voice instruction with him. She also recommended such instruction for other gifted African American musicians. Before leaving the French capital to return to the United States, she formulated a philanthropic initiative to raise money for promising Black musicians to pursue study in Europe. Her inspiration came from a realization that some Black musicians of considerable talent could not financially support themselves in Europe long enough to gain sufficient benefit from their studies. In contrast, she noted that some white singers of lesser potential, "being assisted by millionaires," could elect to remain overseas indefinitely. She wrote to the *New York Age* detailing her philanthropic plans: "It is my intention to assist some of the young musicians of the race in studying abroad by establishing a foreign scholarship."[65] She secured the assistance of Henry O. Tanner, who not only wholeheartedly supported Hackley's initiative, but also agreed to serve as trustee for a fund to be held in a Paris bank for distribution to scholarship recipients. Ida B. Wells also pledged her support, and journalist Noah D. Thompson agreed to serve as secretary for Hackley's organization.[66]

Trip to London

Hackley left Paris in late summer of 1907. She traveled from France to England and then made the Atlantic crossing onboard the aging SS *Westernland*, departing from Liverpool on 11 September and arriving in Philadelphia on 23 September. She immediately began organizing a series of concerts intended to help finance her newly inaugurated Foreign Scholarship program and to raise money for a second trip to Europe. Advertisements for her concerts of the 1907–08 season mentioned her studies with de Reszke and thus she took advantage of his name as a compelling credential and inducement for prospective audiences. She also promised attendees that she would deliver lectures about her Parisian experiences. In addition to soliciting donations for her scholarship initiative, she realized income from concert ticket purchases and the sale of autographed photographs.

Having met her fundraising goals less than a year later, Hackley left for England in November 1908. Once again, she planned to study with a renowned pedagogue while overseas. She chose to audition for William Shakespeare, England's acclaimed oratorio tenor. In addition to a successful career as a vocal soloist, the multifaceted Shakespeare earned glowing reviews as a composer, pianist, and choral conductor. He taught at the Royal Academy of Music, at Queen's College, and in the studio located in his home.[67] Hackley faced a competitive audition as, like de Reszke, Shakespeare exercised considerable discretion when choosing his students. Although he never achieved the celebrity status enjoyed by de Reszke, Shakespeare maintained exacting standards; therefore, an audition for him would have been no less challenging. For, as Shakespeare unequivocally insisted, "I think that out of 100 voices [students of singing] accepted at academies, they ought to send away 90, as being not physically capable of producing the grand effects required even if they were trained."[68] However much discernment he exercised during the audition process, those students he accepted into his studio could count on his cordiality, attentiveness, and devotion to his art. As described by respected New York music teacher Herbert W. Greene (1851–1924), Shakespeare's "ease of manner and hearty geniality were most magnetic," particularly in the presence of his students.[69]

Shakespeare toured the United States, coast to coast, beginning with an inaugural appearance in New York's Mendelssohn Hall on 4 January 1900. Although he performed a few solos from oratorio warhorses, the main attraction for these events consisted of lectures about, and demonstrations of, elementary vocal techniques.[70] A review of his concerts in *Etude* magazine noted that Shakespeare's "ideas are simple enough and he has been teaching them to Americans directly or by proxy for many years." Indeed, Shakespeare offered US audiences what amounted to lessons in the fundamentals of singing. From London, he sent articles to the US press and these published items provided the "proxy" instructional opportunities referred to by Greene in his review. During private lessons, however, Shakespeare employed a methodology he deemed most "applicable . . . to those whose voices are already highly developed." Hackley, a regular reader of *Etude*, probably noticed the observations regarding Shakespeare's preference for experienced, mature singers as private students.[71]

Most likely, Hackley took lessons from Shakespeare at the private studio he maintained in his London residence. In contrast to the luxurious surroundings of de Reszke's palatial estate, Shakespeare lived in considerably smaller and far less ostentatious circumstances. Shakespeare's "compact little home," as the press described it, reflected his means and taste. Students were taught in "the little room at the back of the house" he owned, furnished with a piano and comfortable but unremarkable furniture. As his only pretense of an upper-class lifestyle, Shakespeare employed a footman, "urbane and noiseless," who ushered students in and out of his teaching studio and residence.[72]

In addition to studying with Shakespeare, Hackley conducted choruses, gave music lessons, and organized concerts. She taught at London's famous Toynbee Hall, an institution founded in 1884 and modeled in accordance with the US settlement house movement. Run by the English Anglican Church, Toynbee Hall offered Hackley a location where she could attend Episcopalian services. The Hall took pride in its mission as a beacon for activities committed to assisting the underprivileged and disenfranchised. Through her association with this influential institution, Hackley deepened her resolve to employ music as a means for improving the lives of African Americans.[73]

Hackley organized concerts at prestigious venues, including an event in January 1909 that took place at the Town Hall of Kensington at which she was the "headliner."[74] Famous for its stunning Italianate architecture, Town Hall attracted renowned performers and well-heeled audiences to concerts and lectures. Owing to her initial success at Town Hall, she was invited back for another performance, on 4 February 1909, to help raise money for victims of the devastating earthquake in Messina, Italy, that occurred on 28 December 1908.[75] A brief review of this event, copied from the *Kensington News*, offered this assessment: "Mrs. E. Azalia Hackley, who is better known in America, . . . is possessed of a genuine soprano voice of the highest quality. She sang the aria 'Bel Raggio' (from *Semiramide*) by Rossini, which was received with much enthusiasm, and Henschel's 'Spring' in which she carried the audience with her from beginning to end." The *Kensington News* did not comment on the other selections Hackley performed.[76] A repeat performance of this benefit event, which featured Hackley prominently, took place at another Kensington venue on 14 February 1909.[77]

Hackley also sang at an event in the opulent Queen's Hall, a venue selected by the most celebrated and discerning of artists owing to it superb acoustics and a large seating capacity for 2,500. Her appearance in Queen's Hall, arranged by government official and ardent music aficionado Sir Charles Stevens and concert violinist Grace Thyme, offered Hackley another opportunity to form associations with persons of considerable influence in London's musical circles. No publicity for this event has been located, but Hackley's performance received persuasive endorsement in the form of a letter written by "a lady that has traveled

Fig. 2.2. Samuel Coleridge-Taylor, photograph autographed on 12 July 1900. Music excerpts in margins are in Coleridge-Taylor's own hand. Courtesy, Royal College of Music, London, England / ArenaPAL.

extensively in the old countries." Mysteriously opting to remain anonymous, the writer of this letter presented, as a credential, confirmation that she had attended numerous performances by Hackley in Paris and London. The writer recalled that when she "happened to be in London," she "saw her [Hackley] advertised to sing at the Great Queen's Hall." She continued, "I knew that if this lady could interest artistic London to the extent that she be invited to sing in a hall where . . . great sopranos won their fame, I knew she must be an artist of more than ordinary capabilities. . . . Perhaps no other woman has done more

Fig. 2.3. Caricature of Samuel Coleridge-Taylor and female admirers. Pen and ink, artist and date unknown. Handwritten text reads: "A distinguished composer escaping from the autograph fiends." Courtesy, Royal College of Music, London, England / ArenaPAL.

for disseminating knowledge and inspiring love for music along its highest and cultured line as Madam Hackley."[78] Other than this information about Hackley's performance at Queen's Hall, no additional documentation survives.

Beyond her association with Shakespeare, Hackley made the acquaintance of two other celebrated English musicians: Sir George Henschel and Samuel Coleridge-Taylor. Henschel, a German native and respected English baritone soloist, composer, and conductor, spent considerable time in the United States in the early years of the twentieth century. Shakespeare must have brought Hackley to Henschel's attention as the two men occasionally shared the stage together. Hackley's vocal gifts impressed Henschel, and she eventually studied his song "Spring" under his guidance.[79]

Hackley also spent time with Anglo-African composer Coleridge-Taylor (figure 2.2). She hoped to convince him to support her foreign scholarship initiative and to agree to accept students funded by her philanthropic efforts. An opportunity to study classical composition with Coleridge-Taylor would have been an extraordinary honor for an African American musician. His pieces, along with his reputation as a teacher, were held in high regard in Europe as well as in the United States. In fact, he enjoyed celebrity status on both sides of the Atlantic (figure 2.3).

Coleridge-Taylor visited the United States three times (in 1904, 1906, and 1910). During his visits, he conducted acclaimed performances of his famous choral cycle, *Song of Hiawatha*, a setting of Henry Wadsworth Longfellow's celebrated epic poem of the same title, written in 1855. For Coleridge-Taylor's US visit of 1904, African American musicians in the greater Washington, DC, area founded the Coleridge-Taylor Choral Society and performed *Song of Hiawatha*, earning enthusiastic reviews. Hackley undoubtedly made his acquaintance at this historic event.[80]

In a letter to the *New York Age*, Hackley identified London as a metropolitan location where African American classically trained musicians could successfully launch their careers:

> London is the Mecca of everything musical.... The time is ripe in London for the debut of a colored musician, if he has the money to put up for it. Perhaps a pianist or violinist would be most timely, but a male singer would also have a fine opportunity [here].... I will never be happy until I can hear a colored musician at Albert Hall (which holds 10,000 persons, by the way).... A musician of merit always receives impartial criticism in London.... If a colored artist can do the work, has repertoire and experience, he can expect fair treatment at the hands of critics.[81]

London's support of musical activities for all citizens, regardless of race or class status, also impressed Hackley. She wrote:

> London believes in music for the poor. There are organizations which for years have supplied the best musicians for the poor sections of London that England has to offer. As a consequence, in the East End [of London], where probably the poorest people in the world are, the audiences are as appreciative of symphonies and classics as the more cultured West End audiences. Explanatory [printed] programs are generally furnished gratis, and the poor in this East district are remarkably intelligent musically. At Albert Hall and Queen's Hall, there is often free admittance to a certain number, especially at the Sunday concerts.[82]

The tradition of offering free concert admittance to London's less fortunate music lovers contrasts practices commonplace in the United States. Generally, only those of comfortable financial means attended US classical music performances; the poor and African Americans were generally unwelcome at these events. Throughout the country, music, especially classical genres, assumed

Fig. 2.4. E. Azalia Hackley. Argent Archer, photographer, Kensington, London, England, ca. 1908. *Chicago Broad Ax* 12 November 1910, 1.

and expressed class and racial hierarchies quite dissimilar to those Hackley encountered in London. Not only did she witness a more enlightened approach to audience development at classical music concerts in London, but she also came to realize that the ability to understand and appreciate European-modeled repertoire did not relate, in any way, to class and race identity. Of course, Hackley would have seen racial minorities in attendance at concerts, so the inference she made regarding the egalitarian nature of London performance spaces extended to her aspirations for all African Americans.[83]

Hackley did not offer direct comments about race relations in London and instead drew conclusions about the English attitude toward Blacks while she resided in Paris. According to her observations, English travelers interacted with African Americans in a more cordial and accepting fashion than did native Parisians. She credited a higher level of educational attainment among the English as an explanation for their tolerance of racial diversity: "I have noticed considerable association between the English and Afro-Americans and I believe that the English in Paris are much more friendly to the Negro than the French are. The English masses are much more educated than the French; they are more liberal in their ideas and they understand conditions in the States better."[84]

During her stay in England, Hackley commissioned London photographer Albert Argent Archer to produce a series of portraits. Archer operated a studio in the Kensington district of London, the fashionable neighborhood where Hackley boarded. He advertised his work as "high-class portraiture" for "high society," yet available for "moderate prices."[85] Archer also specialized in hand coloring and journalistic photography of automobiles and buildings, and he also photographed the coronation of King George V in 1911.[86] It seems likely that Hackley intended to use Archer's images of her to assist in furthering her career, as the distribution of portraits, especially to newspapers and periodicals, epitomized the hallmark of an established artist and was a routine practice of successful white performers. For her studio session with Archer, Hackley wore an outfit with an ample white lace collar, which presented little contrast to her light skin. In the single surviving Archer portrait, Hackley's rather thin lips, heavy eyebrows, and wire-rimmed spectacles reinforce her pensive, downward gaze. She selected the photograph shown in figure 2.4 more than any other to appear in the press of her day, and it became the image by which the newspaper and periodical reading public knew her best.

Hackley had originally planned to remain in London until late 1909 or early 1910. However, health problems forced her to return to the United States sooner than anticipated. She departed Southampton, England, onboard the SS *St. Paul* and arrived in New York on 5 June 1909.[87]

Trips to Cuba

In March 1912, the *New York Age* announced that Hackley had again left the country and was "spending a few weeks in Cuba." In letters she sent to Black newspapers, she expressed unbridled fondness for the Cuban people and culture: "Cuba is entrancing. No one can adequately describe Havana and its charm. From the moment one enters the beautiful harbor until the last glimpse of this fascinating tropical city one is enthusiastic and desires to return as soon as possible."[88] In the locales she toured, she observed cordial race relations and happily concluded that "white and colored live in perfect harmony." She felt that readers of her letters "will not wonder at my being so enthusiastic over the extreme cleanliness and equality [in travel accommodations] shown in Cuba to those of my race."[89] Of the prevalence of persons of African heritage in Cuba, she observed that "the majority of the population is black or of mixed blood." In contrast to the US treatment of mixed-race persons, Cubans afforded light-hued Blacks more favorable status. For, as Hackley noted, "the mulatto must be very marked [with obvious indications of African ancestry] not to be treated as white." Given this assertion, we might speculate that Hackley, light enough to have passed for white, may not have been regarded by native Cubans as an African American.[90] She cautioned, however, that even as Cuban Blacks had "escaped political prejudice," she nonetheless feared "they will never be permitted to rule," that is, to hold influential government appointments.[91]

Hackley's viewpoints regarding Cuban race relations belied the reality of racial strife and injustices widespread within the island nation. In her letters to the US press, she neglected to mention the inhumane treatment of Black workers in sugar cane fields and the tobacco industry or the ensuing bloody "Negro Rebellion of 1912," also known as the "Armed Rising of the Independents of Color" or the "War of 1912." In the wake of these tumultuous upheavals, wealthy white land, business, and plantation owners increased their abuse of Afro-Cubans and invoked racist social and political provocations, mirroring those of the US South. However uninformed or naïve Hackley may have been about the escalation of racism in Cuba, she appeared to know something of the ongoing and heated debate as to whether or not the United States should annex Cuba. The press regularly issued remarks by racist white political anti-annexationists who feared the admission of Cuban persons of color into the overall US population through annexation. Yet, pro-annexationists envisioned Cuba as an additional southern state where the white population could dominate economically and socially. In addition, discussion ensued in the press concerning Cuban racial unrest resulting, in part, from the Platt Amendment (1901), which ostensibly prohibited annexation but permitted the United States to intervene in Cuban affairs, both politically and militarily.[92]

Hackley returned to the United States in 1912 and visited Cuba again the following year. The *Chicago Defender* reported that she gave a series of concerts in Havana, but no additional information about these performances has surfaced.[93] During this second visit to Cuba, she sent an informative letter to the *New York Age* in which she finally acknowledged escalating tensions in Cuban race relations. She wrote:

> The color question is beginning to be agitated among the Cubans, in fact, it is assuming huge proportions. I understand that recently a manifesto was read in one of the large tobacco factories, to the point that Cuba did not desire any Negroes from anywhere to enter Cuba. I am told that already families are breaking up, and that the fairer [racially mixed family] members are leaving to advance their interests and incomes [elsewhere]. Americans are prone to utter many senseless remarks, and the white Cubans are [also] very thin-skinned. I cannot remember how many times I have heard [white] Americans [visiting Cuba], both men and women, say, "I can't stand to see all colors mixing."[94]

Another Trip to Paris

In June 1914 Hackley traveled to Europe, again, to pursue additional music instruction and to concertize and teach. Given her appreciation of the friendly reception of African Americans in London, it might be expected that England would be her destination of choice. However, in London, she had experienced recurring episodes of respiratory illness that she blamed on the city's infamous fogs, so she decided to return to France. As she noted, she deemed the "dampness... of the English atmosphere particularly unfavorable to singing voices."[95] Clearly, her lessons with Jean de Reszke must have proven most satisfactory and fulfilling, and she sought a place, once again, in his studio.[96]

Hackley encountered chaotic conditions in Paris as the city prepared for the armed conflict that eventually erupted into World War I. Not surprisingly, she found it difficult to arrange any recitals, and no newspaper accounts survive to confirm she ever performed publicly during this Parisian residency. However, she did manage to make a recording of her singing, and de Reszke undoubtedly assisted her in arranging this session. She wrote to W. E. B. Du Bois about her studio experience and indicated that she had worked with a "new company" but did not disclose its name. Most likely, the company was Pathé Records, a Parisian firm that produced both the older, more perishable wax-cylinder format and innovative, durable discs. For her studio session, Hackley performed some of her favorite songs, including "Last Rose of Summer," Stephen Foster's "Old Folks at Home," "Comin' Thro' the Rye," and Henschel's "Spring."[97] Although Hackley sent many copies of her recording back to the United States, she claimed she did not know their whereabouts. She informed Du Bois, "I meant to look into the matter but the mobilization of the troops made me forget everything but to get back to America."[98] Unfortunately, no copies of her recording have ever been found. Nonetheless, Hackley was probably the first African American artist to make a recording abroad.[99]

The potential danger Hackley faced as Paris prepared for war forced her to cancel plans for travel to the Netherlands, Switzerland, and Germany.[100] She wrote letters to African American newspapers in which she described the heightened fear of violence and armed conflict that gripped Parisians. To the *Cleveland Gazette* she sent this postcard message: "Aug. 1, 1914. Greetings! Things are interesting even though the war scare is on. We [US citizens] are held in Paris. There are lots of 'us' [African Americans here] from Howard [University] and etc."[101] The African Americans she associated with during this trip included Roy W. Tibbs (1888–1944), a graduate of Oberlin College Conservatory of Music and a pianist and faculty member at Howard University; artist Henry O. Tanner; Helen Hagan (1893–1964), an aspiring concert pianist; and author Jessie Redmon Fauset. By September 1914 the press expressed anxiety about Hackley: "The music lovers of the country and all interested in real race leadership are greatly concerned for the safety of Mme. E. Azalia Hackley, who is in the beleaguered city of Paris."[102] A subsequent bulletin offered some reassurance of her well-being: "The versatile and brilliant Mme. E. Azalia Hackley is writing some fine newsletters from Paris and 'sizes' up the delicate situation [in Europe] with a degree of skill and courage not excelled by any writer who has endeavored to handle the issues growing out of the most deadly conflict the century has ever seen. But, as versatile and as brilliant as Mme. Hackley has long been known to be, who would have ever pictured her in the role of war correspondent?"[103]

Not surprisingly, transportation back to the United States in 1914 proved difficult for many US citizens to secure. Nonetheless, Hackley managed to book a return trip rather expeditiously, and she departed from Le Havre, France, onboard the *S. S. Rochambeau* and arrived in New York on 7 September 1914.[104] The outbreak of war precluded another European excursion for Hackley for the foreseeable future. After recovering from her return voyage, she organized a series of tours during which she presented folk song festivals and patriotic celebrations. These programs occupied her for the ensuing years, and her activities in this regard increased dramatically after the United States entered the war in 1917.

Travel and Racial Identity

No discussion of Hackley as a consummate traveler would do justice to her experiences, commentary, and legal actions without further consideration of how she self-identified, racially, and how others responded to her appearance and attendant racial ambiguity.[105] Such analysis and speculation help illuminate her relationship with the overarching, recalcitrant, and inextricable connections among travel accommodations, segregation, gender, and race. Photographs of Hackley depict a woman whom activist Fannie Barrier Williams would have classified as a "white Negro." According to Williams, an individual who embodied this identity represented one of the most provocative and disquieting "paradoxes of American life." She offered this explanation:

> The people to whom this term [white Negro] is applied are not Negroes according to the principles of ethnology and are not white according to understanding and usage of that term in the United States. Although American in nativity, language, interests and appearance, the status of these people is shifting, anomalous and embarrassing to themselves and everybody else. Wherever their race identity is known, their right to live and act is challenged either by white or colored people. They seem to be a hopelessly disturbing social factor, because they may be either black or white by their own election or force of circumstances. The only

sanction for insisting upon the status of these people as Negroes is the uncompromising American antipathy to anything related to the Negro race.[106]

As a young adult, Hackley readily recalled how her mother, Corilla Smith, instilled in both her daughters a strong sense of pride in their African heritage. Smith's task must not have been an easy one as Hackley attended predominantly white schools, and thus she surely experienced temptation to suppress her racial identity when in the company of fellow students. Yet, as Hackley stated, emphatically, she considered herself "pre-natally [sic] marked for everything black." As a result of her mother's inculcation of race pride, Hackley claimed to feel "color hungry" when "among pale faces."[107]

Hackley's mixed-race appearance attracted considerable attention, and she admitted to "being stared at" rudely in public.[108] According to Fannie Barrier Williams, any person who lacked clear racial specificity existed as a "hopelessly disturbing social factor" and thus could count on the penetrating gaze of those in their proximity. The very presence of a "white Negro" created a public spectacle of sorts and stirred up no little amount of social anxiety. Racists feared the possibility that a person with attributes similar to those of Hackley might successfully pass as white and thus elude, altogether, the carefully monitored system of Jim Crow segregation, especially when traveling. As one newspaper noted of the angst whites felt regarding light-hued African Americans: "We find these saddle-colored Negroes and some lighter than the saddle[-colored] . . . more objectionable to the whites than the black men because the line of distinction was not so pronounced."[109]

Hackley's wavy hair and light skin caused a stir in the press, and newspapers printed items that fueled speculation about her racial heritage. She wrote of two such incidences during which her racial identity came to the fore while she was on tour sometime in 1914. In one incident, a Black clergyman alluded to her ambiguous racial characteristics when he introduced her to a recital audience with the quip, "There isn't much of her on our side, but what there is, is all for us."[110] She related another comment about her appearance, made after a performance, when a woman approached her and sarcastically remarked, "'Why, are you Madame Hackley? I thought Madame Hackley was a big black woman.'"[111] Attempting to set the matter straight, the *Indianapolis Freeman* described Hackley as "almost white."[112] Occasionally, the press misidentified Hackley's race altogether, as when *New York Age* columnist James H. Hogans reminisced about an incident when railroad personnel mistook an elegant and fashionably attired Hackley for "some Spanish or Italian countess."[113] Chicago's *Broad Ax* went a step further and offered a comparison of Hackley's skin hue to that of another celebrated singer and audaciously asserted she was "not nearly so dark in complexion" as the internationally renowned opera star, Jeanne Gerville-Réache.¹¹⁴ Photographs of Gerville-Réache leave little doubt as to her white heritage, as her "pale complexion, jet black eyes and hair" closely resembled those of her Caribbean father and Spanish mother, neither of whom claimed African ancestry.¹¹⁵ With this comment, the *Broad Ax* issued a challenge and warning to southern racists—one that questioned their supposed infallibility when determining a person's racial heritage. For, as observed by journalist and historian Ray Stannard Baker, "Southern [white] people who take pride in their ability to distinguish the drop of dark blood in the white face, are themselves frequently deceived. Several times I have heard police judges in the South ask, concerning a man brought before them: 'Is this man colored or white'?"¹¹⁶ The deception to which Baker referred inspired this detailed assessment of race designation:

> I had not been long engaged in the study of the race problem when I found myself face to face with a curious and seemingly absurd question: "What is a Negro?" I saw plenty of men and women who were unquestionably Negroes, Negroes in every physical characteristic, black of countenance with thick lips and kinky hair, but I also met men and women as white as I am, whose assertion that they were really Negroes I accepted in defiance of the evidence of my own senses. I have seen blue-eyed Negroes and golden-haired Negroes; one Negro girl I met had an abundance of soft straight red hair. I have seen Negroes I could not easily distinguish from the Jewish or French types; I once talked with a man I took at first to be a Chinaman but who told me he was a Negro. And I have met several people, passing everywhere for white, who, I knew, had Negro blood. Nothing, indeed, is more difficult to define than this curious physical color line in the individual human being. Legislatures have repeatedly attempted to define where black leaves off and white begins.¹¹⁷

Newspapers also suggested that Hackley could have successfully passed for white, permanently—a possibility that particularly rankled and unsettled racists. For instance, a white newspaper, the *Philadelphia Times*, admitted that she might readily cross the color line undetected: "She is a light mulatto, so light, in fact, that she could easily pass for a white woman."¹¹⁸ Hackley's friend, Marie A. D. Madre, confirmed that "during all of her [Hackley's] professional life the color question has played a tantalizing temptation." Madre recalled many "offers" for Hackley to "cross the color fence and lose identity with her race" in order to further her career, had been proposed.¹¹⁹ Just such a suggestion came from Black journalist William Milton Lewis, who alluded that, for the sake of her career, Hackley "may have to leave the race altogether, and, if so, a pardon may well be granted her."¹²⁰ A one-time student of Hackley, Kate Johnson, echoed Madre's observations and added that, regardless of the potential to pass as white, Hackley remained "true to her Race, and often [when I was] discussing the matter with her, she would say, 'if I am going to be an educator, it will be with my own people.'"[121] The *Philadelphia Tribune* reported that Hackley, "unlike most of our people who can pass for white, . . . always advertises her color in most of her speeches."[122]

Hackley sneered at African Americans who, especially when in a foreign country, "became inoculated with passing fever" and were thus "guilty of what is said to be the besetting sin of man—representing himself to be what he is not."[123] Moreover, she felt that those who passed for white for an indefinite period of time shirked their ultimate responsibility and obligation to Blacks as "no one can lift the race unless he stays in it."[124] However, her overseas trips enabled her to escape US racism and to enjoy more relaxed and tolerant environments. To be sure, while in Paris, she associated with many African Americans, yet she pursued professional activities overseas, such as studying with de Reszke and Shakespeare, and concertizing, that placed her squarely in a privileged white milieu. She also called attention to a disquieting prevalence of Parisian racist attitudes and behaviors that, if somewhat moderate compared to those common in the southern United States, nonetheless occurred more often than some press accounts admitted. Furthermore, while in Cuba, Hackley may have been identified and treated as white by the native population as she claimed the people she encountered tended to categorize as Black only those persons who possessed unequivocal African racial characteristics.

Hackley also conflated issues of race and gender in her comments regarding train travel. She admitted to occasionally purchasing first-class tickets to ride in a "ladies'" car; these cars, always reserved for white females, were off limits to smokers and tobacco chewers—persons whose close proximately she avoided. Even as she persistently decried passing, or what she constituted as the denial of one's Black identity for lengthy periods of time, she nonetheless found the occasional deceit of racial obfuscation, enacted in the South, to be a potent tool of resistance in certain instances. Such actions of defiance while traveling by train reveal a significant dimension of her activist agenda, in which she sought to disrupt race proscriptions associated with the segregated southern rail system. Therefore, we can assume that she boarded whites-only train cars intentionally, as a mode of protest and as a way to debunk southerners' claims of their unerring ability to identify African ancestry.[125] Mary Church Terrell also boarded cars reserved for whites and vociferously defended such conduct: "People who are discriminated against on account of race, color, or creed are justified in resorting to any subterfuge, using any disguise, or playing any trick . . . if it will enable them to secure the advantages and obtain the rights to which they are entitled by outwitting their prejudice-ridden foes."[126] However, at times, Hackley attributed her presence on white cars to misidentification of her race by railroad personnel. According to the *Philadelphia Tribune*, such errors occurred quite often, as "the majority of trainmen have mistaken her for a white lady and always ushered her into the white folk's car." As the paper elucidated, "she often told them [railroad personnel] that she was a colored woman and wanted to go with her people; [on such occasions] they would say to her, 'No, you are not and you will have to ride here; that car is for N*****s.'"[127] Nonetheless, Hackley did not politically agitate or lecture in favor of the dissolution of Jim Crow laws and practices. Instead, she campaigned for cleaner and safer facilities for African Americans, in pursuit of *de facto* "separate but equal" accommodations. Even as she criticized Black passengers for their contributions to the unacceptable conditions she encountered in Jim Crow trains and depots, she laid ultimate blame on white railroad officials and the railroad industry in its entirety for not only allowing filth and litter to fester but, most importantly, for refusing to attend to the safety of Black female passengers.

It seems telling that Hackley's railroad activism surfaced and gained momentum after her first overseas trip. Foreign travel presented her with altogether different and extraordinarily compelling perspectives regarding race relations. Her experiences in other countries convinced her to lend her famous name and celebrity status to the fight for improved Jim Crow travel accommodations. Her legal proceedings against the southern railroad industry received national publicity as the Black press shared with readers her philosophy of defiance, resistance, and active engagement. Although her racially ambiguous appearance permitted her to travel in foreign locations with ease, comfort, and without Jim Crow humiliations, she nonetheless denounced African Americans who sought to pass as white, especially in more racially permissive locations. While overseas she did not attempt to shirk the racial responsibilities she held fast to, especially in Paris where she performed African American spirituals and readily identified as Black.[128] In addition, she circulated among the artistic and musical elite of Paris and London and astutely took full advantage of the opportunities a more enlightened urban populace offered. Thus, her experiences as a traveler, both domestic and foreign, helped shape her evolving activist agenda. Even so, Hackley's foray into more overt protest against the demeaning treatment she endured on Jim Crow cars proved short lived. After she returned from Paris in 1914, she did not rejuvenate her defiant actions, nor did she launch any further legal complaints. Instead, she refocused her energy and concentrated on wartime patriotic music and spectacle in Black communities.

CHAPTER THREE

New Thought Activism

Hackley spoke to audiences of the ways African Americans could harness the powers of mental concentration and telepathy as means to deflect and transcend the devastating effects of racism and segregation. She encouraged each person to nurture and exude what she called a "somebody" persona, characterized by evident self-confidence, race pride, and a commitment to optimistic thinking. Accordingly, she wrote that "if one has been unfortunate enough to be born without the fine points of a somebody, he can observe and cultivate these points."[1] To facilitate this process, she urged audiences to embrace principles and practices associated with the New Thought Movement. This was revolutionary thinking in her day, and she was, most likely, the first African American activist to advocate tenets of this ecumenical nexus of liberative beliefs and traditions. Of equal significance, her adoption of New Thought and its emphasis on self-reliance and personal responsibility obviated, in her mind, the need for collective political agitation and militancy.[2]

New Thought History

The New Thought Movement, founded in New England in the mid-nineteenth century, offered an eclectic and syncretic spirituality incorporating elements of Judeo-Christianity, US Transcendentalism and Asian traditions. Early New Thought followers espoused an evolving catalogue of practices including, but not limited to: mental healing, psychic phenomenon, thought concentration, mesmerism, and telepathy. Although Hackley advocated principles associated with this movement, she did not abandon Episcopalianism and instead, elided the denomination of her formative years with New Thought tenets. She also interwove her musical and activist agendas with New Thought practices.

The rise of New Thought emanated from the teachings of Phineas Parkhurst Quimby (1802–66) and his influential protégé, Warren Felt Evans (1817–89). As a young man, Quimby, often referred to as the "Father of New Thought," suffered from tuberculosis, and his chronic ill health resisted the best efforts of medical practitioners. He eventually turned to spiritual and psychic strategies to effect a lasting remission from the ravages of disease. Following the success of his unorthodox methods, he codified and disseminated his experiences with mystical approaches to medicine and wellness, thereby establishing many of the early premises of New Thought.[3] He promoted the belief that negative thoughts, coupled with a dearth of metaphysical spirituality, caused illness. When purged of the deleterious effects of pernicious mental processes, the mind could, according to Quimby, orchestrate and sustain the well-being of an individual.[4] Evans also suffered from recalcitrant health problems and sought treatment from Quimby. He later studied the techniques of mind healing with him and assisted in disseminating his mentor's methods. A prolific author, Evans expounded upon principles regarding the "correspondence of body and soul" and the "causal relation of disordered mental states to diseased physiological action." Like Quimby, he practiced guided meditation and mental concentration as means to combat corporeal fragility.[5]

By the twentieth century, New Thought followers numbered in the millions worldwide.[6] Leaders of the movement published hundreds of articles, pamphlets, and books attesting to the enormous breadth, accessibility, and adaptability of the movement's tenets.[7] The eclectic nature of New Thought and the movement's lack of strict doctrine unquestionably contributed to its widespread appeal. As a loose collection of affirmations and practices, the movement's principles consist of traditions and literature culled from an ever-expanding number of sources, including spiritualism, paganism and Judeo-Christianity, along with Hindu, Buddhist, and Yoga teachings. In confirmation of the movement's composite content, historian Horatio Willis Dresser (1866–1954) acknowledged that New Thought philosophers "ransacked the Christian Bible and the scriptures and literature of all nations, in search of brief, specific statements tending to enforce ideals, and make them habits of life."[8]

Early New Thought followers eschewed the postponement of happiness often thought to be attainable only after biological death, and instead condoned and sought financial reward, and physical, mental, and emotional comfort and satisfaction during one's lifetime. Founding adherents believed that the riches of a bountiful life came as a consequence of optimism and concentrated thought, or what was often referred to as "thought force" or "right thinking." For New

Thought practitioners, the pursuit of prosperity did not constitute selfishness or avarice. Therefore, one could cultivate wealth and good fortune without fear of recrimination, the threat of eternal punishment, social or religious condemnation, or ostracism. Succinctly put, New Thought followers reject the concepts of sin, guilt, and damnation.

African Americans and New Thought

Many historians consider US New Thought to be a white movement as no known persons of color served as its earliest philosophers and practitioners. However, Hackley found New Thought literature and practices to be highly adaptable, and she infused her writings and lectures with distinctly African American interpretations and applications of the movement's principles.[9] In activist initiatives, New Thought yielded, for her, a spiritually grounded, liberative, supple, and racially specific response to segregation, racism, and issues of African American identity. For example, she believed that "because of his color" each person of African heritage was singularly and uniquely attuned to the power and potential of mental and psychic phenomena, and thus she considered the practice of New Thought particularly apropos to the needs of the Black population.[10] New Thought followers could harness such potential in two ways: first, through the engagement of the highly personal process of mental concentration, and second, through the conviction that one's individual thoughts assume a communal function. Beyond consideration of the empowering influence of an individual's mental capabilities, common thoughts or yearnings sometimes merge to form a shared, collective consciousness. Hackley fervently believed in the existence of this phenomenon among African Americans to the extent that she credited enslaved people with bringing about "their own freedom" through "concentrated, united thought."[11]

By the late nineteenth century, some African Americans questioned the efficacy of organized, traditional religious denominations in the struggle against unremitting racism. They found it increasingly difficult to reconcile the promise of heavenly salvation with the earthly reality of intractable and humiliating conditions imposed on Black citizens.[12] Painfully aware of these sentiments, activist Anna Julia Cooper cautiously interrogated the function of religious observance in Blacks' lives when she wrote, in 1891, "Religion ought to be (if it isn't) a great deal more than mere gratification of the instinct for worship linked with the straight-teaching of irreproachable credos. Religion must be life made true; and life is action, growth, development—begun now and ending never."[13] W. E. B. Du Bois offered poignant observations about religion in *Souls of Black Folk*, in which he acknowledged the "peculiar wrenching of the soul [and] a peculiar sense of doubt and bewilderment" encountered by African Americans as they contemplated the role of religion in a racist society. He posited that this "ethical paradox" of African American life threatened to limit the offices of religion to expressions of bitterness and vindictiveness "instead of worship," and spirituality to more of "a complaint and a curse, a wail rather than a hope, a sneer rather than a faith."[14] Toward the end of his life, he admitted that organized religious observation gradually assumed less personal significance for him: "From my 30th year [ca. 1898] on I have increasingly regarded the church as an institution which defended such evils as slavery, color caste, [and] exploitation [of persons of color] in labor and war."[15] However, he acknowledged the incontrovertible presence of "the deep religious feeling of the real Negro heart, [and] the stirring, unguided might of powerful human souls who have lost the guiding star of the past and seek . . . a new religious ideal." With the prediction that "someday the Awakening will come," Du Bois condoned avenues of innovative spiritual and religious observances that facilitated the acquisition of worldly empowerment.[16]

The New Thought movement held forth the potential for a "religious ideal" and an "awakening" of which Du Bois so eloquently wrote. Correspondingly, Hackley came to realize that organized, traditional religious practices, especially those associated with the white population, could not be relied upon, exclusively, to further the cause of racial uplift. Those African Americans who embraced New Thought in the early twentieth century found reassurances in the movement's validation of transcendent thinking, the righteousness of worldly achievement and fulfillment, and the legitimacy of acquiring money and material success.[17] Hackley cited the potential of a more ecumenical spirituality to better meet the unique and pressing needs of Black citizens when she wrote that "the religion that does not help toward the advancement of this persecuted race, and does not win the admiration and respect of other races, is not the religion" for African Americans.[18] She encouraged her audiences to become more personally involved in ecumenical uplift efforts rather than engage solely in conventional worship and prayer as solutions to racism. The emphasis on self-reliance, a tenet of New Thought derived from US transcendentalism, also occupied Hackley. "As a rule," she argued, "colored people expect entirely too much help from God." Instead, she insisted, "we must help ourselves more."[19]

In general, early New Thought leaders expressed a commitment to inclusivity and nonsexism, especially noticeable in the number of women who served as spokespersons. This level of tolerance appealed to those African Americans who had begun to feel disillusioned with the treatment of Blacks within some traditional white belief systems and churches. Even as New Thought founders did not overtly invite persons of color into their circle, they nonetheless expressed egalitarian sentiments. As one writer, Charles Brodie Patterson (1854–1936), confirmed: "New Thought is not a church, a cult, or a sect. It recognizes no limitations of any kind, creates no barriers between man and man: it asks no allegiance to creed, form, or personality, and is as much for one race as for another.... There can, therefore, be no spirit of judgment, controversy or condemnation of any other body of people" in New Thought.[20] Similarly, Horatio Willis Dresser remarked, "our New Thought Movement teaches a still wider inclusion:... its open-armed welcome to those of every class, creed and color."[21]

Even as Hackley disseminated New Thought ideology, she maintained an affiliation with the Episcopalian faith throughout her life. When, as a child, her family relocated to Detroit, she attended St. Matthew's Episcopal Church. After her marriage in 1894 and her subsequent move to Denver, Hackley and her husband became members of the Episcopalian Church of the Redeemer, considered to be the most exclusive and influential Black congregation in that city.[22] In Philadelphia, she became a member of the Episcopal Church of the Crucifixion. While in Paris, she associated with St. Luke's Episcopal Church and the Episcopalian affiliate, the Holy Trinity Lodge. In London, she frequented Toynbee Hall, a settlement house under the aegis of the Anglican (Episcopal) Church of England.

Fortuitously, Hackley visited or resided in metropolitan areas where New Thought flourished—Detroit, Denver, London, and Chicago. One significant New Thought leader, Rev. Margaret C. La Grange, not only established the First Church of New Thought in Detroit and edited a New Thought periodical, but she also served as the elected bishop of the newly inaugurated New Thought diocese of Michigan.[23] It seems likely that Hackley, who spent most of her formative years in Detroit, knew of La Grange's work and may have attended her lectures or services conducted by her. While residing in Colorado, Hackley must have known of Denver resident Nona Lovell Brooks (1861–1945), often referred to as the "prophet of modern mystical Christianity." Brooks moved to Colorado in the early 1880s, and her ordination as a minister in the Church of Divine Science, a subdenomination closely aligned with New Thought, occurred in 1898. That same year, Brooks, along with two of her sisters, founded the Denver Divine Science College and the Church of Divine Science.[24]

New Thought was well established in London by the time Hackley visited the city. According to Thomas Troward (1847–1916), one of London's New Thought leaders, the movement arrived from across the Atlantic as "a spiritual invasion from America" and rapidly attracted countless followers. While in London, Hackley resided near the Higher Thought Centre, a flourishing New Thought institution in the Kensington neighborhood where she boarded.[25] She also associated with Asian and Middle Eastern mystics and claimed to have made the acquaintances of many "Turks" and "Hindoos" in London. Their eastern philosophies fascinated and inspired her, and the Yogic breathing techniques she learned from them later served as a fundamental component of her pedagogy.[26]

New Thought thrived in Chicago, a city Hackley frequented. At one point she maintained a residence in Chicago and established a music school, the Normal Vocal Institute, there as well. Two significant New Thought leaders, Emma Curtis Hopkins and William Walker Atkison, spent considerable time in Chicago. The charismatic Hopkins established a center of New Thought in Chicago in 1886 and Hackley would have had ample opportunity to become acquainted with her work.[27] Atkinson studied with Hopkins and, through her encouragement, relocated to Chicago where he became a preeminent lecturer, writer, and publisher of New Thought periodicals and books.[28]

Of the principles associated with New Thought, none served a more universal and communal function than the practice of telepathy and its constituent, "thought suggestion." As a resolute proponent of the power of thought force in its many manifestations, Hackley advocated the use of telepathy and routinely informed readers and audiences, "I believe thoroughly in thought suggestion."[29] Additionally, she told audiences how mental impressions could be transferred over great distances and that this phenomenon took place even during sleep as the subconscious mind could also send and receive thoughts.[30] New Thought writers often likened the power of thought transference to radio transmission and wireless telegraphy, as developed in the late 1890s by inventor and electrical engineer Guglielmo Marconi (1874–1930).[31] Hackley marveled at the ability to "send thoughts miles away" in the form of "currents or waves of electricity" exactly as "Marconi sends messages through the air."[32] She sometimes addressed audiences about the contributions of electrical impulses to telepathy, such as in one of her popular lectures, described as a "demonstration of Human Electricity and its control."[33] Her insistence that African Americans possessed acute receptivity to telepathy caught the attention of arts critic Minnie Adams, who noticed and commented on Hackley's "extreme sensitiveness to surrounding vibrations of thoughts and feelings."[34]

Hackley also acknowledged, and cautioned audiences about, the role played by the transference of negative thoughts, and she taught that such abuse of telepathic powers contributed, substantially, to the perpetuation of racism: "Riots, political agitations and race prejudices are all evidence of the power of strong projections of [negative] thought. . . . Race prejudice is the result of the vibrations of hate and anger sent out [telepathically] by strong minds." To deflect the negative mental vibrations of racism, she recommended concentration on positive thoughts and the employment of telepathy to disseminate such impressions: "We must teach our minds to act upon the minds of others," she exhorted. She vehemently expressed a conviction that "strong thoughts of peace and love" could "counteract the overwhelming tide of [racist] thought against us."[35]

Hackley recommended that each person should conduct a personal inventory of character, morality and integrity. This "self-valuation," as she called it, would disclose both positive attributes and negative characteristics, representative of one's "higher" and "lower" selves, respectively. The knowledge gained from this evaluative process could then be implemented as an informational tool in the practice of New Thought in order "to learn restraint, how to govern and control" oneself and to "accumulate sufficient will power" for personal and racial "advancement." Those who exuded positive thought vibrations engaged the higher self predominantly and thus manifested what she called "a Somebody valuation." Conversely, those controlled by negative thought exhibited a "Nobody" self-identity, persona, and correspondingly weak posture. "At first meeting one is judged either a Somebody or a Nobody according to external evidence," she informed audiences. In her assessment of facial expression and posture, she stressed the relationship of appearance to the state of one's inner mind: "One is really a Somebody or a Nobody according to the control she has over her mind," she wrote. Thus, "those with whom one comes in contact will take each at his own valuation, the Somebody valuation or the Nobody valuation. It is simply a question of which [valuation] one prefers" and projects. Beyond appearance, she told audiences, "there is a Somebody and Nobody voice and laugh. There is a Somebody and Nobody tone in singing."[36] After lecturing about the virtues of self valuation and guiding her audiences through a few exercises in posture, she informed them, "You now have the poise of a Somebody ... and if one *is* a Somebody, his carriage should imply that fact [italics original]."[37]

The cultivation, reception, and transmission of psychic magnetism provided another source of empowerment for New Thought followers. In her lectures, Hackley insisted that African Americans possessed a specialized capacity to exude a "mysterious indescribable hypnotic influence" in the form of "personal magnetism" that could be generated, accessed, and projected to advantage.[38] This phenomenon existed as a universal attribute among African Americans, Hackley insisted, as "every one of us has a magnet which attracts others for good or evil, and which is attracted by good or evil." To this assertion she added this aphorism: "A great deal of success in life comes from winning people through Personal Magnetism." As the New Thought concept of concentrated, positive thought existed in a mutually reciprocal relationship with telepathy, Hackley noted, "one attracts the kind of vibrations that one sends out.... The magnetic, energetic, hearty person brings [positive] things about because he projects a stronger vibration of [optimistic] thought, will power and personality."[39] In other words, and, as Hackley advised, "vibrate the things you desire to receive."[40]

Hackley also made references to *prana*, a Hindu concept and Sanskrit word for "life force" or "vital energy." New Thought philosopher William Walker Atkinson wrote of *prana* as existing everywhere, and the ability to engage in controlled and deep breathing enhanced the potential to inhale large quantities of this atmospheric essence. According to New Thought philosophers, through the practice of Yogic breathing techniques, an individual absorbs energy and nourishment from *prana* for the brain. Atkinson credited *prana* with contributing to an improvement in overall health and enhancing the ability to think positively and engage in mental concentration.[41] Hackley acknowledged the function of *prana* as "that precious unseen something . . . taken from fresh air" ultimately responsible for "generating vital force" and "personal electricity."[42]

Hackley informed her students and audiences of her belief in the central function of the solar plexus as an anatomical structure responsible for enhancing intelligence and brain function. Atkinson wrote of the solar plexus as "a most important part of the Nervous System, and that it is a form of brain. . . . It radiates strength and energy to all parts of the body, even the upper brain, depending largely upon it as a storehouse of Prana."[43] New Thought lecturer and author Elizabeth Towne also appreciated the power of the solar plexus as "another form of intelligent will." According to Towne, anyone who breathes correctly and deeply "appropriates intelligence" from the solar plexus.[44] Hackley concurred and likened the solar plexus to what she identified as "a second brain." She focused considerable attention on its primacy in breathing and singing and informed audiences that the solar plexus both stores and "calls forth energy and power when needed." Commenting on the role played by the solar plexus in the attainment of success, she happily observed that "there are many colored people who already know about the wonderful powers of the solar plexus [and] that [Yogic] deep breathing increases its influence."[45]

Hackley proposed to audience members that they energize psychic phenomena in order to bring about inner transformation and to combat external adversity. In addition to employment of telepathy, New Thought proponents also believed that thought could manifest itself as a visible or tangible presence. Thus, New Thought enthusiasts claimed that "thoughts are things" as all mental activity produced palpable vibrations and observable results.[46] Hackley often spoke of the results possible through thought force, such as the attainment of a fulfilling and abundant life and a sense of racial empowerment. Additionally, concentrated thought facilitated emotional balance, and Hackley encouraged all to "discipline themselves to gain self control over such habits as . . . inertia, anger" and other destructive and enervating attitudes.[47] This transformative process could only be initiated by exercising the strength of the will and of the mind, as summarized in her aphorism, "We may become whatever we WILL to become."[48]

As an advocate of mental healing, Hackley promoted the principle that concentrated thought could triumph over disease and emotional turmoil. She cautioned audiences that "impure thoughts, angry thoughts, unhappy thoughts, jealous thoughts, and cowardly thoughts will arrive, but they must be driven away. Health suffers from these thoughts." Negative mental states also contributed to systemic health problems, as "an organ may become exhausted from the rush of blood caused by impure thought." To stave off the pernicious effects of negative thinking, she encouraged each individual to "resist the temptation to scatter . . . [one's] vital forces"—a reference to the deleterious consequences of lapses in concentration on optimism. She lamented that "many have not learned the secret of preserving their bodies" through the application of positive thought force.[49]

Uplift Eugenics

During the late nineteenth and early twentieth centuries, the US eugenics movement ushered in the practice of enforced sterilization of disabled, addicted, and impoverished persons and those with genetically inherited conditions. Some applications of eugenics followed a blatantly racist agenda with the intention of greatly reducing or eliminating, altogether, certain minority populations. With an awareness of the atrocities committed in the implementation of eugenics and its practices, it becomes difficult to acknowledge the existence of any favorable results emanating from policies remotely resembling the control of heredity and reproduction. Although analyses of the reception and strategies of eugenics extend far beyond the present discussion, it should be admitted that contemporary views on heredity contradict, in some ways, historical public and scientific opinion and practices.

New Thought enthusiasts and racial uplift activists forged philosophical links with the eugenics movement. Since New Thought advocates of the early twentieth century approached all bodily functions, including reproduction, as extensions of mental powers, they considered certain eugenic principles as not only potentially advantageous but also readily attainable through the practice of thought concentration. In turn, racial uplift leaders explored the possible benefits of enlightened or positive eugenics, along with empowered pregnancy, birthing, and parenting. Drawing on her national prominence as an uplift activist and a pioneering New Thought leader, Hackley wrote and lectured about her views on reproduction, parenting, and controlled heredity.[50] Her views tend to correspond with those promoted by W. E. B. Du Bois. For Du Bois and his circle, the very existence of what he referred to as a "Talented Tenth" intrinsically related to the philosophy of uplift eugenics.[51] In one of his signature moments of elitist thinking, Du Bois recommended painstaking discernment when selecting someone to marry, as "a rising race must be aristocratic; the good cannot consort with the bad—nor even the best with the less good."[52] Hackley adopted a similar viewpoint on the issue of spouse selection, and she established a consideration of "fitness" as the ultimate criteria for choosing a potential parent. Accordingly, she recommended that each Black woman should "aim to marry a man mentally and physically fit to be the father of her children."[53] Du Bois consistently singled out members of the Talented Tenth as individuals who should be encouraged to have large families, as "the negroes must try to make the deserving and fit among them as numerous as possible."[54] He endorsed the preservation of the most desirable African-derived characteristics, and he urged the reproductively fittest of Blacks to "conserve" their "physical powers," "intellectual endowments," and "spiritual ideals" through prolific reproduction and responsible parenting.[55] Conversely, he recommended that an unfit strata of the Black population, identified by him as a "submerged tenth," should be discouraged from reproducing. He characterized members of this group as the "lowest class of criminals, prostitutes and loafers" and those "untrained" or "poorly educated."[56] Hackley also supported the component of uplift eugenicist philosophy that sought to limit the number of children among the submerged tenth. She leveled this complaint about irresponsible reproduction and parenting at men, saying that "an immoral, vile-tongued, untruthful or diseased father is a curse to the race."[57]

To demonstrate and disseminate, widely, the benefits of uplift eugenics, Du Bois and other African American leaders sponsored baby contests. These events established a means of identifying the salient characteristics of exceptional infants, by displaying babies endowed with an appealing appearance, vigor, robust health, and inquisitiveness.[58] During the 1910s and 1920s, Du Bois published popular special issues of the NAACP's *Crisis* magazine, each entitled *Children's Number*. These issues featured photographs of exemplary "prize" babies who had won NAACP-sponsored contests.[59] The *New York Age* also participated in the business of showing and evaluating babies, but with slightly altered goals. The judges at one such event downplayed physical appearance in favor of showcasing healthier infants. They impressed upon *Age* readers the "main idea of the contest" as, in actuality, "*better babies*, not beautiful babies [italics original]."[60] The organizers of another series of exhibitions, held in Washington, DC, emphasized healthy babyhood as a central requirement in the improvement of the African American population as a whole with the slogan "Better babies build a better race!"[61] Hackley subtly expressed confidence in the New Thought approach to uplift eugenics as, in her estimation, "the percentage of physical deformities in colored children is lessening."[62] With this comment, she also tacitly endorsed the practice of holding baby contests as these events brought to the attention of the white population the efforts of African Americans to subscribe to the ethics of responsible reproduction. Like many proponents of uplift eugenics, Hackley issued statements that left no doubt as to her sympathies, especially evident in her call for African Americans to "improve" their "racial stock."[63] To prospective mothers, she issued this memorable and, in her day, popular catchphrase: "The cry of the hour is a better breed of babies."[64] But such declamations only added to the already slippery slope for Hackley and other Black leaders as their opinions treaded precariously close, at times, to those held by racists who interpreted an interest in eugenics among African Americans as yet another confirmation of their belief in limiting or controlling reproduction among minorities.

By way of justifying uplift eugenics and prudent reproduction, Hackley offered a simple, if cryptic, explanation in which she aligned racial inheritance to plant propagation: "The colored race comes from several lines of white ancestry, and as fruit is grafted to a finer degree of species, so the colored race will some day show its latent powers."[65] On the surface, this statement reads as an unsettling valorization of white hereditary influences in the evolutionary and genetic history of African Americans. So, too, Hackley revealed her unapologetic allegiance to the colortocracy of the Talented Tenth, its membership consisting, predominantly, of racially mixed persons with lighter skin. But, in her reference to "several lines of white ancestry," she also obliquely identified the source of mixed-race persons in the United States—the sexual exploitation, rape, and impregnation of female enslaved people by white males. With her horticulturally inspired creation metaphor, she also attempted to disrupt the grip of binary racial designation of her day—that one was either Black or white—by recognizing the presence and significance of mixed-race heritage and persons. In this regard, we should also recall Du Bois's somewhat veiled reference to the possibility of a mixed-race heritage among ancient Egyptians: "It is still a mooted question among scientists as to just how far Egyptian civilization was Negro in its origin; if it was not wholly Negro, it was certainly very closely allied."[66]

Even as Hackley laid claim to the contributions, in African American genetic history, of a multiracial evolutionary process, she resolutely disapproved of racially mixed marriages, known in her day as "amalgamation" or "miscegenation." Arguably the most enthusiastic endorsement of interracial coupling among African American uplift eugenicists originated with Thomas Wyatt Turner (1877–1978), a professor at Tuskegee and Hampton Institutes and Howard University. Turner sought a middle ground in the debate surrounding controlled reproduction, as elucidated in his philosophy of "assimilationist eugenics." To further constructive interaction between the races, he supported mixed marriages as expressions of racial cooperation, especially as, in appearance, the children of such unions modeled an ultimate manifestation of assimilation, or race blending.[67] However much Turner and other scientists favored mixed marriage, the topic nonetheless became one of the most contentious components of uplift eugenics. The debate centered around whether or not interracial marriage should be promoted, tolerated, or even permitted. In many locations, this argument raised a moot question as sexual relations, marriage, and procreation between Blacks and whites were illegal. These laws not only sought to constrict reproductive autonomy among Blacks, but they also imposed a method for reducing, or eliminating altogether, the number of mixed-race babies. The very suggestion of interracial marriage agitated racists, who not only found the idea of intimacy between members of different races abhorrent, but they also expressed anxiety about the resultant increase in the population of African Americans with light skin. Such offspring, they feared, would be more difficult to identify as Black, and therefore such individuals could subvert efforts to enforce Jim Crow laws.[68] Certainly, Hackley's ability to ride in whites-only train cars confirmed that light-hued African Americans could and did bypass the rigid segregation rules maintained by the southern railroad industry.

Thus, interracial marriage and parenting loomed as a double-edged sword for African Americans. Blacks who opposed mixed-race reproduction did so because they feared attendant dilution of African-derived physical features. By extension, this loss of racial identity and purity could ultimately lead, ostensibly, to race suicide—a distant prospect, to be sure, but one that fueled debate about intermarriage. An impassioned statement on marriage between races, articulated by Rev. Alexander Crummell (1819–98), set the rhetorical standard for arguments in opposition to mixed marriages and parenting. Crummell, a venerated Episcopalian clergyman and race leader in Washington, DC, wrote of mixed-race marriage as tantamount to eventual extinction of Black Americans:

> Do the indications point to amalgamation or to absorption as the outcome of race-life in America? Are we to have the intermingling of our peoples into one common blood or the perpetuity of our diverse stocks, with abiding integrity of race, blood, and character? . . . The gross and violent intermingling of the blood of the southern white man cannot be taken as an index of the future of the black race. . . . The race-problem cannot be settled by extinction of race.[69]

Hackley sided with Crummell's opposition to marriage between Blacks and whites. In her advice regarding the selection of a spouse, she counseled each Black man to select, as a bride and as the mother of his future children, "a woman of his mother's race—a Colored Woman."[70] She remained committed to the preservation of African-derived physical features, and she did not espouse Turner's definition of, and aspiration for, assimilationist eugenics.

In contrast to other uplift eugenicists, Hackley infused her endorsement of discretionary procreation with New Thought principles. In her view, the responsibility of controlling heredity, and birthing and raising healthy children rested, substantially, with a mother's practice of mental concentration.[71] Additionally, and as an attendant obligation, a woman needed to exercise prudence when deciding who would father her children as a prospective father's thoughts could also affect heredity and prenatal development.[72] The quest for "better babies," Hackley explained, required that thought power be harnessed as the primary determining influence throughout a woman's pregnancy and a child's formative years. The importance of introducing New Thought to children could not be overstated, and she advised mothers that "colored children should be taught that Thought will improve their good points and will eradicate any objectionable points.... The colored mother should put success in the child's thoughts and teach it to believe in himself and his race. It is the duty of every mother to preach success."[73] She encouraged mothers to demonstrate to their children how to engage in New Thought practices at a young age, such as the ability to send and receive thought, to focus on the power of positive thinking and, most generally, to "think rightly."[74] She added a sense of urgency to the implementation of uplift eugenics and New Thought parenting, stating that "it is time for the colored race to look into these things and prepare for the future colored child."[75]

Although Hackley lectured and wrote about motherhood, she did not do so from experience as she had no children of her own. Nonetheless, she celebrated motherhood as the "privilege to carve the destiny of a race" and to "see lines of ancestry influenced and advanced by her [a mother's] thoughts." Hackley's reference to what she termed "child culture" not only reiterated a mother's responsibility to raise children appropriately by following New Thought principles but also to employ strategies and methods "unhampered by [undesirable] inherited mental or physical tendencies.... Through the exercise of will power she [a mother] may conquer inherited tendencies and even command nature."[76] For Hackley, the obligation to control thought in order to ensure a healthy baby began at conception. She believed that an expectant mother's thoughts influenced an unborn baby and hence profoundly affected its future:

As mental impressions are as active during the night as in the day, no prospective mother should carry unpleasant thoughts to bed. The sub-conscious mind receives the bad thought at bed time and acts all night under this influence. Its forces affect the same as [do] thoughts during the day.... Strong thoughts of disgust and hatred, if not controlled during the pre-natal period are liable to leave disastrous affects. The aim [of a pregnant woman] should be to train herself to change any thought which will create a physical disturbance.... Often the unborn child's little organism is flooded with shocks of passion and disturbed by nervous movements which cause unsound mind and body.[77]

The Inward Sculptor

Beyond safeguarding health and self-esteem, thought force also functioned as a "sculptor" of physical appearance, attractiveness, and conduct. New Thought followers borrowed the concept of a mental sculptor from US transcendentalist Henry David Thoreau, who wrote: "We are all sculptors and painters, and our material is our own flesh and blood. Any nobleness begins at once to refine a man's features and any meanness or sensuality to imbrute them."[78] In his adaptation of Thoreau, New Thought philosopher Henry Wood (1834–1909) offered this interpretation: "Thinking is an engraving-tool, and by its skillful wielding we project ideals into high relief.... I am a sculptor and thinking is my chisel."[79] Hackley referred to this application of concentrated thought as an "inward sculptor," described by her as follows:

> Real beauty is carved from within and the inward Sculptor is always at work. One may buy artificial teeth, hair and limbs, but no cosmetics or massage will cover up the ravages of [negative] Thought.... Every Thought leaves its imprint and every emotion leaves its manifestations.... Lines appear on the face as an index of interior troubles.... A little colored girl who wants to be pretty should be taught ... the power of the inward Sculptor, Thought, and its controlling and cultivating forces.... She may have everything in life that she wills, if she will only guide this inner workman.

Hackley also reminded audiences that "because people think, feel, and act, they leave marks of these in bodily lines and habits." The face, in particular, reflected the workings of one's inward sculptor and thus displayed a "bulletin board" of thoughts and emotions. Hackley reinforced the relationship between the inward sculptor and attractiveness with this epigram: "To be beautiful, one must fill her mind with beautiful thoughts."[80]

Hackley's assertion that one's face can be likened to a "bulletin board" reveals her familiarity with physiognomy, an ancient pseudo-science and diagnostic tool. Founded on the notion that physical characteristics correspond to one's mental state, physiognomists analyzed facial features, along with head, body, and behavioral attributes, as a means for evaluating personality and determining intellectual potential. Although Hackley expressed reservations about certain tenets of physiognomy, she agreed, in principle, with the premise that facial expression and posture communicated crucial information about mood and self-image: "Every face tells a tale and we read character from the physical form—the head, the backbone, the eye, the mouth, the chin, or hand. The uplifted eye, the corners of the mouth, the manner in which one eats or stands, in fact every movement has a special meaning, which may be easily read. The body is like a camera; it always tells the truth."[81] However, she disagreed, philosophically, with physiognomists who insisted that certain physical traits present at birth predetermined, incontrovertibly, an individual's eventual place in society's hierarchy. Such an interpretation not only deemed observable features to be immutable, but it also invariably linked African-derived facial characteristics, hair texture, and dark skin with low intelligence, immoral conduct, criminal behavior, and sloth. These spurious findings provided justification for the relentless degradation of Blacks as biologically and genetically inferior beings. Hackley sought to upend the deleterious influence of racist physiognomy by encouraging Blacks to take pride in the very traits denigrated by whites and to employ the New Thought strategies of telepathy and thought force to resist and deflect racist interpretations of these traits.

Hackley derived inspiration for one of her popular lectures, entitled "Racial Characteristics," from the biblical verse Jeremiah 13:23. The verse reads: "Can the Ethiopian change his skin or a leopard his spots? Then may ye also do good that are accustomed to do evil" (KJV). To endow this verse with more relevance to African Americans, Hackley offered her own version: "If one were to ask, 'Can a leopard change its spots,' the reply must always be 'No.' But if one were to ask if the Negro could change his appearance, through himself, his own will power, the answer would be, 'Yes,' because the Negro has a thinking brain. He may become as attractive as he wills to become."[82] Through mention of the Bible quotation's reference to "spots," she foregrounded the ability of African Americans to define their own standards of attractiveness and intellectual interests.

Many other references to Jeremiah 13:23 circulated in the early twentieth century. As these references received widespread press attention, they contributed, substantially, to contemporaneous discussions regarding racial identity and race relations. That Hackley knew of these references, as did her audiences, must be assumed. Arguably the most widely read appropriation of Jeremiah

13:23 appeared in the writings of Thomas Dixon, Jr. (1864–1946), a popular southern-born author, lecturer, lawyer, and ordained Baptist minister. Dixon derived thematic implications from Jeremiah 13:23 for his fiction debut, the virulently racist novel *The Leopard's Spots: A Romance of the White Man's Burden—1865–1900*.[83] An avowed and dogmatic physiognomist, Dixon offered an interpretation of Jeremiah 13:23 in which he summarized three themes central to his argument: first, African American "spots" always denoted biological and social inferiority; second, these features were unalterable; and third, African Americans could not be educated:

> The Ethiopian can not change his skin or the leopard his spots.... If a man really believes in equality, let him prove it by giving his daughter to a negro in marriage. That is the test. When she sinks with her mulatto children into the black abyss of Negroid life, then ask him! Your scheme of education is humbug. You don't believe that any amount of education can fit a negro to rule an Anglo-Saxon or marry his daughter.... Can you change the colour [sic] of his skin, the kink of his hair, the bulge of his lips, the spread of his nose, or the beat of his heart, with a spelling book? The Negro is the human donkey. You can train him, but you can't make of him a horse. Mate him with a horse and you will lose the horse and you get a larger donkey incapable of preserving his species. What is called our race problem is simply God's first law of nature—the instinct of self-preservation.[84]

Beyond his censure of racial intermarriage, Dixon refused to hold white males responsible for the prevalence of mixed-race individuals and instead laid blame on the supposedly uncontrollable sexual lasciviousness of Black females. Not surprisingly, his outrageous interpretation of Jeremiah 13:23 received considerable highly condemnatory attention from the Black press along with African American writers and activists.[85]

Hackley explored the implications of the biblically derived term "spots" in her lectures, many of which provided content for her only book-length publication, *Colored Girl Beautiful*. She commingled "spots" with the New Thought processes of the inward sculptor to assemble a response to racist interpretations of Jeremiah 13:23, such as those promulgated by Thomas Dixon and his following. She designated "spots" as "objectionable racial characteristics," that is, as subjects of unceasing ridicule by racist whites.[86] The list of characteristics Hackley cited as most often denigrated by whites included African-derived physical features along with certain conduct such as clownish antics and indolence. Admittedly, and in a most literal sense, her use and connotation of "objectionable racial characteristics" present a troubling reference to racist labeling and stereotyping while simultaneously seeming to privilege white expectations and standards of appearance and conduct. Yet, the readers of her published comments about spots and "objectionable racial characteristics" were the same people who may well have attended her lectures, so these words were not new to them. Nonetheless, she thought it her responsibility as an activist, armed with knowledge and experience gleaned from years of travel throughout the United States and overseas, to inform her audiences of the dangers inherent in continuing to ignore, or remaining apathetic to, the significance whites placed on the term "spots." Yet she also reasoned that if whites found African features deserving only of derision, then these were the very attributes Blacks needed to claim, proudly, as unique and their own.

Hackley's seeming allegiance to certain physiognomic principles and methods belies the fact she knew full well the limitations of such practices, especially as they failed to account for the facial features of African Americans who had attained success and leadership status. A brief perusal of images found in the vast catalogue of facial characteristics cluttering physiognomic publications of the early twentieth century reveals a total absence of analyses of African features as representative of appealing personality traits and intellectual attainment.[87] Furthermore, racist physiognomists, such as Thomas Dixon, considered facial features and their implications unchangeable, so much so that innate characteristics "trapped" a person at birth, literally and metaphorically, and thus their future must and would unfold accordingly.[88]

Hackley admonished audiences for tolerating, and engaging in, certain behaviors such as those associated with blackface minstrelsy, especially public displays of buffoonery. She also castigated those Blacks whose immoral conduct, chronic unemployment, and criminal activities fueled the unceasing diatribe of racist propaganda and opinion. As a conservative race leader, she feared that such conduct, if unabated, would excite racist vituperation, foment hostility, and greatly impede the progress of race advancement. Her stance echoed that of W. E. B. Du Bois who proposed: "The first and greatest step toward the settlement of the friction between the races—commonly called the Negro Problem—lies in the correction of the immorality, crime and laziness among the Negroes themselves, which still remains as a heritage from slavery.... [O]nly earnest and long continued efforts on our own part can cure these social ills."[89] During lectures on the subject of conduct and decorum, Hackley occasionally segued into what the press called her "strong sense of humor," sometimes embellished with hyperbole.[90] Her remarks in such instances drew criticism from journalist Sylvester Russell, who wrote: "Her disposition appeals to comedy; she has even been molded for *soubrette* [comic opera] work and that is why she delights to chew on the substance of vocal literature and other extremes which lead to commonplace humor and sarcasm of a kind which causes society to frown upon her eccentricities [italics original]."[91] Hackley even baldly warned audiences that indecorous behavior and idle gossiping could, potentially, "broaden" noses, cause lips to "hang" and "thicken," and "mouths to widen."[92] The very mention of distorted facial features in this context reads as a bizarre cautionary tale. By employing this rhetorical strategy in such instances, she appeared to act in a patronizing manner toward the Black masses. Still, however much she introduced humor into her talks, the potential of facial deformations, as described by her, would have proven momentarily unnerving to her audiences. A calculated risk to be sure, such a tactic may well have jolted her listeners out of a state of complacency, thereby increasing receptivity to her activist message. She evidently felt that audiences needed to be verbally prodded, occasionally, in this manner. An editor for the *Chicago Defender* agreed:

> Some of our worthy [journalistic and activist] brethren seem to have taken exception to parts of Madam Hackley's heart to heart talk[s].... There are always two ways of looking at things and the right way is to give every one the benefit of the doubt. We as a people need plain unvarnished things told to us, and especially when said by one of our own. The truth may hurt. No one really cares [wants] to be told of their shortcomings, but mistakes are only the stepping stones to success. Would there were more Madam Hackleys.[93]

Hackley insisted that Blacks needed to wrestle with "objectionable racial characteristics" themselves as whites could not be trusted to alter their denigrating associations of an African appearance and Black identity with inferiority. She asked of audiences, "Has the Negro any spots?" and responded by saying that "other people think so." Her solution to unremitting racist derision involved New Thought practices and the corrective and restorative capabilities of the inward sculptor: "If these so-called spots will interfere with his [an African American's] future success in life, then let him eradicate them with the Inward Sculptor—Thought."[94] Still, as Hackley cautioned, pride in African-derived racial characteristics also mandated an appropriate and unswerving commitment to the uplifting influences of education, moral conduct, and honest employment. In addition, the deflection of racist stereotypes required consistent individual attention to thought concentration as the paramount generative force behind the mechanism of one's inward sculptor. Such efforts did not entail purchasing skin and hair products purported to alter features inherited from African ancestors as such practices constituted a type of disguise and an expression of racial self-denial that Hackley vehemently discouraged.[95]

Hackley also addressed the imperative of quality education for all African Americans. She supported the establishment of separate institutions for general education and musical training for African Americans, but, unlike Booker T. Washington, she did not endorse or encourage appeals to white philanthropists for financial assistance. To fund her foreign scholarship program and her Normal Vocal Institute, she turned to Black communities and institutions, especially churches and civic organizations, for donations. Although she occasionally accepted complimentary attention from influential whites, she regarded the sentiments and intentions of the white US population as a whole with skepticism. At best, she reasoned, most whites remained ambivalent about the possibility of Black success with uplift initiatives; at worst, they resorted to racist violence and strict enforcement of Jim Crow laws to maintain dominance. In addition, and as demonstrated by the popularity of Dixon's novels, racists underscored their deep-seated prejudicial convictions with vicious propaganda in the press, literature, and film, and on stage. Thus, as Hackley exhorted audiences, each Black person bore an individual responsibility to achieve a personal sense of human wholeness. She considered such a quest to be a private mental process for each individual to undertake and one she deemed preferable to collective and overt political agitation or militancy.

Hackley counted on her audiences' ability to readily wend their way through her lectures and prose and sift out intended constructive and activist context. Listeners and readers familiar with her uplift agenda undoubtedly expected her to segue, occasionally, into sarcasm, heavy-handed humor, and hyperbole. However, she usually conveyed her message in a straightforward manner, without meandering or resorting to satire. She delivered just such a lecture in Washington, DC in 1912, as part of a performance reviewed by Lester A. Walton of the *New York Age*. In his review, Walton stated that Hackley's lecture "made a hit" with him "because it was full of optimism and taught the Negro to think something of himself." He continued, saying that "she believes that the racial characteristics we possess should be regarded as blessings and argues that the wide mouth, big nose and other strong physical characteristics with which we are marked should be turned to good purpose." To Walton, "her talks" were actually "far more beneficial than her singing" for racial uplift as through lectures "she inspires and kindles a flame of hope."[96] Even in moments of sarcasm, Hackley did not intend her remarks about "objectionable racial characteristics" to be interpreted as pejorative observations about African American racial heritage. Instead, she encouraged her audiences to take pride in their appearance and, more generally, in the uniqueness of their African ancestry and African American history. As one audience member recalled, "she told the Negro not to be ashamed of their mouths and noses."[97] The *Philadelphia Tribune* noted, of her popular lecture, "Racial Characteristics": "in a humorous manner she told her audience how to be a 'Somebody' and although she made them laugh, she also made them think, and in a pleasant manner brought home certain truths to them which they will not soon forget."[98] Of Black skin, Hackley wrote: "Is the dark skin a spot? Oh, no, it is his [an African American's] history, his strength, as was Samson's hair. Because of his color he has powers and forces which could get him anything he desires in life."[99]

In the face of the onslaught of racist propaganda proliferated by Dixon and his sympathizers, Hackley encouraged all Blacks, especially those who could pass for white, to remain steadfastly committed to an African American identity and to the cause of uplift. She lectured about the beauty of African-derived features and how pride in them contributed to race loyalty and a positive self-esteem. To charges of Black intellectual inferiority, she responded by harnessing the principles and vocabulary of New Thought. As a direct challenge to Dixon's denial of the benefits of education for Blacks, Hackley supported access to quality publicly funded schools for all African Americans. Of the relationship between education and the inward sculptor, she observed that "in examining the pictures of the graduates from the different schools, we find that Thought is changing the noses as well as the mouths."[100] In other words, the photograph of an educated African American presented an outward manifestation of an intellectually engaged individual whose facial expression radiated the positive effects of education along with attention to the workings of one's inward sculptor. She often used an image of Booker T. Washington to illustrate how his facial features reflected his accomplishments and success: "I like the mouth of Booker T. Washington. It has a stiff upper lip, [and] a determined, straight line between the lips. . . . The corners of his mouth go upward in hope and faith, not only faith and hope in the project [of establishing and sustaining Tuskegee] but faith in himself. He set his lips together and never thought of another thing but Tuskegee, and, of course, Tuskegee had to be."[101]

In a stinging rebuke of Dixon's writings and influence, printed in the Black press, a correspondent praised the influence of education on African American "spots": "Can a leopard change his spots?" the writer asked, and then replied: "Yes, yes he can. I have changed mine. I was ignorant, without ambition, and careless of both mind and soul. But I saw my danger and my need. I decided to be a man. I am a man, even if my color is black. I graduated from college. I have built a home. I have saved my money. I have a wife and little children. . . . Yes, sir, the leopard can change his spots!"[102] Hackley would have wholeheartedly endorsed this writer's assessment of the contributions of education in countering racist applications of physiognomy and negative connotations of "spots."

Give to Get

New Thought followers practice the reciprocal "Law of Giving and Receiving," a core principle derived from transcendentalist Ralph Waldo Emerson, who wrote: "Serve and thou shalt be served. If you serve men, you cannot, by any hiding or stratagem, escape the remuneration."[103] Hackley codified this tenet as "give to get" and, throughout her career, she spoke of the personal rewards attainable through charitable and philanthropic initiatives, and an abiding spirit of generosity. She advised:

> The first rule is "GIVE TO GET." . . . If one measures or doles out his services, he receives in like proportions. When one gives, he should receive "heaps" and "heaps" in return. The first habit then, to get, is [actually] the habit of "giving," and to persist in giving big efforts if big returns are expected. One should never be stingy. Stingy people grow less and less in efficiency and in every way because they lack "hope." . . . It has happened, during all of my life, that I have been "giving" (of myself) just because it gave pleasure to me. There was no plan but I have always noticed results. Favors, friendships and other things more valuable than money were showered upon me in proportion to the efforts which I had put out.[104]

For Hackley, as for New Thought followers, giving and receiving represented yet another means for achieving personal happiness and a positive self-image. "By helping others we help ourselves," she commented, and she urged that "we must learn to give, give, give, in order to receive."[105] She pursued a number of philanthropic and community projects intended, as she noted, "to help some race, charitable or church effort." Of the services and expertise she contributed to various causes, she emphasized the following: "I have taught individuals gratis; have organized musical societies, choruses, orchestras, gratis; have given operettas, musical dramas, cake sales for charity. I have also made new dresses and have made over old dresses for people. I have trimmed hats, dry cleaned clothes, gloves, and other articles for people, all gratis. Nothing has been too much trouble in order to show my interest and good will."[106] She formulated her most ambitious philanthropic project in 1907 during her first residency in Paris, when she announced the inauguration of her Foreign Scholarship Association. With the intent of facilitating overseas study for promising African Americans, she remarked, "I would like to be one of those to help some of the talented young musicians of the race 'to have a try at it.'"[107] In a letter to comedy duo Bert Williams and George Walker, she elaborated, "I have resolved to try to help a few of them by starting a musical scholarship. As I will be so busy the next two years, re-earning what I have spent abroad, I feared it would make the effort too tardy, if I waited until my return [to the United States] in the fall, and this is why I am starting it in Paris. Perhaps, if I can get enough people to pledge at once, I could offer the [first] scholarship to [violinist and composer] Mr. Clarence Cameron White late next fall, or early in the winter [of 1908]."[108] Hackley also raised funds for a second scholarship, awarded to composer and pianist Carl Rossini Diton, who eventually studied in Germany.[109] Prior to her return to Philadelphia, Hackley secured the assistance of several well-placed acquaintances who agreed to assist with the promotion of her scholarship project. Her friend Henry O. Tanner not only wholeheartedly supported this initiative but also agreed to serve as trustee for a fund to be held in a Paris bank for scholarship recipients.[110] Activist Ida B. Wells sponsored social gatherings at which she solicited scholarship contributions.[111] The respected journalist Noah D. Thompson agreed to handle correspondence and press notices for Hackley's organization. Hackley also raised money for scholarship recipients by performing a series of recitals at which she collected donations, sold autographed photos, or charged admission.[112]

Among the many supporters of her scholarship program, W. E. B. Du Bois and Atlanta's Rev. Henry Hugh Proctor applauded her initiative and assisted with fundraising. Proctor wrote letters to subscribers of Hackley's effort to request payment of donation pledges. In one such letter, he reminded Du Bois to submit his payment as promised:

> A letter from Mrs. E. Azalia Hackley is at hand. She asks that I help uphold Atlanta's fair name by reminding the subscribers to the fund for a "Foreign Scholarship" in Music that the money is now needed. Mr. Clarence C. White [Hackley's first scholarship recipient] sails [for Europe] in June [1908] and Mrs. Hackley wishes to hear from me by June 3rd or 4th. Will you, as a subscriber, kindly remit to me at once [the] amount of subscription [you pledged] that it may be accounted for and forwarded [to Henry O. Tanner in Paris].[113]

Du Bois devoted considerable space to Hackley's scholarship program in his annual report of racial uplift projects, published by the historically Black Atlanta University. He distinguished Hackley's Foreign Scholarship Association and its goals as "most remarkable" and offered this detailed assessment:

> Mrs. Hackley, who herself has an unusual voice and was trained abroad, said, in taking up her work in 1907: . . . "If we encourage our young people generally throughout the country, every five or six years some one of them will leap out of the circle of mediocrity and push his way to the front and perhaps represent us

musically as we have never been represented. If the colored musicians in each place would unite as enthusiastically as people do to start a new church, or establish a lodge, there could be some one helped each year. Who is doing anything for a colored genius? Well, of course, the race is comparatively poor, but there are some wealthy ones, and we could help a couple a year, at least, if we tried."

Thereupon, Mrs. Hackley established what she called the Foreign Scholarship, and induced two hundred or more colored people to contribute [money to fund] a scholarship of two or three hundred dollars a year. In the pursuance of this plan Mrs. Hackley has sent her first beneficiary abroad during 1908–09 in the person of Clarence C. White, a violinist of rare ability; the next beneficiary is to be Carl R. Diton; three hundred dollars to be raised for him. In her last report, Mrs. Hackley says: "In June I finished the last payment of the five hundred dollars I had promised to Mr. Clarence White, to assist him in his studies abroad for one year. Mr. White sailed for London in June 1908. It has been a difficult task to collect this amount, but it has been accomplished, and the scholarship establishes a precedent. I am highly gratified with all the results. If those who have contributed could understand how arduously Mr. White has worked, and how much he has improved in his playing, they would be as pleased as I am."[114]

In expression of appreciation to generous donors, Hackley wrote: "I am so grateful to all those who have believed in and helped this Scholarship Fund. I will always treasure the kind letters assuring me of loyal support."[115]

Hackley's espousal of New Thought principles set a precedent for the Harlem Renaissance era. Even as the press neglected to acknowledge her role in introducing New Thought to Black audiences, the movement nonetheless gained momentum among African Americans in the 1920s and beyond. Two New Thought leaders of the 1920s merit mention: Marcus Garvey and Rev. Garland Anderson. Garvey infused his unique philosophy of racial self-reliance with New Thought ideology, and he lectured and wrote of its singular utility for Blacks. During the late 1920s and continuing for a decade, Anderson, an ordained New Thought clergyman, lectured throughout the United States and in England, and he contributed to the already enormous catalogue of New Thought literature.[116] Although neither of these activists credited Hackley with pioneering the dissemination of New Thought tenets among Africa Americans, her philosophy resonates in their writings. More recent Black advocates of New Thought include Father Divine (Rev. Major Jealous Divine, 1876–1965), Rev. Johnnie Colemon (1920–2014), and Rev. Ike (Rev. Frederick J. Eikerenkoetter, II, 1935–2009). Cultural and literary historian Trysh Travis has added Oprah Winfrey to the list of prominent African Americans who find solace and empowerment in New Thought. As a celebrated media star, Winfrey engages her immense audiences in a racially defined hybrid faith interwoven with the New Thought practices of positive thinking and an incontrovertible belief in the righteousness of leading an abundant life.[117]

CHAPTER FOUR

Music Education and Racial Uplift

For an interview printed in the *Indianapolis Freeman,* Hackley reiterated her long-held conviction that "a solution of the race question" resided "in the depths of the throat where the musical notes are shaped."[1] She believed music making held forth the potential for more cordial interaction between races, as "everyone recognizes what singing does to break down color prejudice."[2] And, confident that music teaching and performance offered employment and income opportunities, she assured audiences that Blacks "could sing themselves to wealth, influence and to power."[3] These statements provide a glimpse of the philosophical underpinnings that energized Hackley's activist agenda, referred to by her as "musical social uplift" or, more simply, "musical uplift." To carry out her agenda, she traveled throughout the country, conducted community choruses, lectured, and taught singing techniques and music appreciation to large audiences. Newspapers welcomed her employment of music education as an activist vehicle and noted, for example, "in all this work Madam Hackley has kept steadily in mind the ultimate object of her effort, the broadening of the culture of her race . . . as a very real means of permanent and useful racial uplift."[4] Teaching, then, assumed a preeminent role at her public events, and a commitment to music education ultimately defined her public persona and professional activities. As her career evolved, she gradually reconfigured her concert events by reducing or eliminating altogether her own performances of classical repertoire and replacing these selections with lectures and music instruction. She later explained, in a letter to philanthropist George Foster Peabody: "As I sang, season after season, I could see that no community was materially benefitted by my singing. . . . I was a petted singer, . . . and when I came off my little pedestal, . . . I decided to give the best years of my life to my race for their musical uplift."[5] The press announced, appropriately, "Madame Hackley prefers to be known from now on as a musical missionary."[6]

Voice Culture

Hackley's unique style of teaching, whether in private lessons, small classes, or large audiences, drew considerable press attention. With evident esteem and enthusiasm, the Black press described how, through an ingenious "series of exceedingly interesting demonstrations," she taught audiences to appreciate and learn the rudiments of formal singing technique.[7] Quite aware of the singularity of her teaching goals, she expressed regret that "few or none of our artists have devoted any of their time or knowledge to the masses of our people to uplift them musically."[8] The *Indianapolis Freeman* lauded Hackley for accomplishing "more than any other colored woman to advance among her own people the art of singing."[9] Another newspaper appointed Hackley "the authority of the race" in all matters related to music education.[10] Of the inspiration for her pedagogy, she wrote: "Our people require fresh, new ideas in cultivating musical soil." She later explained why she developed a new method of music instruction specifically for African Americans:

> The race needs something much more than all it has had that we may educate the future fathers and mothers that may play and sing, as examples to the coming generations. A singing or playing parent is very likely to create a singing or playing child.... A race may only be advanced through competent teachers who have a definite end in mind. The race has now reached the place where it needs some standardized musical plan.... We need a school vocal music [text]book,... a standardized short, simple method of voice culture and light [music] reading combined.[11]

However unique, Hackley's instructional philosophy and methods nonetheless followed some of the principles associated with "voice culture," a common descriptive term for the teaching of singing in her day. Yet, unlike most music teachers, Hackley did not envision voice culture as applicable only to the more talented students of singing. Rather, she set out "to prove the value of voice culture to the masses."[12] In the nineteenth and early twentieth centuries, voice culture pedagogy encompassed the study of vocal production with due attention to such ancillary considerations as diction, elocution, oratory, breathing, and posture. Most teachers of voice culture also required students to become familiar with what pedagogue David Clark Taylor called "the operation of the voice" through the study of "the sciences of anatomy, mechanics, acoustics [and] psychology."[13] Hackley was first introduced to this traditional interpretation and application of voice culture at the University of Denver, where she majored in voice performance and music education. While at the university, she studied singing with George F. Brierley, whose teaching philosophy embraced strategies "plain and yet scientific, enabling pupils to understand every principle of the vocal art, and giving them possession of a method which preserves and beautifies the voice, removing all wrong vocal effort and developing nature's form, giving ease and comfort in the use of the voice."[14] Hackley's studies in the more technical aspects of singing under Brierley's guidance encompassed these areas of concentration:

> The study of [the] union of [vocal] registers; study of the physiology of vowels and consonants; study of solfeggio and application of words to music; exercises for obtaining agility and flexibility of voice; thorough exercises in scales, major and minor; the chromatic scales and arpeggios; study of the movements and embellishments suited to the different styles of singing; study of English, German and Italian songs; [and] preparation for the concert, opera and oratorio [stage].[15]

Yet, few teachers of voice culture could agree on even the basic principles of singing instruction, and hence many practitioners and students came to deplore the loosely defined state of the discipline's philosophy, characterized by pedagogue Henry Holbrook Curtis as "a tangled skein of theories."[16] To complicate the situation even further, some 150 voice-culture method books were published between 1880 and 1920.[17] When Hackley began teaching singing technique, she encountered a veritable battlefield of voice culturalists quite ready and willing to besmirch each other's reputations at the slightest provocation or hint of competition. As Edmund Shaftsbury reluctantly admitted, "it is the delight of professional elocutionists and voice trainers to ridicule the theories of everybody excepting the particular one which they advocate. . . . The holy attitude of horror assumed by some teachers . . . at the erroneous methods of others is quite impressive."[18] Fallacious claims and arguments abounded in the world of teachers of singing, thus creating the pedagogical and philosophical morass in which Hackley found herself. Moreover, a surprisingly large number of singers advertised their services as teachers of voice culture without appropriate training in healthy pedagogical strategies. For, as *Etude* magazine columnist J. Harry Wheeler summarized, "In no department in the curriculum of musical instruction are found so many imposters and ignorant teachers as in that of voice-culture."[19] Voice teacher Lutie A. Gunn concurred and added that "one hardly knows where to go to secure safe instruction" as too many teachers remained insensitive to the reality that "the vocal cords are the most delicate of all musical instruments." Gunn warned that lessons with an incompetent teacher could cause a potentially promising voice "to become greatly impaired, bad habits formed, and prospects ruined beyond repair."[20] J. Harry Wheeler extended this argument and cautioned aspiring singers that "an ignorant teacher not only fails to improve the voice, but often ruins it, and also the health of the pupil."

For activist purposes, Hackley favored a more transparent approach to singing instruction than what she encountered at the University of Denver. In her instructional booklet, *Guide in Voice Culture*, she summarized a philosophical standpoint that clearly embraced accessibility and avoided harmful methods:

> This "Guide" is neither a scientific nor a literary treatise. Its sole purpose is to be *helpful*, in a *tangible* way. It has been compiled from talks given to classes. It is designed to help those who have not the means to study, [and] those who have studied and would like to teach, but do not know how to impart their knowledge.... There is nothing in this "Guide" which can confuse, or harm [one's vocal anatomy]. Special voices need, of course, special training, . . . but the "foundation work" is about the same for all voices, and after the pupils have gained some control over their *breathing apparatus*, . . . the shaping and polishing [of the voice] can begin [italics original].[21]

Hackley rightly sensed students' intimidation when faced with the seemingly daunting task of learning to sing in a more formal, cultivated style, especially if such an endeavor required the memorization of anatomical vocabulary and attendant functions. From the myriad of techniques associated with opera and the concert stage she spent years perfecting, she isolated only the most fundamental skills and transformed these into simple exercises. In this way, she eliminated the anatomical and subjective references that characterized private lessons with many voice teachers. Her emphasis on approachable "foundation work" nonetheless mandated diligent attention to what she referred to as the "three requisites" for achieving competence as a singer: "the first is brains, the second, breath, and the third, voice."[22]

Hackley set rigorous standards for private students, and she informed them that self-discipline and a strong work ethic were essential in the successful study of singing. To these requirements she added: "I can never make you a great singer without an education.... To interpret the great songs, a singer needs imagination and ideality and discrimination as well as other mental equipment."[23] She required students to read about music history and learn to appreciate appropriate instructional and performance repertoire. To both music teachers and performers, she recommended the study of the fine arts in general, with a focus on "the great paintings and works of art, and lives of great composers." She considered the ability to read music as a necessary skill, and she expected students to be capable of, and amenable to, memorizing their music. Yet, in spite of the exacting standards she set for prospective students, Hackley remained conscious of the fundamental fact that she needed to convince aspiring singers that they did, in fact, possess the potential for success under her tutelage. As part of her strategy, she identified specific African American physical features she deemed particularly advantageous for singers. She routinely reminded students and audiences of the African-derived characteristics that enhanced vocal production, such as "a large mouth with a high roof and large, fine, hard teeth, . . . a large nose with big nostrils, . . . a large post-nasal cavity, . . . and wide bony [facial] formation." In her dissemination of the New Thought practice of positive thinking, she encouraged her students' feelings of self-worth, evidence of which she looked for in facial expression and posture.[24] She approached correct, deep breathing not only as an integral component of singing but, and of equal importance, also as a New Thought strategy for achieving mental acuity and overall physical wellness. In a conversation with Cary B. Lewis of the *Indianapolis Freeman*, she noted that "the effort of concentration in deep breathing while singing is helpful in forming correct habits along other lines." She assured students that the study of music not only would benefit their "mental and moral outlook," but also "physical health will be improved under action of deep breathing and the power of song."[25] Deep breathing also assumed activist significance for Hackley: "The practice of deep breathing is invaluable in the matter of resistance," particularly against the ravages of racism. As she insisted, "deep breathers are seldom mentally weak because deep breathing develops Will power [and] . . . Personal Magnetism."[26] Still, she occasionally expressed frustration with some students who did not always respect their innate vocal gifts, and she warned against abuse of the voice by "screeching or yelling."[27] She also criticized female students who wore confining garments, such as corsets, as their "tight lacing" contributed to poor breath control and compromised vocal production.[28]

Hackley derived her instructional strategies for teaching breath control from "old East Indian breathing exercises" introduced to her by Yoga mystics with whom she associated during her London residency.[29] She began lessons in Yogic breathing by telling students to assume a comfortable standing position in which they could maintain erect posture for an extended period of time.[30] To help singers learn to inhale quickly and deeply, she developed accessible preliminary warm-up exercises. She selected yawning—a motion familiar to all students—as the introductory lesson in a series of uncomplicated activities. By yawning with a relaxed jaw, students could inhale rapidly or "gasp" and thus actually experience an appropriately open throat. Efficient breathing also required what she called "correct interior [internal] conditions," the presence of which could be ascertained by sensing a corresponding fullness in one's chest and abdomen. Hackley informed students that if executed correctly, her yawning exercises also engaged the "muscles around the waist, in the back, and at the joining of the upper arms and front of the shoulders." She described "the whole secret" to attaining this desired physical phenomenon as tantamount to "being excited by a surprise, or a start or a gasp" and then "holding the muscles [in a] contracted [position] long enough to feel a 'hollowing out' sensation." In other words, to vocalize correctly, a singer needed to strive for utmost relaxation in the jaw and throat while making rigorous demands of the torso muscles.[31]

The next phase of Hackley's instructional sequence, after successful completion of yawning and breathing exercises, consisted, not surprisingly, of vocalizing. Starting with the syllable "ah," she coached students to sing long tones in a descending chromatic pattern and then to progress to arpeggios. She accompanied students on the piano as they worked through these exercises. Careful attention to matching pitches with the piano also served as a remedy for sliding or slurring up or down to the desired note—something she considered "a bad habit not to be tolerated." Hence, even when working with large groups, she impressed upon all present the importance of being aware of correct intonation. She approached this fundamental concept kinesthetically, by encouraging students to ascertain whether or not their jaws, throats, and abdominal muscles were appropriately positioned and engaged to produce an in-tune note.[32]

Hackley devoted considerable instructional time to the role of the diaphragm in singing—a strategy common in voice lessons. To teach students about the diaphragm, she developed her own anatomical vocabulary and referred to the diaphragm as a person's "electric dynamo." As she elaborated, in New Thought terms, "down in our bodies each of us has an electric dynamo which sends out, or may be taught to send out, currents or waves of electricity."[33] The activation of this anatomical "dynamo" required a singer to learn the location and function of the solar plexus, or what Hackley called the "electric button." The process of accessing one's "electric button," she explained, could only occur "when the diaphragm dome is depressed or contracted, [and] the air rushing in pushes against the soft spot [electric button] under the chest bone." When a singer activated their solar plexus, the resultant "electric line" connected the internal participants in the breathing process via a "current" that rose from its origin in the diaphragm and then communicated with the throat and vocal cords.[34] To assist singers as they learned how to engage the diaphragm and solar plexus, she recommended the following sequence of exercises which could be practiced at home:

1. Practice ten "gasps" with mouth open, shoulders down, and swelling out all around the waist, fixing the mind's eye on the "electric button." Hold as long as possible.
2. Practice ten "gasps" fixing the mind's eye on the "dimpling" of the muscles of the back. Shoulders down. Hold as long as possible with mouth open as in a yawn.
3. Practice ten "gasps" closing the mouth as if saying "oo."
4. Begin on middle G and exercise [vocalize] down to middle C. Get the electric button ready and then sing "oo" right on the "button" as if you were a ventriloquist. Do you feel the "hollowness?"
5. Select words of two, three and four syllables and string these [words together] on the electric button. Keep sounding "oo" before and after each word to prove [confirm] the complete hollowness and looseness of the throat, tongue and lips.
6. Recite poems or hymns in the same way until you obtain perfect control over the breathing muscle.[35]

Physical culture, a late nineteenth-century approach to fitness and strength training, also assumed a role in Hackley's teaching. She envisioned deep breathing, singing, and physical culture as completely inseparable. When executed correctly, her warm-up exercises produced an awareness of the sheer physicality of singing.[36] In fact, she intended her exercises to engage the entire upper body, as did physical culture.[37] When her students spoke of fatigue after lessons, she responded, "Ah! Yes, the muscles ache. If you were using [lifting] dumbbells [weights] or performing any simple exercise in calisthenics they would ache also."[38] Some students expressed disbelief and amazement at the exertion required to sing correctly, stating, "I never knew voice culture was like that." To such comments Hackley replied, "Well it is. It is physical culture."[39] One of Hackley's students, Zelma W. George, studied voice culture with her as a girl and later recalled the very physical nature of the exercises through which Hackley guided her. George also alluded to the comprehensive approach of Hackley's teaching strategies and added: "Madame Hackley . . . would teach you to sing scales, enunciate, breathe correctly, sing softly as well as loudly and she would demonstrate all this! She was, oh, she was great for me at the time. And I was really young then."[40]

Community Music

Hackley's method of teaching large groups of students owed a debt to her London teacher, William Shakespeare, and his work with audiences. As described by journalist and critic Herbert W. Greene, Shakespeare taught the fundamentals of singing at his concert events when he toured the United States in the early twentieth century. Greene noted of Shakespeare's pedagogy that "his platform [stage] has been a piano stool; his auditorium a studio; his audience a pupil."[41] This same philosophy and strategy also typified much of Hackley's teaching career as she, too, occupied a piano bench while she taught large audiences of aspiring singers. As Atlanta journalist Louise Dooly described Hackley's methodology, "a piano was her first aid, and seated or standing, she used it with equal ease, although in most of the songs merely to provide the pitch."[42]

In her work with audiences, Hackley became a celebrated and tireless leader in the community music movement that spread coast to coast in the early years of the twentieth century. Influential pedagogue Peter Dykema (1871–1951), an important advocate of community music making, encouraged the organization of amateur choruses designed to enhance the appreciation of singing among the general population. As this movement gained momentum, it actually succeeded in "democratizing" music, that is, making music performance accessible and available to all citizens, regardless of musical aptitude.[43] Another provocative endorsement of community music and choruses came from composer Arthur Farwell, who articulated the philosophy to which Hackley adhered when she taught audiences to sing. Of the incalculable value of community choruses, Farwell wrote,

> All the inspiration and exaltation that the individual artist [such as Hackley] had alone will now suffuse the whole community.... When the community becomes the artist, every individual becomes a *part of a mighty artist*. Each does that part of the art work which he can, the whole can be perfect only by his doing his share, however little that may be.... The little talents of individuals, bound together in one common effort, make the genius of the people.... [E]very community, no matter how remote or obscure, is rich in unsuspected ability and talent of innumerable sorts.... And I have not failed to notice the happiness which is given them to find that they could do so, and especially to find that they were forming an indispensable part [of the effort],... such as they had never before dreamed of [italics original].[44]

On a theoretical level, the community music movement's philosophy of amateur choral singing held forth great appeal for Hackley. Under her direction, a community chorus became a totally welcoming ensemble, free of competition, elitism and hierarchy: "A community chorus is not a singing society.... It is absolutely democratic. It includes all who want to come together for the joy of singing without [a] *voice trial* [an audition] and *without [membership] dues* [italics original]."⁴⁵ However, as most white conductors of community choruses tended to ignore the musical aspirations and talents of African Americans, Hackley promoted her own events. Accordingly, she remarked that "the white community [music] directors are simply afraid to give a cordial invitation to the Negro—who is the singer of them all, either individually or with chorus representation. . . . [Therefore] colored community choruses must be organized. . . . If they [community choruses] are good for the whites, they are good for us."⁴⁶ She emphasized the need for self-reliance in the effort to spread the growth of choruses as "each [Black] community must advance itself through its own [musical] efforts."⁴⁷ Hackley also acknowledged the prevalence of gender bias in the world of conducting: "There are very few female chorus conductors among the musicians of our race, but those who occupy this unique position are as capable as men."⁴⁸ Even as she became an innovative proponent of community music making, her priorities and programming decisions reflected the more specialized needs and interests of African Americans. Specifically, she harnessed music teaching and learning to disseminate and implement racial uplift rhetoric and ideology. Her approach to community music events placed more emphasis on instruction as, owing to racist budgetary inequities, most schools in Black communities could not afford to offer music classes.

Hackley attended the National Conference on Community Music, held in 1917 in New York City, representing Chicago's Black musicians. The lack of a Black presence at this gathering disappointed her as she was one of only two African American delegates in attendance. At this meeting she made the acquaintance of many influential community music specialists including Arthur Farwell and Peter Dykema. The many presentations, lectures, and concerts she witnessed invigorated her own commitment to the community music movement. She later wrote: "The community [music] movement is sweeping the country. Hundreds of community choruses are forming everywhere. Everywhere the people of all kinds and conditions are coming together to express themselves in song. Why and why now? . . . Because, in song, differences are forgotten and the spirit which all people show in common comes forth as a creative power for the shaping of the community and the nation."⁴⁹

Hackley strove to make her musical uplift events entertaining and fulfilling, saying that "it has been . . . oh so satisfying to leave the colored people proud and happy."⁵⁰ Throughout her career, she promoted music as the ultimate mode of cultural expression among African Americans and music education as a powerful agency of uplift and activism. Music also reinforced community and family solidarity and helped Blacks achieve and nurture a sense of self-worth.⁵¹ Owing to her preference for working with large groups of students, she became famous as "the vocal teacher of ten thousand."⁵² As she explained,

"I started out to educate 12,000,000 colored people," the approximate number of African Americans during the 1910s.[53] She often organized events in expansive venues, with participants sometimes numbering in the thousands; her audiences became large classes of students. In accounting for her famous sobriquet as a teacher of thousands, journalist Cary Lewis observed that in 1911 alone, "she visited seventy-five colleges and schools for colored youth in various parts of the country."[54] Another journalist offered this glimpse of her frenetic schedule:

> During the past year [1912] Madame Hackley has taught voice culture to over sixty thousand colored people. For instance, in Norfolk [Virginia] the other day, direct from an all-night trip from Danville [Illinois, she went] to one school at 9 a.m. and [then to] three others [that day and taught] until 3 p.m.; she instructed over 1,600 children. . . . In one day in Chattanooga [Tennessee] she taught as many as 3,000, going directly from a train and giving lessons in five schools. . . . In Wilmington, N.C., over 1,600 were reached [taught by her] in one day. . . . In Augusta, Ga. [she taught at] three colleges [and] two large schools . . . instructing over 2,000 in one day.[55]

By 1914, Hackley claimed to have taught singing to large groups at over 500 African American schools.[56]

Hackley's method of organizing events drew upon the very fiber and essence of African American communities and their institutions, especially newspapers, churches, civic associations, and schools. As journalist Eloise Bibb Thompson reported, when Hackley "enters a town for a professional engagement, she visits every school for the purpose of giving half hour to hour lessons to the students" and to excite enthusiasm for future community projects.[57] Hackley anticipated her arrival with announcements placed in local papers and then visited churches and schools to recruit singers and teach classes.[58] Of a particularly arduous recruiting effort, she described to George Foster Peabody how she had endured "piping hot air" to give lengthy presentations at "five crowded churches" in one day, informing attendees of her plans to organize community choruses.[59] She also coordinated publicity and supervised the printing of programs and promotional materials. In this way she maximized her relationship with local Black businesses and thus enhanced advertising opportunities and ticket sales.[60]

The press showered Hackley with glowing reviews of her choral performances and community music events. For example, the *Afro-American Ledger* declared her "without peer as a director of large choruses."[61] Another accolade came

Fig. 4.1. E. Azalia Hackley with her Harlem Chorus. Hackley is seated in the front row, fifth from the left. *Musical America* 26 (December 1917): 13. Courtesy, Kelvin Smith Library, Case Western Reserve University, Cleveland, Ohio.

from Lucien H. White, an arts critic for the *New York Age*, who distinguished Hackley as "the one person to whom the most credit should be given" for the promotion of African American community music making. White further remarked, "there was no one who took up the work of going into the different cities of the United States—north, east, west and south—organizing the people of the communities into choral bodies for the purpose of singing . . . until Mme. Hackley came along and gave unstintingly of her time and money to that effort."[62] Hackley approached community events as uplift initiatives with multigenerational potential and significance. As one journalist confirmed, "the members of her 'classes' often ranged from 3 to 70 years of age."[63] On her success in this regard, she noted, "The children that I taught . . . ten or more years ago have grown to manhood and womanhood, and many to fatherhood and motherhood, and my following has increased threefold. One must always calculate on the future and aim to secure his following."[64] Even a few white community music leaders applauded Hackley's extraordinary skill as a conductor and producer. For example, John C. Freund, the founding editor of the popular periodical *Musical America* admired her determination, artistry, and ingenuity. In an address he gave at a performance of the Harlem Chorus (figure 4.1), founded and conducted by Hackley, he praised her "splendid efforts . . . to bring music back to its own place in the lives of the people."[65]

Normal Vocal Institute

In 1912 Hackley announced plans to establish a normal institute in Chicago, primarily for training music teachers, but also for the purpose of offering free or reasonably priced music instruction for all of Black Chicago. Sources differ as to exactly when she officially opened her Normal Vocal Institute, but the year of its inauguration was probably 1915. Most likely, it was the second community music school in the country established exclusively for Black students and the first founded by an African American.[66] Not long before the Normal Vocal Institute began operations, David Mannes and Natalie Curtis Burlin had already established the Music School Settlement for Colored People, in New York City, and appointed composer J. Rosamond Johnson, Hackley's friend, as principal. Johnson's famous brother, James Weldon Johnson, suggested to Hackley that she give strong consideration to relocating to New York to work with J. R. Johnson at the Music School Settlement rather than opening her own institution.[67] To be sure, Hackley's institute did not altogether duplicate the services and instruction offered at the Music School Settlement as she offered voice culture and teacher training, whereas Mannes and Burlin provided private lessons and classes for instrumentalists and singers but no instruction in pedagogy for prospective teachers.

To house her school, Hackley acquired an expansive brick building in Chicago.[68] She proposed to enroll only those students who had earned a high school diploma or its equivalent and could demonstrate some proficiency on piano.[69] In addition to teacher training, the Normal Vocal Institute offered instruction in piano, music theory, singing technique, deep breathing, and foreign-language diction. Hackley charged students a membership fee of twenty-five cents per week rather than tuition, yet voice culture classes were free. If students could afford to pay, they were also assessed an additional five cents per week to help offset expenses for the building's heat, water, and electricity. She asked students of limited means who could not afford fees to volunteer their time cleaning the building and assisting with general upkeep of the grounds. The fee requirements drew some negative publicity, but she assured Chicago's Black residents that she did not operate the institute as a money-making venture and instead intended her school to serve as a provider of an essential community service.[70]

Initially, Hackley experienced success with her institute and attracted a sufficient number of students. The school depended, especially, on an increase in enrollment during the summer months when teachers who wanted to study music pedagogy and take private or class lessons had time off from their academic-year duties. In a letter to James Weldon Johnson, Hackley expressed satisfaction with early enrollment numbers and referred to her school affectionately as "a dear."⁷¹ Owing to her continuing schedule of performances and extensive travel, she needed assistants and she appointed local musicians Pauline James Lee, Helen Abbott Sayres, and Delia Martin Waring to teach in her absence. Her sister, Marietta, fulfilled administrative and budgetary responsibilities.⁷² To meet mortgage payments and to fund the institute's scholarships, Hackley used donations, lecture and performance fees, money raised from sales of photographs and pamphlets, and she also taught private lessons at two dollars apiece. Proceeds from sales of the illustrated booklet about Hackley written by her friend Marie A. D. Madre also helped defray expenses.⁷³ Unfortunately, financial problems and Hackley's frequent absences soon took their toll on the institute. During the summer of 1918, budgetary shortfalls forced its temporary closing.⁷⁴ By 1919 Hackley's health had deteriorated, compelling her to suspend the school's operation permanently and sell off the property.⁷⁵ The *Broad Ax* also blamed Chicago's Blacks for the closing of Hackley's school, claiming they "utterly failed to rally to her support."⁷⁶

Teaching Repertoire

In her *Guide in Voice Culture*, Hackley included three examples of popular songs she deemed appropriate for students: "The Last Rose of Summer," "Comin' Thro' the Rye," and Stephen Foster's "Old Folks at Home" (often called "Swanee River" or "Suwanee River"). She provided the lyrics and notated melodies of these songs, but no piano accompaniments. Her rudimentary instructions for practicing these songs addressed breathing technique, some hints about diction, and reminders to spend extra time on the wider, more challenging melodic intervals. Admittedly, her inclusion of Foster's "Old Folks at Home" raises concerns owing to a line of its lyrics—"still longing for the old plantation"—and use of the pejorative word "darkies." By way of explanation for including this song in her instruction booklet, Hackley wrote that "each teacher has his pet song or exercise" and that this song was "so familiar, a pupil can gain a quicker idea of what is expected from him."⁷⁷ As offensive as Foster's lyrics seem today, it is important to remember that this song remained enormously popular among African Americans in the late nineteenth century and well into the twentieth. Several famous Black performers routinely programmed this song, notably bass Paul Robeson, sopranos Sissieretta Jones and Elizabeth Taylor Greenfield, the Hyers Sister of musical theater fame, and the Fisk Jubilee Singers. A review of a concert by Marian Anderson at which she programmed "Old Folks at Home" confirms the enduring popularity of Foster's song. For the finale of a recital in Jackson, Mississippi, on 20 October 1941, she invited all present to join her in singing "Old Folks at Home." The press described the unexpected and amazing response to Anderson's request: "Fully three thousand persons lifted their voices and almost lifted the steel rafters. . . . It was a thrill that will long be remembered. . . . [S]uch a thing had never happened before [and] . . . it had been a great spiritual experience for everyone to rise so far above his prejudices."[78]

The meager offerings of teaching repertoire in *Guide in Voice Culture* notwithstanding, Hackley strove to provide students with as many compositions written or arranged by African Americans as possible. However, she found it difficult to obtain copies of these pieces owing to publishers' discriminatory practices:

> It has come to my notice that several . . . really ambitious compositions might have been given [performed before] the public but for the obtuseness of some of the leading publishers of the day who . . . shy [away from] anything savoring of the classics from colored composers. These publishers do not realize that we have a race of ten million musically loyal people with money in their pockets, and yearning to be educated in a higher class of music. . . . I am convinced that if [Anglo-African composer Samuel] Coleridge-Taylor had lived in America, much of his music would never have been published.[79]

Nonetheless, a few African American composers of classical genres succeeded in securing publishers for their works. Acclaimed baritone soloist and composer Harry T. Burleigh, with more than 200 vocal works to his credit, acquired the services of the Italian firm Ricordi for many of his pieces. Hackley praised Burleigh as a gifted composer of "the really good songs of the day, . . . enjoying popularity among the best singers." She often programmed Burleigh's compositions for voice and used them as teaching repertoire. In addition, she recommended "the folk song harmonizations of Mr. [R. Nathaniel] Dett and Mr. [Carl Rossini] Diton" for aspiring singers and seasoned artists alike.[80] Because classical song literature written by Black composers had yet to receive widespread publication, Hackley assigned her more advanced students selections found in Henry Krehbiel's *Famous Songs*, a collection of some fifty art songs by famous and lesser known composers.[81] Hackley considered all the songs in this anthology to be "standard classics which every singer ought to know." Krehbiel included a few English-language pieces in his collection, but most of his selections represented Italian, French, and German composers, their original lyrics supplemented with English translations.[82] Hackley required her private students to memorize this repertoire, a traditional practice among voice teachers. To learn classical solo literature, especially pieces with non-English texts, she advised students to vocalize melodies on a syllable such as "ah," and to work on intervals and rhythm separately, before attempting to sing a song through with its lyrics. To commit lyrics to memory, she suggested writing out words and learning them "as you ride in the street car or walk along the street. Place a copy [of them] in [the frame of] your [dresser] mirror, or pin a copy near your work. Write and rewrite the words many times, if necessary." For additional information about solo song repertoire, she recommended that students obtain copies of music magazines, especially "*Etude* and *Musician*, and read all you can."[83] Finally, she urged her students to "go to hear the great singers in concert programs." Such events could become learning experiences, Hackley advised, if students acquired copies of the music to be performed and made notations in the scores during the recital.[84]

African American spirituals, or what Hackley referred to as "folk songs," comprised a substantial portion of her instructional and performance repertoire. She considered this genre and its attendant interpretive practices as crucial for the enrichment of race pride. As she commented, "to get the most out of their lives," Blacks "must be made to know, appreciate, and sing their own song, a song that has come from the soul of a toiling, hopeful people—an extract of their jubilation, their apprehensions, and their achievements."[85] As teaching pieces, spirituals promised "a revelation to the colored singers themselves," she stated, as, by learning these songs, aspiring singers could most readily "realize their vocal powers." She routinely taught spirituals at schools, "so that children may hear and love them," and come to recognize "the difference between these original songs and those sung by [blackface] minstrels."[86] Beyond her goal of cultivating an appreciation for spirituals, she also carefully outlined specific requirements for their authentic performance. She singled out the presence of "charged vocal current" as a component of voice production she considered unique to African Americans and one absolutely essential to the performance of spirituals. As she did not think white singers possessed the requisite technique, vocal timbre, and anatomy to sing spirituals effectively, she cautioned them to avoid this repertoire. "Unless the vocal cords are strong, the large tone, the enthusiasm and abandon [demanded of these songs] will exhaust many [white] singers. The Negroes sang these songs from their hearts. Unless [white] soloists also sing them from 'the heart' they fail to satisfy audiences."[87] For Hackley, the word "abandon" accurately described a level of spontaneity and improvisation that characterized the cultural expressiveness of African Americans. She specified the vocal qualities necessary for effective performance of spirituals, including the possession of innately resilient vocal cords, the power and flexibility of which could produce exceptional richness and volume.

Hackley's interpretation of spirituals mandated, exclusively, African American cultural practices and unswerving dedication to the preservation of an historical and collective consciousness. These requirements can be appreciated as follows: First, in the early twentieth century, Blacks were still temporally close to the institution of slavery, so close, in fact, that the ability to accurately reproduce the performance practices associated with the time period of these songs' origin remained indelibly imprinted in African American cultural memory. Second, as Hackley believed that Blacks obtained their emancipation through the New Thought phenomenon of mental concentration and telepathy, they also possessed the capability to mine, from their collective consciousness, the true performative, spiritual, and aesthetic meaning and nuance of folk songs. Third, because these songs emanated from an institution and history so indescribably and profoundly dehumanizing, only those who possessed the racial characteristics that once identified them as enslaved people could reproduce the emotionality intrinsic to spirituals. For Hackley, African American folksongs communicated the innermost passions and dreams, spirituality, and intellect of Blacks. Moreover, these songs constituted an original American music genre, and for this reason alone, their legacy and the memory of those who originally sang them needed to be preserved for posterity. The *Cleveland Gazette* praised teachers, such as Hackley, who were stalwartly committed to the preservation of spirituals:

> Efforts are being made to give students such a love for these beautiful utterances of an enslaved and deeply religious race, that they might strive to gather up and preserve that emotional expression which is likely to be lost in the transitory period through which the colored people are passing.... [T]hese old songs, squeezed as they were, out of the hearts by the pressure of slavery, are a part of his history that we cannot afford to lose—a breaking forth from bondage of that which could never be enslaved—the genius of a race.[88]

Hackley taught spirituals using performance practices she heard at Hampton and Tuskegee Institutes, Fisk and Howard Universities, and other historically Black institutions. In a description of the Fisk Jubilee Singers' performances of spirituals, conductor John Wesley Work noted that the ensemble eliminated every musical element that threatened to detract from this genre's intense emotion. Lyrics sung in traditional dialect, while not an imperative practice, nonetheless proved effective, culturally sensitive, and accurate and thus promised to accentuate a song's original ethos. In their interpretation, the Fisk Jubilee Singers became celebrated for polish, sincerity, and precision, and they set the performance standards for spiritual repertoire.[89] Hackley foregrounded musical attributes of spirituals, particularly their repetition of words, sometimes set to complex rhythms, with harmonic underpinnings often improvised, even in choral renditions.[90]

Although spirituals were well known to Hackley's audiences, their study and performance did not always meet with approval. Even with Du Bois's widely read endorsement, "Of Sorrow Songs," in *Souls of Black Folk*, spirituals had become "repugnant" to some owing to their association with enslavement and recollection of "the misfortune of a race."[91] An article in the NAACP's *Crisis* elaborated on this point, lamenting that "the young Negro of to-day does not know nor is he interested in the songs of his fathers. He is rapidly forgetting the spirituals."[92] One of Hackley's friends and former students, A. Merral Willis, initially concurred with this viewpoint. Willis recalled that during his student years at Howard University, he and his fellow singers in the institution's choir "rebelled whenever we had to sing spirituals." Hackley admitted, to the *New York Age*, and to James Weldon Johnson, that large-scale choral performances of this repertoire in 1915, conducted by her at the Chicago Coliseum, may not have taken place at all owing to a "hard fight" and resistance on the part of singers to the performance of African American folk songs.[93] Willis was one of innumerable singers who eventually came to love spirituals after having rehearsed and performed them under Hackley's direction and guidance. He ultimately became a strong supporter of her mission to preserve these songs and use them as teaching and performance repertoire, especially after he heard her speak "convincingly of the meaningfulness and deep heritage of the Negro's folk music."[94] Another avid singer of spirituals, G. H. P. Ganaway, stated that "enlightenment and pride" should never obscure the memory of these songs as they "gave happiness to our parents . . . when everything seemed dark and dreary in the days of slavery. . . . It would seem as though it would be a pleasure for us as the younger members of the race to glory in those things that gave them so much pleasure when nothing else could."[95] As observed by the *Washington, DC Bee*, Hackley "has not permitted the race to overlook nor look down upon the cherished 'folk song,' typical of the Negro people's earlier period of development, and which she has idealized to such an extent that they rank among the truest forms of music known to the American continent." At no point did Hackley deny that spirituals were "reminiscent of the plantation days of the Negro people." But she also viewed this repertoire as empowering, as a vehicle for nurturing race pride, and as unequivocal evidence of resiliency, determination, and resistance. Additionally, and as mentioned above, she believed that only African Americans could authentically perform these songs, "given . . . the natural fervor of the race that feels the full force of the spirit of the [folk songs'] music."[96]

A compelling, detailed, and carefully reasoned assessment of Hackley's interpretation of spirituals came from Jane Judge, a respected white journalist who wrote for the Savannah, Georgia *Morning News*:

> Negro folk music, with its haunting minors [modal tonalities], its strange, rolling melodies, echoing and re-echoing each other, its harmonies that no white voice can compass [perform them] that express something deeply poignant, was heard last night at a folk festival at the auditorium sung as it has never been sung before. For, to the natural instinct of the Negro for song and to the traditional interpretation of the old spirituals which those who have been nurtured in them possess, was added the touch of art. Azalia Hackley of Chicago, who trained and directed the large chorus of 250 voices, men, women and children, used her musical genius and trained ability to dignify this interpretation, not changing its character in any way, but making it more beautiful and ideally nearer, one might believe, to the emotions these old songs express and to the religious spirit from which they sprang. An admirable musician herself, the chorus under her hands sang with a purity of tone, a precision and control that did not lessen the fervor and abandon which gave color to these Negro spirituals. Their marvelous range, the antiphonal characteristic which marks so many of them, the amazing harmonies that give them a thrilling quality, were as striking and as stirring as when they are sung by untutored voices, but the voices of these singers had been trained by a skillful teacher so that the traditional music of their race might be reinterpreted and brought forth in new beauty. Her accompaniments, exquisitely harmonized, were themselves a revelation. Usually the old spirituals are spoiled by any attempt to accompany them on the piano, the accompaniment making the voices, with their unusual scale, sound off the key, but this was not so last night with those numbers that Azalia Hackley accompanied, for she was able to make her music sound a part of the singing, with its unusual intervals, its minors, its weird harmonies. One of her most striking and most beautiful accompaniments was played to the song of "Little David [Play on Your Harp],"... music and voice alike producing the sound of the harp in a marvelous way. It was a remarkable piece of imitative singing, quite exquisitely done with its delicate pianissimo and musical cadences.... The swelling volume of the chorus, following the searching cadences of the solo, was most musical.... Several of the folk songs were new to Savannah audiences, but they had their unmistakable quality that give the music of the Negro race its distinguishing marks.[97]

Judge drew attention to Hackley's facility with choral conducting, and her compelling engagement with traditional African American repertoire and interpretive practices. For the performance Judge reviewed, Hackley had recruited a sizeable, multiaged, amateur chorus that, to a less qualified musician, would be an intimidating and unwieldy ensemble to prepare for any occasion or event. She evidently brought to Savannah a wealth of aesthetic goals, pedagogical strategies, and rehearsal techniques she harnessed to shape the sound of this large chorus. In addition, she wrote or improvised her own accompaniments and also played them convincingly and unobtrusively while she conducted. And finally, she drew upon her extensive knowledge of traditional African American performance practices, such as "call and response"—referred to as "antiphonal characteristics" by critic Jane Judge—as typified her folk song concerts. As indicated in Judge's review, Hackley assigned a leader within the chorus to intone the "call" or solo, to which the chorus sang the "response." Thus, Hackley prioritized the Black voice and its conventions—an especially noteworthy strategy as her approach to performing this literature lay outside Eurocentric stylistic and interpretive expectations. Her evocations of Blackness through vocal teaching and performance bring to mind the astute analysis of African American music practices and authenticity elaborated upon by composer, performer, musicologist, and critic Ollie Wilson (1937–2018). Wilson wrote of the ways African American musicians reiterate a core of pragmatic and spiritual beliefs that interacts with and reflects the singularities of their life experiences and history. The musical expression of these beliefs draws upon a rich "kaleidoscopic repertoire of elements and practices" Wilson traces to African sources. These practices include a "heightened sensitivity" to "immediateness of expression," as manifested in improvisatory technique and passages. Wilson also observed, in Black performance, the tradition of valuing music as a "ritualistic, interactive, communal activity." Wilson's concept of African American music making as "multidimensional" and "heterogeneous" assumes the presence of a spiritual underpinning and purpose in its musical elements and lyrics.[98]

Choral Repertoire

Hackley did not altogether abandon European-derived vocal works, and, in fact, she included such pieces in her instructional methodology, notably those selected from Henry Krehbiel's anthology. She also taught classical choral pieces to large ensembles, especially selections from these well-known oratorios: George Frideric Handel's *Messiah*, Felix Mendelssohn's *Elijah*, Franz Joseph Haydn's *Creation*, John Stainer's *Crucifixion*, and Charles Gounod's *Gallia*. She found this repertoire particularly appropriate for some historically Black schools, especially Hampton Institute and Fisk and Howard Universities, where students were more experienced with formal choral singing and the reading of music notation. From Handel's *Messiah*—probably the most familiar of the works listed above—she recommended these movements, in particular, for student choruses: "And the Glory of God," "Surely He," "All We Like Sheep," and the work's most beloved number, "Hallelujah."[99] Gounod's *Gallia* proved especially effective for less experienced choirs owing to its largely homophonic texture. Hackley conducted several performances of this work while overseas. Stainer's *Crucifixion* offered the added benefit of hymns interspersed throughout the score of a level of difficulty quite appropriate for some of Hackley's audiences to join in singing with her choruses.

In her *Guide*, Hackley did not limit her advice to soloists as she also made recommendations to choral directors. She began by reminding choral conductors that, unlike in solo singing, vocal individuality must be suppressed in ensembles as even one conspicuous voice could spoil the desired effect. "Whenever a single voice is heard above the others," she advised, "it should be singing an obbligato, or solo part, otherwise, it should blend with the other voices." She also endorsed a rehearsal activity in which choir members speak the words in their notated rhythmic configuration before actually singing them in order to concentrate on diction. The clear declamation of final consonants not only helped with diction, Hackley wrote, but it also assisted with deep breathing. In her choir rehearsals, she conducted lessons in voice culture, especially using yawning exercises as a strategy that promised to greatly improve overall sound and conserve valuable rehearsal time later on.[100]

Musical Missionary

In comments she made to newspapers, Hackley drew attention to her role as an activist "musical missionary." Certainly, her commitment to community music education and her belief in its benefits to health, spirituality, and morality evoked a missionary-like purpose. Her lectures and demonstrations in voice culture could be viewed as sermons, of sorts, thus serving as an actual religious or spiritual experience for many of those who attended her programs. Furthermore, it becomes difficult, at times, to disentangle her employment and promotion of New Thought principles from those of a more purely musical or pedagogical nature. When combined with her commitment to the New Thought conviction that positive thinking can transcend the most seemingly insurmountable challenges in life, her approach to, and goals of, music education assumed powerful activist dimensions.[101]

As an innovative pedagogue, Hackley assimilated numerous European-derived philosophical principles and pedagogical strategies and adapted them to better meet the needs of Black communities. She offered these details about the comprehensiveness, breadth, and interdisciplinarity of her approach:

> The proper study of voice culture will help children spiritually, morally and physically, through the control of the will power, the emotions and the muscles; that this study will also cause a general knowledge of other thoughtful refining studies; that voice culture will correct the tendency toward tuberculosis and other diseases, because it teaches the value of fresh air, the care and cleanliness of the body, and gives occupation for the dangerous idle hour.... Because the Negro is vocally gifted, much of the time spent on technical training (to which he is naturally inclined and which he absorbs easily) could be spent in directing him toward the appreciation of the beautiful in nature, art, poetry, literature, and the study of psychology and kindred subjects which would cultivate his [powers of] observation, taste, thought, will power, etc.[102]

Her teaching methodology enabled innumerable African Americans to experience and benefit from some of the instructional practices she found so essential to the development of her own musicianship. She explored commonalities between singing instruction and physical culture as manifested in engaging muscles of the upper body during intense breathing exercises. In Hackley's era, physical culture surged in popularity, and she contributed to its appeal by publicly advocating deep breathing as a safeguard against disease.[103]

Hackley made use of ordinary, everyday motions and activities (such as yawning and gasping) to help students and audiences appreciate and excel in the art of singing. Teaching, for her, and learning, for her students, became empowering, satisfying, and entertaining. Under her guidance, students could begin to make connections between seemingly incongruent repertoires, especially African American spirituals and European classical concert works. Her ability to render the materials and methods of music education accessible to all Black citizens made her absolutely unique in her day. The intricacies of musical social uplift depended solely on African American communities as uniquely supportive sites for cultural expression. Thus, ultimately, Hackley's mission as a community music educator became inextricably linked with the strivings and goals of racial uplift.

CHAPTER FIVE

World War I Activism

Hackley arrived in Paris in July 1914, just prior to the outbreak of World War I. She wrote letters to African American newspapers in which she described a city bracing for armed conflict. "War is in the air!" she exclaimed to the *Indianapolis Freeman*. The intense "war scare" escalating all around her reflected the passion of Parisians anxious to settle an old score with Germany: "The French ... have been preparing for war ever since their loss of *Alsace* and every mother's son is itching to fight *Allemagne*, or Germany, as we call it."[1] Military personnel and equipment crowded Parisian streets as the threat of war loomed: "Troops, war wagons, red cross wagons and the blast of the bugle add to the war exhilaration," Hackley observed. Other parts of the city remained eerily quiet as "crowds gathered at Parisian railroad stations and street corners to read government notices posted everywhere.... Silence reigns as the people are thinking of what war means. There is that strange stare that one sees [only] in the eyes of foreigners.... All along the streets the silent groups [of people] and [their] hushed tones tell of suppressed tension." She found the Jardin du Luxembourg, where she often strolled, "almost deserted," its "rows of trees and many monuments seemed like sentinels,... more like a cemetery than a park."[2]

When Hackley returned from Paris, she encountered a brewing controversy among Black leaders about the United States' possible participation in the European war. As the inevitability of increased American presence in the war materialized, many African Americans came to view US involvement as crucial to the future of race relations. Some reasoned that if they enlisted for military service, thereby helping to protect and promote US interests abroad, such demonstrations of patriotism would foster respect and appreciation from whites and thus inaugurate a new era of racial cooperation. To convince Blacks of the correlation between the European conflict, German aggression, and the dismantling of racism in the United States, W. E. B. Du Bois wrote in 1914 that the future of Black America would best be served by an Allied victory:

> Many colored persons, and persons interested in them, may easily make the mistake of supposing that the present war is far removed from the color problems of America.... This attitude is a mistake.... Indeed, considering the fact that black Africans and brown Indians and yellow Japanese are fighting for France and England, it may be that they will come out of this frightful welter of blood with new ideas about the essential equality of all men.... [A German victory] means the triumph of every force calculated to subordinate darker peoples, [and] would mean a crucifixion of darker peoples unparalleled in history. As colored Americans, then, and as Americans who fear race prejudice as the greatest of War-makers, our sympathies ... should be with France and England; not that they have conquered race prejudice, but they have at least begun to realize its cost and evil.³

Ordinarily a staunch critic of white treatment of Blacks, Du Bois urged readers of the NAACP's *Crisis* to "forget our special grievances" with whites, "while this war lasts," and temporarily halt political and rhetorical agitation against racism. After the United States declared war on Germany, Du Bois issued his most vehement statement about race relations during armed conflict. In an essay published in the *Crisis*, he called for African Americans to "close ranks with our own white fellow citizens" as a means toward securing the eventual relaxation of segregation and disenfranchisement after the cessation of fighting.⁴

By asking African Americans to put aside, however temporarily, their "special grievances" with the dominant white population, Du Bois appeared to appropriate the apolitical stance associated with followers of Booker T. Washington's philosophy. Du Bois's "close ranks" essay drew harsh criticism from some Black leaders who argued that the sacrifices of African Americans in a European war effort would accomplish little, if anything, to eradicate racism.⁵ Most notably, William Monroe Trotter, the outspoken editor of the African American newspaper *Boston Guardian* and usually an unflinching ally of Du Bois, accused him of betraying "the cause of the race."⁶ In another decidedly acerbic reaction, the esteemed Washington, DC, clergyman and activist Rev. Francis James Grimké censured Du Bois with this comment: "The greatest enemies to true democracy are not in Germany or Austria, but here in these United States of America: and the sooner that fact is recognized the better it will be, not only for the country but for the whole world. The most pressing, present need in this country today is the safe-guarding of democracy here. If it were safe-guarded here, our forces would be worth ten fold more abroad.

The democracy we glory in at home, to our shame, is a democracy in which black men have no rights."⁷

During the Great War years, Hackley adroitly sidestepped the war debate. Her reticence to voicing an opinion on race relations and the war should not be construed as disinterest or ambivalence, however. While she carefully distanced herself from confrontation, she tirelessly organized community events at which Blacks could express and celebrate patriotism in music and pageantry. Within the context of what William Jordan identifies as the wartime "accommodation-protest continuum," Hackley's strategy constituted a supple, nuanced, albeit complex, position with which she sought balance between the constrictions of segregation and aspirations of improved race relations. As Jordan so astutely observes, if African Americans closed ranks with whites, they anticipated some improvements in their circumstances and broadening of political rights but not necessarily a termination of white dominance. Conversely, if certain Black leaders refused to moderate their critical rhetoric and postpone their egalitarian objectives, they risked dire institutional and economic consequences along with total withdrawal of cooperation and sympathy from whites. Du Bois formulated and adopted his version of patriotic discourse as an attempt to derail white obsession with racism and discrimination, assuage anxieties regarding Black loyalty in time of war, and elicit promises of eventual enfranchisement and full citizenry.⁸ Ultimately, Du Bois could not have hoped for a more effective messenger of Black patriotism and loyalty as Hackley conducted patriotic pageants throughout the country, with extraordinary conviction and persuasion.

On the surface, Hackley's promotion of patriotism through music performance and pageantry would appear to represent an unequivocal endorsement of Du Bois's viewpoint. Yet, in actuality, her response to Du Bois's call to "close ranks" involved subtle acts of resistance not entirely congruent with the sentiment of his message. In particular, she did not "close ranks" with whites in her choice of war-time music as she programmed, almost exclusively, pieces written or arranged by African Americans for her events. Nor did she invite whites to perform in her celebrations. Many of the songs she selected for her war-time productions featured lyrics that paid homage to African American military service, sacrifice, and courage. Additionally, the pageants she directed celebrated African ancestry and African American history and culture. Nonetheless, she clearly sympathized with the plight of the French as she had witnessed, first hand, the urgency of a country preparing for conflict and self-defense. She was also acutely aware that some African Americans remained in Paris and, potentially, in harm's way, especially those with whom she had formed lasting artistic associations and friendships.

Folk Song Festivals

In an effort to bolster Black support of the Allied cause, Hackley organized patriotic events in numerous large cities coast to coast. Although her events were unique and of her own design, she clearly experimented with ideas borrowed from other forms of entertainment, such as festivals and pageants. In a genre she referred to as a "folk song festival," she introduced elements associated with similar white community extravaganzas, such as music, poetry recitations, and dramatic oratory. Her festivals also included large-scale choral performances, occasional solo songs, and, sometimes, one or more of her famous "vocal demonstrations." By this time in her career, she had come to regard festivals as a more effective means to carry out her agenda of musical social uplift. For festival repertoire, she relied, almost exclusively, on spirituals.

Hackley's audiences quickly came to expect spirituals at her wartime performances, and she included several at nearly all her events, chosen from among such famous and enduring songs as "Roll, Jordan Roll," "Steal Away to Jesus," and "Swing Low Sweet Chariot." During the war years, spirituals assumed added significance as audiences increasingly came to view them as expressions of hope and of the ideals for which the United States went into battle.[9] To these sentiments, Hampton Institute faculty member Natalie Curtis Burlin added, "The nobler music of the Negro, the prayerful Spirituals, should form the basis of a battle-hymn in this war wherein the black man, side by side with the white man, fights for the larger liberty of humanity. . . . For this music sprang from men who best know how to value freedom, and I feel that their songs, as well as their lives, are their immortal gifts to Freedom's cause."[10] Whether sung by Hackley as solos or performed in choruses under her direction, her interpretations of spirituals elicited glowing reviews. As one critic wrote, "Oh! The indescribably sweet music of these songs. I had often wished I could hear a really great singer render these songs and was rejoiced when I noticed that the program of Mme. Hackley contained a group of these songs, for I knew that she would sing them better than any other singer in the world. And she did." Praising her interpretation at this performance for its "soulful beauty" and "magic power," this critic made special note of the silence that fell over the mesmerized crowd after Hackley's last note faded away.[11]

Some of Hackley's most successful folk song festivals took place in 1915 at the Half-Century Anniversary Exposition and Lincoln Jubilee. The Jubilee lasted three weeks (22 August through 16 September) during which Hackley conducted daily choral performances of spirituals.[12] These events, held in Chicago's Coliseum, celebrated the fiftieth anniversary of the cessation of the Civil War and the ratification of the Thirteenth Amendment, which ended slavery.

Ex. 5.1. E. Azalia Hackley, "Carola: Spanish Serenade" (Detroit: Hackley, 1918), mm. 24–30.

As chronicled in the Black press, exposition organizers intended to "bring together the positive proofs of the achievements of the American Negro" as represented by "every agency which interprets the actual life of the Negro . . . and the real fundamental facts which have made his progress possible."[13] During her daily performances, Hackley conducted choral renditions of spirituals and debuted her only known original composition, "Carola." Hackley wrote the lyrics and music of "Carola" while she toured Cuba, and the song's rhythmic underpinning reflects a recognizable Afro-Cuban *habanera* pattern, articulated in characteristic dotted figures. The piano gently supports the lyrics, which evoke a nostalgic lullaby (excerpt 5.1). Hackley often accompanied herself when she performed solo song literature, and the uncluttered texture of her piano writing rendered "Carola" particularly suitable for this performance practice.[14] Although she seldom performed the virtuosic showstoppers associated with her earlier solo career, she regularly programmed the lilting and soothing "Carola," and it became a staple for her wartime festivals and pageants.

Hackley performed a particularly well-received folk song festival in Washington, DC, in 1916, at the historic and spacious Metropolitan AME Church. According to the press, the church was "packed to the doors" and "all of cultured Washington turned out *en masse*" for this event. Hackley received a stellar review, and the *DC Bee* lauded her as "one of the wizards of the times as a teacher and director."[15] Her friend J. Rosamond Johnson made a special guest appearance at this concert, singing some of his own compositions. In an impromptu speech, praised lavishly by the press, he "paid lofty tribute to the unselfish labors of Mme. Hackley for the musical uplift of the Negro people." The *DC Bee* printed the entire lengthy program that included a rousing patriotic grand finale in which everyone present sang "America."[16]

Pageantry

As the United States became more overtly involved in the war effort, Hackley added elements of pageantry to her festivals and increasingly focused her energy and creativity on patriotism. Of her entry into the world of pageantry, she wrote: "The time has come for pageants. . . . The word pageant means a spectacle. It suggests action, something that our people like. Spectators enjoy the pomp and the ceremony. They crane their necks during the processional and recessional and when it is over they go home happy with the memory of a beautiful motion picture. . . . It [pageantry] gives all the people an opportunity to participate."[17] Hackley's pageants bore some resemblance to those associated with the pageantry craze that swept the United States during the early twentieth century. The leader of this movement, William Chauncey Langdon (1871–1947), founded the American Pageant Association and established and promoted guidelines for the standardization of pageantry as a legitimate artistic, dramatic, and community genre. Beginning in the 1910s, dozens of communities nationwide produced pageants that recalled historical events and celebrated the legacies of persons of special significance to a particular locale. These productions, often enacted outside, involved large numbers of participants and drew huge audiences.[18] Although Langdon made claims about pageantry's inclusiveness owing to the genre's depiction of Native American culture (albeit patronizingly), the American Pageant Association did not welcome Blacks as members, nor did the pageant movement acknowledge

African American historical events, persons, or issues.[19] In particular, Langdon ignored the pioneering contributions of Rev. Henry Hugh Proctor and W. E. B. Du Bois to the history and development of US pageantry. Proctor produced his musical pageant, *Up to Freedom*, in Atlanta, in 1912 and again in 1913, as part of Georgia's Colored Music Festival. Configured in three acts, Proctor's pageant depicted not only Black Americans' African heritage, but also their struggle to conceptualize and attain an African American–defined destiny devoid of white domination and exploitation. Du Bois shared with Proctor, a friend and fellow Fisk University classmate, a fascination with the pageant genre. In his pageant, *The Star of Ethiopia*, premiered in 1913, Du Bois staged a massive extravaganza that called for hundreds of participants, lavish scenery, and elaborate costumes. Du Bois's prologue and five scenes portrayed a glorious African past and rich cultural heritage, intended as a potent counternarrative to the racist notion that African Americans came from a barbaric, uncivilized, and backward continent.[20]

Although surviving reviews reveal frustratingly little detail about the actual configuration of Hackley's pageants, it seems reasonable to assume she included at least some plot development, oration, dialogue, or scenic enactment. However, we do know she incorporated elements associated with the US pageant genre in her wartime events, such as large numbers of participants, flags, banners, costumes, marching bands, audience participation, and symbolic ritual. More significantly, and in keeping with the goals of musical social uplift, she paid homage to the cultural expressiveness of Blacks and the richness of their ancient African heritage. She approached pageantry as a community and amateur endeavor, without the use of complicated scenery or other expensive theatrical accessories. Of her efforts, she expressed cautious optimism in the success of the pageant movement among the Black American population: "It is my hope that ... pageant[s] may be produced in every city and town in the country ... by some church, school or other organization, in order that, as never before, the world may recognize not only our worth and advancement, but our determination to be a real part of the best community life wherever we may chance to live."[21] A review of Hackley's "Queen's Pageant," held in Washington, DC on 24 April 1917, offers some insight about her approach to pageantry, especially her love of spectacle and celebration of African heritage:

> Amid the fanfare of trumpets and the emblazoned banners of heraldry, ... [Hackley] gave a demonstration of a patriotic devotion to America and her new found allies that left no doubt in the minds of the most skeptical that the loyalty of the Negro is 100 per cent. The occasion was a spectacular "Queen's Pageant" and was given under the auspices of the [Washington, DC] Bethel

Literary and Historical Association, with Mme. E. Azalia Hackley of Chicago, as director-general, and Miss Marie A. D. Madre, president of the Bethel Literary, as business manager. The spacious edifice [Metropolitan AME Church] was richly decorated with the American colors . . . entwined with . . . the insignia of France and England. Fifteen governments were represented by "Queens" and following them in the pretty historical [processional] were members of their trains—lords and ladies in waiting, chamberlains and color [flag] bearers. . . . [The queen of] "America" led the procession, closely followed by . . . "England" and . . . "France." The house rang with cheers as the united throng sang "The Star-Spangled Banner" and joined in with [the queen of] "America" who had reached the center of the stage. . . . [The queens sang] a stanza of "God Save the King" and . . . "The Marseillaise," the audience standing throughout. The heartiest applause was given when the three "queens," on the main section of the rostrum, with graceful sweep, entwined the "Stars and Stripes" . . . with the "Union Jack" of Great Britain and the tri-color of the French Republic. It was a thrilling and dramatic scene. . . . The most signal individual triumph of the evening was achieved by . . . a picturesque and vivid portrayal of "Africa" and . . . [the] life-like assumption of the role of the "Queen of Sheba." She had . . . the largest entourage—lords and ladies—[and] . . . was awarded by being crowned by "America" as "Queen of Queens," winning the first prize of the pageant. . . . "Japan" and . . . "China" were attired in the unique garb of their native lands and gave characteristic evolutions with fans and parasols. . . . Mme. Hackley gave an informal talk on pageants and their historical significance, and explained why she had . . . abandoned prima donna work in favor of pageantry, showing the wonderful power of the latter in impressing the story of international progress and unity of peoples.[22]

In this pageant, Hackley audaciously explored the possibilities of a context imbued with a gendered and racialized interpretation of global relations and governments. Her portrayal of an idealized and feminized world in which Black queens held positions representative of national sovereignty dominated the visual and ritualistic narrative. To Hackley, the veracity of "international progress" and "unity of peoples" could most effectively be represented by assigning leadership roles exclusively to women of African heritage. The crowning of the Black queen of Sheba as "Queen of Queens" endowed Hackley's spectacle with an irrefutable biblical reference and time-honored sanctity.[23] Her emphasis on female leadership and Afrocentrism contrasted dramatically with white pageants as these tended to feature white male heroes of history, allegory, and legend, along with female roles largely confined to the portrayal of women in the domestic realm.[24] Hackley's focus on female empowerment in her "Queen's Pageant" brings to mind a provocative assertion made by pioneering pageant

Fig. 5.1. Atlanta Auditorium and Armory, ca. 1916. Courtesy, Georgia Archives, Vanishing Georgia Collection, ful0183.

author, director, and suffragist Hazel MacKaye, who wrote: "through pageantry we women can set forth our ideals and aspirations more graphically than in any other way."[25] In subsequent pageants, Hackley returned to a similar worldview, in which she dramatized the communal, celebratory, and nonconfrontational ethos she associated, singularly, with women of African ancestry.[26]

On July 1 and 2, 1918, Hackley produced what the press referred to as "monster" pageants. Consistent with her accommodationist approach to race relations, she did not protest the seating requirements at these events, and white and Black audiences, each numbering in the thousands, sat in racially segregated sections on opposite sides of the cavernous Atlanta Auditorium Armory (figure 5.1). These performances featured hundreds of participants and included 100 African American military personnel from nearby Camp Gordon.[27] Paying tribute to those fighting overseas, Hackley's program included a "Procession of Countries" led by marching soldiers carrying the flags of Belgium, Canada, China, Cuba, England, France, Greece, Ireland, Italy, Japan, Russia, Spain, and several African countries. Following the entrance of military personnel, over 500 children, dressed in international costumes, filed into the armory. Children's choirs, one comprised of African American boys and the other of girls, sang "Rule, Britannia, Rule" and "The Wearin' o' the Green," respectively.[28]

Several weeks later, in August 1918, in Detroit, Hackley organized a pageant that attracted a huge audience of 3,000. For this event, she conducted a large community chorus of adult singers, a girls' choir, and a mixed children's choir. A critic enthusiastically lauded the astounding results she achieved with amateur choruses, adding, "Never in the history of musical life in Detroit was such singing heard, and the fact that all songs, used either in solo or ensemble, were compositions of members of the Race, added novelty as well as producing remarkable enthusiasm." The press acknowledged the significance of Hackley's wartime patriotic events as they had "grown to be a part of the national life of the Race throughout America."[29]

Wartime Pageant Repertoire

Hackley's performance repertoire underwent a dramatic change after she returned from Paris in 1914. She all but eliminated art songs, virtuosic pieces, and arias from her concerts. In place of the repertoire audiences had come to expect from her, she programmed patriotic and sentimental songs, marches, and spirituals. All her wartime pieces were either arranged or written by the best-known Black composers of her day, especially Harry T. Burleigh, Bob Cole, Will Marion Cook, R. Nathaniel Dett, Carl Rossini Diton, James Weldon Johnson, J. Rosamond Johnson, and Clarence Cameron White. Not only did she hope that her endorsement would aid the careers of these and other Black composers, but she also believed their music communicated something uniquely optimistic and empowering to audiences.

The crowds at many Hackley pageants thoroughly enjoyed a comic song she frequently programmed entitled "It Takes a Long, Tall Brown-Skin Boy to Make the Kaiser Lay His Weapons Down" (excerpt 5.2). The title and lyrics of this tune were actually a wartime parody of the hit song "It Takes a Long, Tall

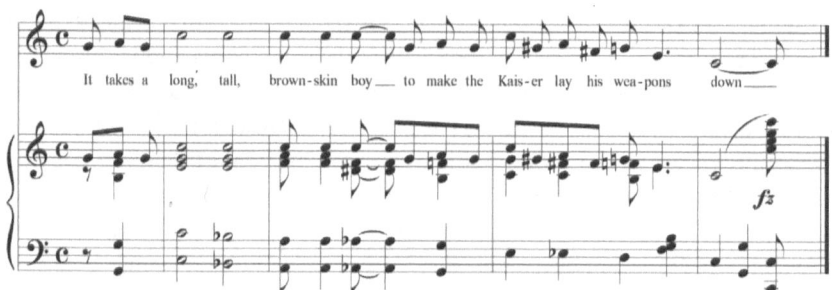

Ex. 5.2. "It Takes a Long, Tall, Brown-Skin Boy to Make the Kaiser Lay His Weapons Down," mm. 35–39. Parody of Will E. Skidmore, "It Takes a Long, Tall Brown-Skin Gal to Make a Preacher Lay His Bible Down" (New York: Stern, 1917).

Ex. 5.3a. Will Marion Cook, "Exhortation: A Negro Sermon" (New York: G. Schirmer, 1912), mm. 1–8.

Brown-Skin Gal To Make a Preacher Lay His Bible Down," written by vaudeville pianist and composer Will E. Skidmore (1880–1959) and lyricist Marshall Walker. That everyone present at Atlanta's Auditorium-Armory could, and did, join with the performers to sing this song comes as no surprise as its melody was already well known throughout the United States.[30] Black soldiers serving overseas also responded enthusiastically to the song's swinging syncopation and adopted it as one of their numerous marching tunes.[31]

Ex. 5.3b. Cook, "Exhortation," mm. 32–37.

Pieces by Will Marion Cook, a successful director, composer, and producer of a number of African American shows on Broadway, appeared regularly on Hackley's programs.[32] Cook's popular solo song "Exhortation: A Negro Sermon" featured lyrics written by Alex Rogers (1876–1930).[33] The singer, imitating a Black clergyman, declaims the biblical verse Matthew 5:39 in dialect.[34] Critics praised the emotional and religious fervor of Rogers's text and deemed it particularly appropriate for wartime performances. In this recitative and aria, Cook revealed his devotion to African American cultural expression as well as his training in the European concert tradition. Accompanied mostly by sustained chords, the lyrics of the recitative section dramatically convey the increasing intensity characteristic of a Black preacher's sermon (excerpt 5.3a). In contrast to the rhapsodic and improvisational nature of the recitative section, the solo voice and accompaniment in the homophonic aria share melodic responsibilities through pitch doublings. The religious fervor of the opening recitative returns, with a concluding and extended "Amen" section (excerpt 5.3b).

Hackley frequently turned to J. Rosamond Johnson for wartime repertoire. Johnson's song "Sence You Went Away" (excerpt 5.4) became a sentimental

Ex. 5.4. J. Rosamond Johnson, "Sence You Went Away" (New York: Stern, 1900), mm. 1–13.

favorite during the war, especially for those whose loved ones served overseas. With dialect lyrics written by Bob Cole and James Weldon Johnson, the song featured catchy dotted rhythms and diatonic harmonies in a standard verse-refrain form.

Hackley also programmed pieces by composer and famed baritone soloist Harry T. Burleigh.[35] Burleigh's song "The Young Warrior," arguably the most frequently performed song of the war, became a Hackley favorite. For the text

Ex. 5.5a. Harry T. Burleigh, "The Young Warrior" (New York: Ricordi, 1915), mm. 33–34; pitches of "My Country, Tis of Thee" in parentheses.

Ex. 5.5b. Burleigh, "Young Warrior," mm. 45–48.

of this song, one of five he composed for World War I, Burleigh selected a poem of the same title written by James Weldon Johnson. The poem tells of a young and newly minted soldier about to embark on his first military excursion. As the soldier bids his mother farewell, he pleads with her to forego tears and, instead, to pray for his moral and spiritual well-being while off fighting. Burleigh composed this song at the outbreak of war in 1914 and it was a hit among soldiers in Europe.[36] Hackley undoubtedly knew of the song's soaring popularity and judiciously added it to many of her events. Critics singled out musical attributes of "Young Warrior" that reinforced the lyric's meaning and contributed, substantially, to its appeal. For example, one journalist likened the song's piano accompaniment to bugle calls that imaginatively captured "the true war spirit."[37] Writing for *Musical America*, A. W. Kramer credited the effectiveness of Burleigh's song to its "martial motif, reiterated throughout." Kramer admired the subtlety of Burleigh's quotation of the first two measures of "My

Ex. 5.5c. Burleigh, "Young Warrior," mm. 56–61.

Country, 'Tis of Thee," which achieved a "surprisingly fine effect" (excerpt 5.5a). In addition, Kramer complimented the song's "declamatory recitative, 'Mother, the lines are drawn,'" as an example of "splendid" compositional technique (excerpt 5.5b), along with the "great climax" that brought the song to a stirring conclusion (excerpt 5.5c).

Yet another wartime favorite of Hackley's audiences was a song written by William Joseph "W. J." Nickerson, entitled "The Colored Soldier Boys of Uncle Sam."[38] Recalling her father's song, Camille Nickerson confirmed how quickly it became a staple at patriotic celebrations. In an interview, Nickerson noted that "Colored Soldier Boys" "was very popular . . . and was sung a great deal. . . . We were so proud, the colored people, that we could take part [in the war effort]. And as badly as they [whites] treated us, we were all agog; we lined up and down the streets to see those colored soldiers who were going to fight for this country. I remember that this song was sung at these celebrations."[39] African American historian Emmett J. Scott observed in W. J. Nickerson's lyrics "a sentiment that is at once eloquent and convincing in their patriotism."[40] The

Ex. 5.6a. W.J. Nickerson, "The Colored Soldier Boys of Uncle Sam" (New Orleans: Grunewald, 1918), mm. 1–12.

introductory percussive motives in the left hand of the piano accompaniment immediately establish a stirring march tempo. Adding to the overall fun of this song, Nickerson instructed singers to imitate bugle calls by buzzing pitches through fingers held up to their lips (excerpt 5.6a). As Hackley often invited audience participation, attendees at her patriotic events could look forward to performing the rousing opening measures of Nickerson's song. In another cleaver gesture, Nickerson included a quote from Stephen Foster's song, "Old Black Joe"—a tune everyone present would have known (excerpt 5.6b).

In 1918, Hackley added Maude Dean Newsom's popular tune "The Black Yanks Did Their Share" to her programs.[41] *Chicago Defender* columnist Nora Douglas Holt described Newsom as a "popular society matron" whose compositions "astounded her many friends."[42] Another writer singled out Newsom's song as one of her "snappiest" pieces, noteworthy for its "remarkably catchy melody and lyrics, . . . of the sort that thrill the hearer."[43] "Black Yanks" featured a martial accompaniment underlying lyrics written by the composer (excerpt 5.7).

Ex. 5.6b. Nickerson, "Colored Soldier Boys of Uncle Sam," mm. 62–78, showing quote from Foster's "Old Black Joe."

Get the Pageant Habit

Following Armistice Day (11 November 1918), Hackley compiled her experiences as a producer of wartime extravaganzas into a book entitled, *A Patriotic Pageant: A Musical and Dramatic Spectacle of Allied Countries*. She secured the able assistance of veteran *Chicago Defender* writer Tony Langston to serve as an agent for publicity and sales of her book.[44] He not only placed advertisements for the book in prominent publications, but he also repeatedly mentioned its title

Ex. 5.7. Maude Dean Newsom, "The Black Yanks Did Their Share" (Chicago: Newsom, 1919), mm. 66–82.

to the Black press.[45] In one of his announcements, Langston credited Hackley for drawing attention to the enormous outpouring of patriotism in Black communities: "the country is seeing the other side of Race life in America as never before." He recommended Hackley's "unparalleled system" of organizing pageants during peacetime, as her approach promised events "full of action, satisfying and educational." "Has your community joined the nation-wide movement to give the Madam Hackley Victory Patriotic Pageant?" Langston asked readers. Sadly, no copy of *Patriotic Pageant* has been located, but advertisements provide clues as to its purpose and scope.[46] According to newspaper notices, Hackley organized her book into fifteen "simple and comprehensive" chapters. She urged communities "to get the pageant habit" and continue the work she had inaugurated.

During peacetime, Hackley recommended pageants as fundraising vehicles and as a means to further community music making. Beginning with strategies for preparing a pageant, she offered guidelines for event directors and predicted success even for those with little or no experience in dramatic productions.[47]

Langston considered Hackley to be the most significant African American community activist during the war years. He credited her "more than any other person in the country" for striving "to create and keep alive the interest in Race music and pageants."[48] In his reflections on wartime community performances, Emmett J. Scott cited the "mesmeric influence of Negro music" as a major factor in the building of "high-grade morale" on the home front.[49] Hackley's events exemplified Scott's and Langston's observations, especially as she relied on African American music and cultural expression to inspire and bolster patriotism. In addition, she continued the revivification of spirituals by insisting on their currency as stirring wartime repertoire.

While Hackley shunned participation in the debate over African American participation in the war, her unequivocal promotion of patriotism helped ease unfounded racist fears of Black disloyalty and potentially traitorous conduct. In addition, she further assuaged white discomfort by yielding to Jim Crow laws that mandated separate entrances and seating for whites and Blacks at the events she produced in the South. If such acquiescence perpetuated the gradualist politics and accommodationism associated with Booker T. Washington, it also coincided with W. E. B. Du Bois's temporary reduction, during the war years, of his customary militant rhetoric. The war did not eclipse Hackley's commitment to musical social uplift; rather, the quest to embolden morale and cultivate patriotic zeal became dimensions of her activist mission. She refused to allow racism to dampen African American expressions of patriotism, race pride, and solidarity or to thwart the fulfillment of community service during the war years. Moreover, she manifested flexibility and resourcefulness in response to wartime pressures by adapting her activist agenda and altering her repertoire to address the needs of Black communities in an unprecedented crisis. Her strategies reinforced the appeal to "close ranks" as her festivals and pageants offered fervent demonstrations to the white population of loyalty and civic responsibility. They also presented incontrovertible proof of the urgent need to respond to the wartime sacrifices of African Americans by ameliorating racism and granting Blacks full citizenry. For, as Tony Langston argued: "The people of the United States must be made to realize that the Race has gone forward unitedly [sic] to victory, and that the time has come when just recognition must be given to exercise our rights."[50]

In her pageants, Hackley showcased African American heritage and expressivity by creating a narrative which celebrated a glorious African past. In the

1920s, Black leaders perpetuated her enthusiasm for large-scale community extravaganzas and spectacle by producing pageants as a means of dramatizing Black achievements and encouraging race pride. In so doing, participants of the Harlem Renaissance continued the struggle to wrench cultural authority from the white-dominated American Pageant Association, and to rescue Black historical figures from anonymity and their accomplishments from obscurity. It is for these reasons that pageantry of the Harlem Renaissance owes much to Hackley and her extraordinary wartime events.[51]

CHAPTER SIX

Writing and Uplift

Not long after her return from France in 1914, Hackley acquired property in Chicago and began preparations to open her Normal Vocal Institute. Almost immediately, the administrative and teaching responsibilities of the institute placed inordinate demands on her time. The fledging school also saddled her with an enormous financial burden, the severity of which convinced her of the urgency to identify a steady source of income. In order to focus on the institute's needs, she gave strong consideration to establishing Chicago as a more permanent place of residence and base of operations. She contemplated ways to replace at least some of the income she realized from touring with lucrative local initiatives she could realistically pursue and sustain. Her success at raising money for her overseas trips through the sales of pamphlets and photographs offered her a strategy to replicate. She decided to publish some of her manuscripts, with a view toward selling copies of them at public events for the benefit of the institute. Newspaper advertisements for her publications along with mail-order sales surely figured into her plans. If this initiative proved successful, she could reduce traveling while still being able to disseminate her activist agenda to as many African American communities as possible.

Hackley corresponded with James Weldon Johnson for advice on editing and publishing her manuscripts. Of this correspondence, ten letters, written in 1915, survive. The tone of Hackley's letters to Johnson confirms that the topic she addressed comprised a portion of an ongoing exchange with him, and one that extended beyond the scope of this extant set of letters. Her decision to consult Johnson for assistance was both timely and judicious. Respected internationally by this point in his career, Johnson had already served as a US diplomat in Venezuela and Nicaragua; practiced law; taught in a public school and eventually served as its principal; published fiction and poetry; and accepted, in 1914, an editorial appointment with the *New York Age*. Johnson and Hackley shared influential mutual friends—including Booker T. Washington, W. E. B. Du Bois, and *Age* editor Fred R. Moore—any of whom would have recommended to Hackley that she consult Johnson about her publishing aspirations. In addition, Hackley was well acquainted with Johnson's brother, J. Rosamond Johnson, with whom she occasionally shared the stage.

Hackley posted her first letter to J. W. Johnson in early June 1915, in Chicago. In her letter, she reminded Johnson, "Some time ago, you said . . . that you would assist me in some of my schemes for my young folks. Well, I have a scheme that is all ready."[1] Her "scheme" actually referred to publication projects she wished to pursue for fundraising purposes. Aside from work with the institute, she planned to use the spring and summer of 1915 to complete some of the manuscripts on which she had been working. As was true for all her writings, her unfinished manuscripts were based on lectures she had given in Black communities, schools, and churches. She provided Johnson with a list of writing projects, along with brief comments about their state of completion:

> *Guide in Voice Culture*—all typewritten and ready for an expert's [editorial] pencil
> *The Colored Girl Beautiful*—half typewritten—3/4 compiled; I can finish [it] in a couple of weeks
> *The Experiences of a Colored Prima Donna*—almost completed but not yet typewritten. Portions appeared in the *N. Y. Age*
> *The Soul of a Colored Singer*—in notes only; dealing with the color question
> *A Thousand Things about Paris*—typewritten and ready, but I do not care to put this out just yet
> *A Jim Crow Car Diary*[2]

Hackley planned to publish an expanded version of her instructional manual, *Guide in Voice Culture* (1909), and had already distributed or published some additional components of its revision. Among these items were a newspaper article, "Foundation of Voice Building" (1911), and various pedagogical pamphlets. Newspapers confirmed the appearance of a pamphlet, "Catechism in Voice Culture," in 1913, although no copy of it has been located.[3] The title of a 1914 pamphlet, "Lesson IV in Voice Culture Given in Colored Schools, Season 1913–14," suggests that Hackley must have released three previous and similar items, perhaps earlier that same year.[4] In a description of "Lesson IV," the *Indianapolis Freeman* mentioned its contents as "a comprehensive study of tone and personality in singing" and noted it "was used extensively in the colored schools of the country during the current year. It has been revised and brought up to date by the author for a wider use among music enthusiasts for 1914. The booklet is neatly printed in tan and brown, and is as tasteful as a *billet-deaux* [*doux*]."⁵ In addition to these pamphlets, she undoubtedly intended to include in the revision of her *Guide* topics upon which she had frequently lectured, namely, those germane to singing, such as "The Cultured Tone," "The Cultured Voice," "The Vitalizing of Tone," "The Model Vowel," and "Illustration in Punctuation."⁶ Work on this revision dragged on, however, its completion delayed by her wartime performance commitments. In fact, three years elapsed before she finally had a "new *Guide in Voice Culture* [ready] to publish," which she expected would "yield" her "a nice income." Even as she stated, "I have been preparing localities for its sale," she apparently did not post advertisements. Again, she reiterated her naïve optimism about expected interest in her revised *Guide* with the prediction, "I should sell thousands of copies."⁷ If she ever actually published this revision, no copies have been found.

All but one of the other manuscripts listed by Hackley in her letter to Johnson fared similarly. Her reminiscences of Paris became the subject of lectures, and one article about her time in France appeared in the *Philadelphia Tribune*.⁸ Presumably, these lectures would have assumed prominence in her proposed publication, *A Thousand Things about Paris*; however, this manuscript also never appeared in print.⁹ She indicated to Johnson that she had given the manuscript *A Jim Crow Diary* to her estranged husband for editing. As Edwin Hackley recalled: "She made voluminous notes of her travels in the South and of her experiences on Jim Crow cars. She sent the work to me for revision and editing which I did and returned it pronto. I never knew what became of the manuscript and why it was not published as intended. I did quite a lot of work on it, and should have liked to see it in print; it was something worthy of public perusal."¹⁰ Edwin Hackley also attempted to obtain a publisher for her book on train travel and consulted with Robert Russa Moton, an administrator at Hampton Institute, about the matter. However, Moton refused his endorsement of the project owing to what he stated was its prohibitively short length.¹¹ A final version of *Jim Crow Diary* was never published. Hackley considered the manuscript *Soul of a Colored Singer* substantially incomplete, while she acknowledged that portions of *Experiences of a Colored Prima Donna* had already appeared in print in the *New York Age* as the series "Hints to Young Colored Artists." With a view toward creating a book from this series of articles, Hackley acquired the assistance of Richard W. Thompson of the *Chicago Broad Ax* who agreed to edit her *Age* articles. At some point, this project, too, was abandoned. Nonetheless, the *Indianapolis Freeman* expressed enthusiasm for Hackley's publication projects and referred to her as "a writer of rare ability and versatility." The paper listed her publications as "various pamphlets on music, vivid stories of first-hand experiences in the war zone in Europe and her series of papers on 'Arts and Artists.'"[12] Most likely "Arts and Artists" was actually her *New York Age* series. In the end, of the items on Hackley's list, only *Colored Girl Beautiful* made it into print.

Hints to Young Colored Artists

However unpolished and rather arbitrarily organized "Hints to Young Colored Artists" may strike contemporary readers, the series nonetheless offers a window into Hackley's sense of her own artistry and the musical world in which she circulated. Of special significance, the series was the first of its kind written by a Black female concert artist and consummate teacher to appear in a nationally recognized and influential African American newspaper. Additionally, this series provided Hackley with an initial attempt at serialized writing with a view toward revision and the expansion of each article into a book chapter.[13]

Owing to her work with the *Denver Statesman* in the 1890s, Hackley had acquired valuable experience as a journalist and newspaper writer. As a result, she knew the value of submitting items to the press, especially for the purposes of activism and publicity. She also sold privately printed pamphlets and the first edition of *Guide in Voice Culture*, sales of which helped fund her overseas trips. Clearly, she anticipated an income from sales of the items she mentioned to Johnson of an amount sufficient to assist with the operational expenses of the Normal Vocal Institute. Yet, even as she insisted that she possessed "a good business head," her desire to publish *Colored Girl Beautiful* before final editing of *Experiences of a Colored Prima Donna* seems ill-advised.[14] After all, she had already completed a substantial amount of writing on the latter title and, in the process, developed important connections with the *New York Age* and editor Fred R. Moore. Both manuscripts—*Colored Girl Beautiful* and *Experiences of a Colored Prima Donna*—were approximately the same length, so final word count was not a factor, especially as Hackley intended to augment the article series upon which she planned to base the latter title. Why she did not pursue, more vigorously, the publication of a book about her life as a concert artist or her many years as a teacher, either of which would have been likely to attract critical attention and sales, remains a mystery. No record has been located to indicate whether or not she consulted Moore regarding the potential for publication of her series of articles, and, moreover, she never mentioned whether or not Richard W. Thompson eventually assisted with any of her manuscripts.

Yet Moore wholeheartedly supported Hackley as she sought to establish herself as a writer. As a seasoned and well-connected editor, he may have already formed an opinion regarding her potential for authorial success. On 17 December 1914, he enthusiastically announced to readers, "The *Age* begins this week the publication of an extremely interesting and valuable series of articles, 'Hints to Young Colored Artists,' from the pen of Mme. E. Azalia Hackley."[15] Moore's introductory comment about the anticipated series suggests he had perused all the articles and rendered his approval of them. It seems likely, given Hackley's enormous popularity, that Moore might have been compelled to compete for her writings with other leading African American newspapers of the day. No record has surfaced regarding whether or not Moore paid Hackley for her articles. In the spirit of cooperation and solidarity among Black editors, Moore sent out word about Hackley's articles, and the *Indianapolis Freeman* graciously welcomed her series with this notice: "Mme. E. Azalia Hackley is not only a charming singer and an engaging speaker but she is showing that she can handle a pen with equal facility as her splendid voice, by her highly instructive and entertaining series of articles in the *New York Age* entitled 'Hints to Young Colored Artists.' Mme. Hackley adds to her recitals of incidents and summary of advice many humorous observations culled from her wide experience in all sections of this country and abroad."[16]

Given Moore's shrewd business acumen and the *Age*'s reputation as, arguably, the nation's most influential and prestigious African American newspaper of its day, Moore would not have consented to publish Hackley's submission of a series of articles without considerable confidence in their favorable reception. After all, this represented a particularly sizeable commitment for him as Hackley had submitted twelve articles with a substantial word count. The *Indianapolis Freeman*, relying on information received from Moore, published confirmation about Hackley's ambitious plans for these articles: "It is understood that the fair diva is to combine these articles in a book later on, that they may be preserved in permanent form. Such a volume should be found in the library of every family where there are young people, for it contains information and counsel valuable to all who must have dealings with the public as a teacher, artist or tourist."[17] By the end of 1914, Hackley was not only a revered household name among virtually all Blacks, but also a public figure whose reputation remained ostensibly unblemished by any prolonged participation in radical racial debates or partisan politics. The title of her article series, referencing, as it did, matters pertaining to artistic pursuits, further reinforced her status as a consummate and esteemed member of the Black elite and therefore likely to attract a readership deemed highly significant and desirable to editors such as Moore. Both Hackley and Moore stood to gain by the appearance of her articles: Moore sought to broaden the *Age*'s circulation and influence, while Hackley always contemplated ways to develop larger and more varied audiences—in this case the approximately 12,000 *Age* subscribers and its innumerable additional readers.

So, too, Moore had already realized positive readers' reactions to items written by Hackley. During his editorship of the *Colored American Magazine* (1905–9) he featured a full-page photograph of Hackley along with her chatty article sent from London entitled "English in England." In addition, Moore published a letter from Hackley, written in Paris and printed in the *Age* in August 1914, in which she described a city preparing for war with Germany.[18] The appearance of Hackley's letter represented a major publishing coup for Moore as he was probably the first editor to print an eye-witness account of Paris on the brink of war, as related by a famous Black American. Similarly, Moore would have been aware of the uniqueness of publishing a series of articles in a major newspaper written by an African American female concert artist.

Hackley's "Hints to Young Colored Artists" also reflected Moore's support of African American arts, especially music. Moore maintained personal connections with the world of music: his sister-in-law, Mattie Lawrence (later Thrift, d. 1907), sang with the Fisk Jubilee Singers, and Moore's son-in-law, Lester A. Walton, served as an arts critic for the *Age*. In addition, John C. Freund, the white founder and publisher of the influential magazine *Musical America* and a mutual friend of Moore and Hackley, provided financial assistance and publishing advice to Moore when he owned and edited the *Colored American Magazine*. Freund continued to support Moore as he assumed publication of the *Age* and helped the newspaper remain financially solvent.[19]

In her article series, Hackley covered subjects she thought would interest *Age* readers, and these topics would have been familiar to those who had attended her popular lectures and concert events. She wisely wrote these articles in an informal and accessible style, free from political controversy. Of her article content, Moore noted, "While all of the articles are justifiably and necessarily personal in atmosphere, there are two other articles [in the same series], 'Being Introduced' and 'Reducing the Ego,' which contain personal references and experiences of a most delightfully intimate nature."[20] In these particular articles, she cautioned aspiring female performers to avoid compromising dignity and respectability in favor of fame or monetary gain. She also dedicated other series articles to voice culture, thereby extending her efforts to make music instruction available to as many Black communities as possible. These articles also served as a vehicle for disseminating New Thought principles, especially noticeable in her mention of "vibrations," the "human electric dynamo," "thought suggestion," and "personal magnetism."

However informal and accessible, Hackley's article series nonetheless exudes an elitist propensity and sense of personal exceptionality. To her, a successful concert artist always needed to remain aware that audiences tended to worship touring performers as if "upon a pedestal," and as "something above the ordinary." To sustain this "illusion," as she called it, she recommended that performers accustom themselves to maintaining a social and professional distance from the public and cultivate a persona of "a person apart."[21] Not surprisingly, she found life as a professional concert artist "a bit lonely at times." Furthermore, on occasion, she clearly lacked empathy and patience with some poorer Black communities that could not offer her a performance space she deemed suitable for a visiting artist. She leveled severe criticism at the management of some Black-owned venues where she sang, especially for issues of cleanliness, ventilation, lighting, and the condition of pianos. Although she did not deny the financial challenges of appropriate building upkeep, she nonetheless expressed exasperation with—even intolerance of—those who did not consider a worthy performance space to be essential for every sizeable Black community.[22]

Colored Girl Beautiful

Hackley anticipated her completed draft of *Colored Girl Beautiful* would require a book of around 100 pages. With only around 21, 500 words, the manuscript was not much longer than her twelve-article series, "Hints to Young Colored Artists," which stood at around 19,700 words. Regarding actual book production, she informed Johnson of her desire to see *Colored Girl Beautiful* "put up artistically" with wide page margins, thick paper, and "rather Elbert Hubbardish in style."[23] To these requirements, she added, "I would like a grayish cover . . . and a classy looking little book, but not expensive."[24] Her choice of a Hubbard-esque format reflected her familiarity with, and admiration of, Elbert Hubbard's famous imprints, known for their sturdy handmade paper and leather bindings. Hubbard produced his books at the press of the Roycraft arts and crafts colony he founded in 1895, located in East Aurora, New York. A prolific publisher, author, and philosopher, Hubbard and his wife, Alice Moore Hubbard, enjoyed considerable popularity among New Thought enthusiasts.[25] Hackley hoped for a first run of *Colored Girl Beautiful* of 1,000 copies to be sold exclusively in Chicago, for $1.00 apiece. She intended to use the proceeds to help pay for the property she had acquired for her Normal Vocal Institute. In addition, she anticipated holding competitions for regional musicians and awarding copies of her book as prizes. Yet, beyond these preliminary ideas, she seemed at a loss as to how to proceed. She sent Johnson a typed copy of a portion of the manuscript and, in a rather pathetic and beseeching tone, asked him for assistance: "Will you help me on this [manuscript] *Colored Girl*

Beautiful, add to, subtract, stretch, condense—whatever you will see fit to do, so it will pass the critics? How much will you charge? Could you begin on what I have already finished?"[26] From these comments, it seems fair to suspect that Hackley was seeking a ghost writer, of sorts, for this project, and one who she felt confident would complete the manuscript quickly, in polished prose.

In his reply to Hackley, Johnson kindly offered support. He reassured her, "I am much interested in your plans and am much inclined in my heart to give you any assistance in my power."[27] He complimented her on the subjects she selected to write about, referring to them, in measured terms, as "readable and saleable." Without elaborating, he cautiously predicted *Colored Girl Beautiful* might become, potentially, "an exceptionally successful book." However, he declined to collaborate with Hackley, stating, "I do not think I could do much toward contributing material to your *Colored Girl Beautiful*. I think it would be better for you to do the complete work, then if you will send a copy on to me I'll be glad to carefully edit it for you and make any suggestions that might occur to me.... I am sure you can make this a very interesting book."[28] Johnson's hesitancy seems quite appropriate. After all, no matter how well Hackley and Johnson knew each other, why did she think Johnson would help her complete a manuscript devoted to female etiquette? Ultimately, however, Johnson agreed to contribute some sort of brief preface by writing "a paragraph or two of foreword for the book."[29]

As this exchange of letters continued, Johnson attempted to divert Hackley by reminding her of the warm reception given her article series, "Hints to Young Colored Artists," which he acknowledged had "attracted the attention of a great many readers."[30] He possessed firsthand knowledge of *New York Age* readers' interests as he had joined the editorial staff of the paper the previous year. Johnson's connection with the *Age* seemed to do little to assuage Hackley's self-deprecating comments, especially her reference to her manuscript as "my poor little effort."[31] In a subsequent letter to Johnson, she wrote of her "hope" that he would "not get discouraged correcting and framing the poorly expressed thoughts." In a rather manipulative manner, she opined she had "no gift of language and no experience in writing," and thus she was giving strong consideration to enrolling at nearby Northwestern University "to study rhetoric and book writing" and to enrich her vocabulary.[32] Still, Johnson continued attempts to bolster her confidence. He informed her, "I have just this week had the opportunity of going over your manuscript *Colored Girl Beautiful*. I am very much impressed with it. I have made one or two suggestions for changes in the text, but I feel that your style and manner of treatment should stand substantially unchanged. However, I shall go over the book again more carefully and critically and suggest whatever I think might be an improvement."[33] He then advised, "Don't study rhetoric at the Northwestern or any other school. You have a good natural style; you need only to continue your reading of good authors for method and vocabulary and to keep on writing. One learns to write only by writing."[34]

Hackley then broached the subject of potential publishers for *Colored Girl Beautiful*. She had initially consulted Hollis Burke Frissell, principal of Hampton Institute, along with his assistant, Robert Russa Moten, for help with identifying a suitable publisher. At first, they agreed to advise her, but the time constraints of intervening administrative duties prevented either Moton or Frissell from working with her any further.[35] Johnson graciously offered to make inquiries among New York publishers on her behalf, yet he counseled, "You might make an advantageous arrangement to publish privately in Chicago." In addition, he reminded her, "There is still another plan worth your consideration, the publication of the book by the *Crisis*; through the medium of the magazine the work would at once be brought to the attention of 150,000 of just the sort of readers you wish to reach."[36] Hackley informed Johnson of her preference for "a white publisher if one can be obtained, and then, I will put an 'Ad' [for *Colored Girl Beautiful*] in the *Crisis*.... I have been advised to have the name of a white publisher [associated with the book]."[37] She did not identify the source of this recommendation. At this point, the correspondence between Hackley and Johnson regarding her writing aspirations and publishing projects apparently ceased.

In 1916 Hackley published *Colored Girl Beautiful* with a white firm, Burton Publishing Company, located in Kansas City, Missouri.[38] Her decision must have been influenced by newspaper articles touting the company's sympathy toward African Americans and detailing the firm's plan to publish a lengthy anthology bearing the working title, *Negro Men, Women and Affairs of Greater Kansas City*.[39] The editor of this anthology, George W. Little, an African American affiliate of Burton Publishing, agreed to solicit and assemble information of general interest, along with biographies and photographs of Black leaders, for the project.[40] The local Black weekly, *Kansas City Sun*, described Little as an "aggressive and hustling newspaper man," well known as a "solicitor and magazine promoter," and thus he needed "no further introduction."[41] For unknown reasons, Little never completed Burton's proposed anthology project.

Nonetheless, it seems likely that Little served as Hackley's liaison with Burton Publishing Company. She initially received promising predictions about sales potential for her book and even claimed that Johnson estimated earnings as high as $10,000.[42] However, Burton ultimately decided on printing only one run, or possibly two, of 1,000 copies each. Thanks to the intervention of Little, or someone on the Burton staff, Hackley got her wish for thick paper and wide margins, but the book, therefore, required more pages than originally planned. Hackley's enormous popularity notwithstanding, the release of *Colored Girl Beautiful* received little press attention. In anticipation of the book's appearance, the *Pittsburgh Press* noted, "It will deal with the subject *en-passant*, will be replete with homely [simple] truths along other and broader lines that make for a rejuvenated and rising race of people [italics original]."[43] For unknown reasons, Burton Publishing Company assigned a publication year of 1916 to Hackley's book, yet it apparently was not released until the following year. The *Age* printed this review, most likely written by editor Fred. R. Moore:

> In a neatly bound volume of over two hundred pages, Mme. E. Azalia Hackley, the noted musical artist, has issued a message to girls, entitled, "The Colored Girl Beautiful." The book has been compiled from talks given to girls in boarding schools and is marked by a frankness and practicality suggestive of intimate conversation. Among the subjects discussed with freedom, tempered with discretion, are: laws of attraction, love, personal appearance, deep breathing, originality, youth and maturity, self-control, relationships with men, religion, school, home, the working girl, the wife, the mother. At times epigrammatic in expression, the author expounds many truisms with a vein of originality that attracts attention. Thus she says, "The beautiful part about the colored race in America is the future. As a mixed race we are underdeveloped. We may become whatever we WILL to become." A very encouraging dictum upon which to base her book. Talking about two attractive periods in a woman's life, she says "A face that reflects nothing is seldom beautiful."[44]

Months later, in an attempt to spark interest in Hackley's book, the *New York Age* issued a second brief notice, in which the paper designated her publication as a "racial book" replete with "beauty hints, . . . not only of physical beauty," but also of "spiritual beauty."[45]

Given the dearth of publicity for *Colored Girl Beautiful*, it seems safe to conclude that neither Hackley nor Burton Publishing Company sent copies of the book to press critics for review, nor was its release advertised. With the financial debts of the Normal Vocal Institute accumulating and her book faring poorly, Hackley was forced to travel extensively and make public appearances to raise money. Oddly, she did not take advantage of these opportunities to promote her book to audiences. Curiously, she failed to follow her own advice so carefully detailed in "Hints to Young Colored Artists." In her article series, she imparted valuable insights gleaned from years of experience related to cultivating and sustaining public interest in, support of, and loyalty to one's creative and entrepreneurial endeavors. Pertinent and applicable to the launch of her first book-length publication, she informed readers of her articles how to attract a following, to welcome publicity in even "the smallest of colored newspapers," and, most significantly, never to underestimate the "value of advertising." She also presumed her reputation as an acclaimed artist and teacher would entice readers, yet she wrote, in "Hints to Young Colored Artists," that it was sheer "folly" to expect that "one's name alone" would "draw." "There must be personal contact," she insisted.[46]

Johnson noticed the press's lack of enthusiasm for *Colored Girl Beautiful*, and he published this brief endorsement in 1917: "There is another racial book, but of a different kind, in that it does not discuss the [race] 'problem.' . . . This book is the 'Colored Girl Beautiful' by E. Azalia Hackley, the well known singer and lecturer. . . . It should prove an inspiration to all who read it."[47] Johnson's announcement did not bolster sales of Hackley's book, and the publicity drought continued. Editor Horace Cayton (1859–1940) of *Cayton's Weekly* could only manage to list the book's title without any mention of Hackley's name.[48] The *Journal of the National Medical Association*, an unlikely location for a review of Hackley's book, offered this brief appraisal: "This is a neat and attractive volume that should be placed within reach of our girls. The talks are hopeful, healthful and inspiring. The author's style is simple and direct."[49] The only other press comment about *Colored Girl Beautiful* appeared after Hackley's death, in Marcus Garvey's *Negro World*, the periodical mouthpiece of his Universal Negro Improvement Association. The *World* reviewer wrote that "in literature Madame Hackley was not inexperienced. Her Book, 'Colored Girl Beautiful' was of valuable information to girls in that the book shows her undying love, respect and confidence in her people. . . . No girl can read her book that she will be inspired too, and taste of the culture that surely was hers and have a larger conception of life and the conduct of experience, an invaluable experience which will, if absorbed, point the way to a more cultured and a more joyous life."[50] The reference to a "joyous life" resonates with the ideals of New Thought to which Hackley returned to throughout her book. It should be remembered that Garvey, who exercised considerable proprietary and editorial control over *Negro World*, often espoused New Thought principles. In fact, he must have known of Hackley's commitment to the dissemination of New Thought in Black communities.

With so little publicity, sales of Hackley's book languished. Eventually compelled to peddle copies herself, she began to sell them for seventy-five cents each, a reduction from the original price of $1.00. In a letter to George Foster Peabody, she complained about a lack of assistance with marketing and promotion and that she was left to handle the distribution of her book on her own.[51] When sales eventually ceased altogether, she gave away many copies.[52] Why did a book written by an acclaimed musician, teacher, and activist fare so poorly, both in sales and critical attention? While definitive answers to this question cannot be determined, contributing factors and circumstances offer clues as to why *Colored Girl Beautiful* failed to bring Hackley the financial remuneration she anticipated. First, to the reading public, Hackley's musical accomplishments did not necessarily warrant the purchase of a relatively expensive (for its time), hard-bound volume with a focus on subject matter quite outside the realm of music, and thus, beyond the author's expertise. And second, there were many other advice manuals in print, along with articles on related topics in newspapers and periodicals, all already popular among African Americans, including those authored by whites.

Ultimately, and for unknown reasons, Johnson did not contribute a foreword or preface to Hackley's book, as he had originally promised. Hackley, therefore, wrote her own foreword. The book's eighteen chapters, she noted in her preliminary remarks, represented but a minute sampling of talks given to students at historically Black schools. In what she described as an "impromptu," "heart to heart," and "very informal" style, she presented to "the daughters of ... colored women" a "new thought" and bits of advice intended to inspire each Black girl and woman to serve as "a beacon light to her home and to the race."[53] She also reinforced her activist message about the status of African American girls and women by referencing, in her book's title, the biblical verse "Song of Solomon" 1:5—"I am black but comely" (KJV).[54] In her title, she conflated the realities of being both female and African American as the narrator of this biblical verse was a Black woman. Her title also anticipated the empowering motto "Black is beautiful." Not until the 1960s would this slogan achieve widespread recognition and use, as a renewed sense of race consciousness inspired African-derived fashion, hairstyles, and sociocultural expressiveness.

Even as Hackley did not shy away from mention of New Thought principles in her lectures and in her article series, "Hints to Young Colored Artists," she approached New Thought tenets in *Colored Girl Beautiful* as complementary to ecumenism and mystical Christianity and not as components of pedagogical strategies or musicianship. As she suggested in her foreword, Hackley cast her activist and philosophical net widely in *Colored Girl Beautiful*. She emphasized the significance of maintaining cleanliness in one's home and in personal hygiene—a component of her conservative viewpoint that reflected an allegiance to Booker T. Washington's philosophy.[55] The biblical Queen Esther provided an example of such conduct and standards for her readers to emulate. She recommended that all Black girls "must be taught the application of the story of Esther to her race. Tell her that each colored girl may be an Esther, especially in all matters of cleanliness, manners, and self sacrifice, to advance and change the prevalent opinion of the Negro."[56] In adulthood, Hackley advised, Black women should aspire to serve the race as mothers for "to assume the position of colored motherhood is the greatest privilege and responsibility than can come to any woman in this age." Such mothers should strive to "make a more beautiful race with the beauty that comes from beauty of character."⁵⁷

Hackley's *Colored Girl Beautiful* faced considerable competition from countless etiquette, advice, child-rearing and self-help books, columns and articles already in print. Without assertive advertising, promotion, and numerous favorable reviews, Hackley hardly stood a chance of competing with other authors and their publications. In spite of this competition, Burton Publishing Company failed to capitalize on the uniqueness of *Colored Girl Beautiful*. Hackley's book was the first of its kind to focus solely on Black girls and women. However, even with a dearth of advertising, publicity, and the lack of a robust marketing strategy, *Colored Girl Beautiful* did not immediately slip into oblivion. In 1920, a chapter from the book appeared in the groundbreaking anthology *The Upward Path: A Reader for Colored Children*. The contents of this anthology comprised what Robert R. Moton lauded as "the best literary works of Negro authors."⁵⁸ The anthology's compilers, Myron T. Pritchard and Mary White Ovington, selected Hackley's chapter "The Home of the Colored Girl Beautiful" for inclusion in their collection. Hackley's chapter shared space with essays, stories, and poetry written by many prominent African American authors.⁵⁹ As Moton explained, "the selections are each calculated to teach a valuable lesson," and "all make a direct appeal to the best impulses of the human." The selection of a white publisher, located in New York City, proved most beneficial for Pritchard and Ovington. Many newspapers across the nation, Black and white, printed reviews of their compilation. Nonetheless, substantial publicity generated by *Upward Path* contributed little, if anything, to the historical reputation of *Colored Girl Beautiful*. Hackley's busy schedule and intermittent illness prevented her from taking advantage of the press attention the anthology received. Moreover, although the publishers of *Upward Path* included a brief biographical statement about each author, they did not mention the title of Hackley's book as the source of her contribution to their literary collection.

It Pays to Be Respected!

Hackley repeatedly returned to the ideals, culture, and politics of respectability, especially in *Colored Girl Beautiful*.⁶⁰ During the postbellum–pre-Harlem era, the expectations of respectability encompassed, among other things, the use of proper manners, regular church attendance, modesty in conduct, and careful attention to grooming and attire. She advised readers and attendees at her lectures that, as a virtue, a respectable reputation was to be cherished and protected zealously. Such a reputation must also never be taken for granted, particularly by those whose forebears were enslaved. For, as Fannie Barrier Williams asserted, prior to Emancipation, "poor slave girls, many of them most beautiful in form and feature, were not allowed to be modest, not allowed to follow the instincts of moral rectitude."[61] Essayist and physician Sarah G. Jones concurred and explained the preoccupation of African American women with respectability as a lingering compensatory behavior emanating from the time of enslavement when white males demanded "compulsory immorality" of Black females.[62] Thus, Hackley presented the pursuit and safeguarding of respectability as a right, privilege, and a lifelong female responsibility. She offered assurance that decorous Black women would reap the benefits of their efforts: "It pays to be respected!"[63]

Yet even as Hackley presented to the public the embodiment of an elite, respectable African American woman who valorized domesticity, family, and motherhood, she was estranged from nearly all of her extended family, had been separated from her husband for many years, and did not have any children. Did her own awareness and self-consciousness about this rather unusual personal history and set of credentials inspire her to publish *Colored Girl Beautiful* before completing her other more musically related writing projects? An answer to this question may never be clarified. Still, the subject matter in her book gave focus to the class-laden and gendered messages of respectability she conveyed to audiences throughout her career. In many ways, *Colored Girl Beautiful* echoed the uplift rhetoric of the Black women's club movement and women's organizations within various church denominations. That she did not take advantage of these organizations and institutions to help build a readership for her book was, in the very least, short sighted. Through her own lack of initiative her book rapidly came to occupy a state of perpetual limbo—as an unheralded and aberrant publication from a woman known to the public as a teacher of voice culture, a consummate performer, an advocate of New Thought ideology, and the progenitor of musical social uplift. In the end, her national reputation did not validate or buoy her efforts to establish herself as a writer or to be recognized as an authority on comportment, etiquette, and child rearing. So, too, her book reads as a lengthy missive of frustration at what she perceived to be the widespread lack of Black adherence to, and appreciation of, the culture of respectability. It seems logical to conclude, then, that *Colored Girl Beautiful* ultimately served very personal and private purposes for Hackley—as a statement of, and vehicle for reinforcing, her own *bona fides* as a moral and dignified African American woman and race leader.

CHAPTER SEVEN

Chronic Illness and New Thought

Hackley's frequent public appearances and hectic traveling schedule belied the fact that she suffered from recurrent ill health throughout her career. In addition to the resultant disruption of concertizing and teaching, her ailments also caused periodic loss of hearing. Determined and stoic, Hackley expended considerable effort to maintain a public image of seeming vitality. Yet, in actuality, she endured the uneasy life of a disabled person, especially owing to her unreliable hearing acuity. We cannot know, for certain, how Hackley viewed her precarious health in light of her allegiance to New Thought, generally, and to the practice of mental healing, in particular. As discussed earlier, she lectured and wrote about the virtues of New Thought tenets and attendant deep-breathing techniques, particularly as regards wellness. She incorporated these principles in her music education pedagogy, and they formed a vital component of her uplift agenda. New Thought also helped her assemble a spiritual underpinning and philosophical framework with which to work toward deflecting the ravages of segregation and racism. It seems reasonable to surmise, therefore, that she realized some solace and comfort from New Thought during her illnesses, and she probably credited its ideology with the remissions she experienced. Yet, even if New Thought ideology proved merely palliative for her, she never publicly expressed doubts about its potential to promote healing and to generate hope and optimism.

Hackley began to suffer from respiratory and throat ailments in the late 1890s when she resided in Denver, Colorado. She blamed these bouts of illness on the city's elevation and severe winters. With her subsequent move to Philadelphia in 1902, she hoped to make a complete recovery. But, by 1904, she had become incapacitated and confided, in a letter to Harriet Gibbs, "I have rheumatism and can hardly walk."[1] Although an archaic term, "rheumatism," in the early twentieth century, connoted more than one debilitating condition, including arthritis, joint disorders, severe inflammation, or a potentially serious auto-immune disease. Not yet forty years old, Hackley already suffered from conditions more commonly associated with the elderly. Whatever the etiology of her ill health at this point in life, she obviously endured chronic pain and compromised mobility.

Hackley first admitted to hearing problems, albeit privately, in 1905. Immediately after a recital in Philadelphia in October of that year, she confided to a friend, Lucille Tate, the general seriousness of a condition involving both ears, noting, "my ear drums pain me." To Tate she also revealed the startling loss of hearing that occurred during the Philadelphia performance: "I could hardly hear my own voice as I sang."[2] However, by early 1906, she had recovered sufficiently to undertake a sea voyage to Europe. Her health did not remain stable, and while she resided in Paris, she became ill. Edwin Hackley wrote to Harriet Gibbs regarding his wife's unspecified illness, stating only that "her health has not been the very best."[3] After her return to the United States in 1907, Hackley apparently recovered and remained well for a time. Yet, during her stay in London, 1908–9, she again struggled with recurring respiratory problems. From London, she corresponded with suffragist Caroline M. S. Severance and elaborated on her condition: "For three weeks I was ill . . . with lumbago [back pain], rheumatism and a cold in my chest."[4] The newspaper reading public learned little about this most recent health crisis save a brief announcement in the *Colorado Statesman*, which read: "She has been quite a sufferer in health since she has been over there."[5] Hackley found the London climate "positively wicked to foreigners," and she added that "the terrible fogs tried to finish me and send me back to America but I am too plucky for that." She confirmed, to Severance, her intention to attend at least a few of London's suffrage events when her health improved. Her hope for a remission proved illusory, and, early in 1909, doctors instructed her to terminate her stay in London and return to the United States.[6] Quite ill at this point, she followed the advice of health practitioners and left England.

Hackley apparently made a rapid recovery after her ocean voyage as no reports of lingering health problems appeared in the press or in her private communications. However, in 1910, she interrupted her travels in order to recover from a cold "and its resultant effects." Her health deteriorated, and the press described her worsening condition as "pleurisy."[7] In addition, she sustained some sort of serious injury in Nashville, Tennessee, when she fell while attempting to board a streetcar.[8] She resumed touring later in 1910, but ill health and impaired hearing again intervened, and she ended her travels prematurely. As the *Broad Ax* reported, she then visited Chicago "for continuous treatment from a specialist for her ear, and for the general condition of her health." The press lamented, "Unfortunately, her stay of one week in Chicago was too short for the ear specialist to give Madame Hackley any relief." In fact, her health problems now mandated frequent intervention, and she admitted to consulting "a specialist in each city she . . . visited."[9]

Hackley's susceptibility to illness continued to impede her professional activities as the 1910s unfolded. In 1911, the press revealed another illness, brought on by the stress of touring, that compelled her to spend a few weeks in Texas seeking treatment and recuperating. By the end of February 1911, the *Broad Ax* happily announced that Hackley was "much improved in health."[10] After many additional months of intermittent rest she was well enough to visit Cuba twice from 1912 through 1913. However, in early 1914, a severe case of bronchitis kept her bedridden for a considerable length of time.[11] Her health improved substantially by late spring of that year, permitting her to sail to Paris, where she remained for some three months. But, in late spring of 1915, a recalcitrant bout of influenza forced her to alter her schedule.[12] In a letter to James Weldon Johnson, she remarked on the lingering physical and psychological effects of this illness: "I lost twenty five pounds of healthy avoirdupois, and my peace of mind. I could not think, much less concentrate." She hinted at a New Thought solution to this most recent health crisis, with the comment: "I'll be in my right mind soon."[13] After a few weeks' rest, she resumed touring and did not experience any health problems for several months. This remission was interrupted when, on 18 December 1916, following a recital in Cleveland, she fell ill with a sudden onset of respiratory distress. When she did not respond to treatment, she traveled to New York City for further medical evaluation. Upon the advice of doctors, she entered the Manhattan Eye, Ear, and Throat Hospital and underwent a "slight operation" to alleviate a "chronic ear condition."[14] The press's mention of a procedure involving one of her ears suggests that she suffered a return of impaired hearing.[15] According to the *Savannah Tribune*, Hackley, now "quite ill with ear trouble," required "confinement and treatment for a fortnight."[16] The *Chicago Defender* anticipated a second surgery for her hearing and throat problems.[17] Hackley must have been emotionally devastated at this prospect as her physicians initially held out hope that another surgery might be avoided, and they had carefully planned her ensuing treatment accordingly.[18] An item in the Denver press confirmed she had, indeed, endured another operation: "The friends of Mme. Hackley will regret to know that she is in a hospital in New York City as a result of an operation in her throat."[19] A "severe cold" and an ear infection hampered her recovery from this procedure.[20] In pursuit of further treatment, she again considered another stay in a New York hospital.

To her sister, Marietta Smith Johnson, she wrote of a frightening episode of total deafness and confirmed that, on her way to seeking medical help, she fell "at the hospital door unconscious."[21] The press lamented that "her condition is serious," and this most recent episode forced her to cancel an important NAACP-sponsored festival in honor of Booker T. Washington, scheduled in New York's Carnegie Hall. That her friend Marie A. D. Madre traveled from Washington, DC to New York to visit her in the hospital only underscored the extent of her health problems.[22] In a letter to another friend, Berena Anderson Sogers, Hackley admitted telling details about her condition: "I am dizzy all the time. My feet fail to find the right spot on the floor and the sidewalk. This is from the ear. The seat of equilibrium and the inner ear ache [are] at the same spot.... I am still deaf in one ear which has [been making] all sorts of sounds [such as] rushing, hissing, and throbbing." In addition, she mentioned being "too deaf and wobbly" to work or travel.[23] Writing to Sogers again, Hackley complained that her "eye jerks with each throb of my ear."[24] Her description of abnormal eye movement, tinnitus, pain, vertigo and deafness suggests she suffered from Ménière's disease, a chronic and, at that time, untreatable, affliction.

Following her release from the hospital in February 1917, Hackley convalesced at "Knoll," the picturesque Cornwall-on-Hudson estate of famed clergyman Rev. Lyman Abbott and his extended family. There she relaxed in Abbott's twelve-room mansion, furnished with the latest conveniences and surrounded by scenic acres of trees and rolling hills. Rev. Abbott's son, Dr. Theodore J. Abbott, served as Hackley's medical advisor while she rested. At this point, Dr. Abbott considered "a mastoid operation" advisable for Hackley's condition.[25] Whether or not this particular procedure ever took place, or what it may have entailed, cannot be determined. A press announcement in late March 1917 indicated that Hackley remained quite ill and still had "not yet recovered from an infection in one of her ears."[26] The *Philadelphia Tribune* informed readers that she "had decided to cancel her engagements for the next month and to remain in the vicinity of Philadelphia that she may avail herself of regular medical treatment from a noted local ear specialist."[27] The imperturbable Hackley refused to slow down, and she not only placed newspaper advertisements seeking students to teach privately, but she also announced her availability to nearby communities for organizing music events.[28] Yet her condition clearly concerned her, so much so that she traveled to Baltimore and entered Johns Hopkins University Hospital to obtain another opinion about her health. Disappointingly, the Johns Hopkins staff failed to offer her any satisfactory treatment, relief, or advice.[29] She left Baltimore and spent much of April 1917 in Philadelphia, quite likely staying at Edwin Hackley's residence, recuperating. While in Philadelphia, she consulted more specialists regarding her hearing impairment.[30] By May

1917 she had recovered sufficiently to travel to Washington DC for a speaking engagement.[31] Her health remained stable for several months thereafter, and she resumed choral conducting, teaching, and lecturing. However, the *Age* reported she "quietly entered New York" sometime in August 1917 for "expert aural treatment."[32] In December 1917 she developed another ear infection, which she blamed on severe winter weather. Owing to unremitting pain, she entered the Manhattan Eye, Ear, and Throat Hospital again, where she remained for two weeks. During this hospital stay, she lost all hearing in her right ear and had to undergo additional surgery.[33]

In 1919, while in Detroit, another illness required Hackley to spend an unspecified length of time at the city's Mercy Hospital. She canceled a series of performances and convalesced at her sister's residence.[34] The Philadelphia press painted a grim picture: "Her physicians say that she will not be able to do anything for about a year."[35] The *Washington DC Bee* noted that Hackley also spent time recovering from an unspecified ailment at the DC home of her friend Marie A. D. Madre (now Marshall).[36] She had already been at the Madre-Marshall residence for two weeks when the press announced that, owing to her health, she intended to remain there for an indefinite period of time.[37] Hackley admitted to Lucien White, music critic for the *New York Age*, that her health had deteriorated throughout 1920.[38] In another letter to Berena Anderson Sogers, Hackley confided she suffered from frequent emesis, kidney disease, and possible neurological complications: "I suppose you have heard how ill I have been since last July [1919] with nephritis. My whole nervous system was poisoned.... [I experience] dizziness and uncertain movements of my feet.... My face on the left side still 'pricks' and 'stings' while my left hand feels as if it were full of pins and needles."[39]

Hackley's health problems extended far beyond those discussed above. Prior to her marriage, she expressed a strong desire to raise a large family. Ultimately, she did not have any children, and it is not known whether she ever became, or attempted to become, pregnant. An explanation for her apparent infertility, offered only long after her death, blamed her inability to conceive on a fall, at around age twelve or thirteen, from which she sustained unspecified internal injuries.[40] Her inability to have children must have been a serious disappointment as she envisioned motherhood as the paramount function and purpose of marriage. For, as she advised, "when a woman enters into the marriage contract,... it is understood that parenthood is to be the chief aim and hope."[41] From this remark, we must conclude that Hackley fully intended to have children but did not know of her potential reproductive limitations before marrying Edwin Hackley.

In addition to physical illness, Hackley experienced severe psychological upheaval at various times in her life. In her later years she vividly recalled her family's abrupt flight from Murfreesboro, Tennessee, in 1870, after racist whites attacked her mother's school and terrorized Black families in the area. Memories of this experience and the resultant relocation to Detroit could only have traumatized her. During her formative years she was subject to the demands of an autocratic and emotionally distant mother, and the caprices of a father who apparently was substantially absent from family life. Her parents' marriage faltered, and they separated when Hackley was in her teens—a critical time for any young person to endure the breakup of one's immediate family. Hackley later made a veiled reference to these unfortunate circumstances when she wrote that "divorce is a terrible 'something.' It is a blight to children and often means their ruin or the blasting of their future."[42] As she suggested, the dissolution of the family she knew as a child caused her considerable angst as a young adult. The problems associated with her parents' separation also affected members of her extended family as, while still living in Detroit, she had little contact with anyone in her family except her sister and an uncle. No documentation has surfaced to indicate whether she ever reestablished communication with other relatives. Not even her marriage to Edwin Hackley in 1894 facilitated a reconciliation as no family members attended the couple's wedding ceremony. Still another emotionally scarring event occurred around 1909 when the Hackley marriage unraveled, and Azalia and Edwin Hackley separated, permanently.

Even during serious health crises, it seems certain that Hackley continued to supplement more conventional treatment by turning to New Thought methods and principles. Occasionally, she attributed her weakening physical health to emotional stress, thus insinuating that her problems emanated from negative thoughts and that a solution could still be obtained from the New Thought premises of mental healing and thought concentration.[43] Toward the end of her life, she blamed racism and the "color question" for her illnesses—another reference to the role she felt thoughts played in physical health.[44] As discussed previously, she ardently believed in the power of thought to overcome physical, mental, and emotional challenges. For her, strong negative thought vibrations traveled contagiously and, if allowed to do so unabated, could cause a myriad of societal and personal problems ranging from racism to illnesses and mental turmoil. To preclude such a possibility, she recommended Yogic breathing exercises as the ultimate method for impeding the flow of negative thought and thus safeguarding one's health.[45]

By the end of 1920, Hackley had recovered to the extent that she felt able to organize a series of appearances on the West Coast. She planned to begin this tour in Seattle with the production of a costumed pageant and then travel south.[46] While in California, just prior to a performance, she collapsed. Within days, the *New York Age* reported she had been found unconscious in San Diego after suffering a "nervous breakdown."⁴⁷ Another newspaper confirmed that her collapse and lingering illness, "caused by the strain of overwork," required a protracted stay at San Diego's St. Joseph Hospital.⁴⁸ Journalist Lucien White blamed this episode on stress initially precipitated by the financial burden and eventual closing of her Normal Vocal Institute.⁴⁹ Hackley's sister traveled to California and took her home to Detroit. By the end of 1921, newspapers described Hackley as "suffering from nervous prostration. . . . Reports have it that the attending physicians give very little hope of her ever returning to the concert stage."⁵⁰ A subsequent item stated that "since the seizure she had in California some time ago, following which she was brought to her [sister Marietta's] home, she has shown little sign of improvement."⁵¹ The "seizure" referred to in this comment could have been a stroke or cardiac episode. During the early twentieth century, terms such as "nervous prostration" or "breakdown" indicated a severe psychological upset and serious illness that prevented attendance to even routine daily activities. A San Diego newspaper reported, "Now it is thought that she is not only physically infirm, but that her mentality is also affected. In fact, it is probable that her mental ailment has affected her physically, according to those who are familiar with her condition."⁵²

Hackley's collapse and resultant invalidism prevented her from contemplating any future travels, and, uncharacteristically, she did not issue any announcements of proposed public events to newspapers. The Black press respected her need for privacy as she struggled to regain her health; few newspapers mentioned her name. As publicity about her diminished, her profile as a nationally respected activist and music educator faded. By September 1922, her health had worsened, and the *New York Age* expressed fear that she had become "a permanent invalid."⁵³ Within weeks of the issuance of this statement, her condition deteriorated even further, and, on the afternoon of 13 December, she suffered a series of cerebral hemorrhages. She lapsed into a coma and died several hours later with her sister, Marietta, and brother-in-law, Joseph Johnson, at her side. Her funeral service took place at Detroit's St. Matthew's Episcopal Church. She was buried at Elmwood Cemetery, Detroit, alongside the grave of her mother.⁵⁴

Owing to chronically impaired hearing, Hackley lived in the socially constructed reality of a person with a disability. Even if she experienced periodic respite from the debilitating loss of hearing, she could never be certain if or when her impairment would return. Such an existence, grounded in a traditional interpretation of sensory deprivation, often assigned an individual the status of inadequacy and inferiority. Furthermore, in Hackley's day, persons with disabilities were often held personally responsible for their condition.⁵⁵ Ironically, New Thought adherents would have promoted just such a sentiment and Hackley may have been convinced that, by accepting even partial responsibility for her hearing loss, she had taken the first crucial step toward a mental and spiritual solution of her problem. For a musician, especially a concert performer, even partial hearing loss is particularly devastating, artistically and professionally. And for an African American woman, already considered inferior by the dominant white society, the situation of impairment compounded an already complicated and tense existence. Moreover, Hackley's prominence and frequent public appearances made it virtually impossible for her to keep such an affliction totally private, much as she endeavored to do. When she eliminated performances of art songs and opera arias from her recital programs, this change in programing must have resulted, at least in part, from hearing problems.[56] The musician who experiences this type of impairment always holds out hope for a more lasting remission or a complete remedy to the problem. Although Hackly retained at least partial hearing in one ear for substantial periods of time, she also accommodated her impairment by altering her repertoire and singing fewer solo pieces herself. She gradually shared the stage with an increasing number of guest performers to fill out her programs and eventually abandoned her solo career altogether.[57] When she changed her repertoire, she programmed pieces with greatly restricted tessitura and therefore reduced the challenge of securing correct pitches. As she usually accompanied herself, she retained tactile awareness of pitch owing to physical contact with a piano and its keyboard. Thus, she could actually "feel" the vibrations of correct pitches and pitch cues as she played the piano while singing. She also believed the accuracy of intonation could be ascertained kinesthetically by employing New Thought principles to develop an acute awareness of the position and tautness of one's diaphragm, rather than relying solely on aural cues to sing correct pitches.[58]

Hackley made public references to "disability" but not in the context of her own illnesses. To be sure, her private awareness of impaired hearing and other health and personal challenges surely informed her comments about the "disabled" nature of African Americans in a racist society. In this regard, she considered an African American child as disadvantaged from birth and as a member of a "persecuted and handicapped" race. She equated "disability" and "handicap" with the imposition of a universal "burden" of racism on, and one shared by, all Blacks. But she also acknowledged the vulnerability of all Black women to the dynamics of the inherited disadvantage of merely being born female. In her nuanced definition of what she identified as a "triple burden," she stressed the imperative of each Black woman to deflect, through employment of New Thought strategies, the relentless bombardment of racism directed at her. The constant and unsolicited attention from whites included not only overt racist behavior but also the sexualized gaze and innuendos of white males. As Hackley ardently believed in telepathy, her comments regarding a Black woman's personal burden also encompassed the potential to perceive the lewd and unspoken sexual thoughts of racists. In addition, a Black woman bore the burden of her race as a whole, including the responsibility to present, publicly, an image of proper feminine decorum and cleanliness, to raise wholesome sons, and to squelch inappropriate conduct on the part of Black males. Therefore, as Hackley concluded, all Black women shouldered a third burden: the overarching presence of constant anxiety regarding the posterity of their race.[59]

In actuality, Hackley spent virtually her entire career overcoming intermittent invalidism and compromised hearing. Yet she insisted on her own humanity and wholeness—as a person for whom illness did not define her or represent physical or emotional inferiority. By maintaining, as much as her health allowed, an ambitious schedule of frequent travel and public appearances, she countered the white Victorian notion of women as innately weak and therefore unfit to work outside the home. She also remained aware of the detriments of revealing any additional information about her illnesses to the press or the public. To do so meant jeopardizing her prominence as an activist, concert artist, and music educator. Furthermore, disclosure of ill health would have tarnished her credibility as a race leader who professed the benefits of mental healing and Yogic breathing techniques. She routinely turned to New Thought's strategies for sustaining wellness, thereby reducing her reliance on overpriced medical care and limiting her exposure to the substandard medical treatment so often meted out to African Americans.[60] Her unswerving endorsement of mental healing and deep breathing in the face of chronic illness and impaired hearing underscored her allegiance to these practices. Ultimately, New Thought yielded for her a compelling alternative for confronting illness and impairment and offered a strategy for sustaining optimism and achieving a sense of a positive future.

CODA

Hackley's career not only exemplified the aspirations and accomplishments of the postbellum-pre-Harlem years, but it also illuminated some of the era's most pressing complexities and contradictions. Hackley tirelessly supported African American music making and believed musical achievement offered both unassailable proof of Blacks' intellectual and aesthetic acumen and irrefutable evidence of racial progress. To meet her activist goals, she interwove music instruction with New Thought ideology to form a hybrid methodology and philosophy. Central to her agenda, she harnessed ways to nurture consciousness of, and appreciation for, African ancestry and racial identity. *New York Age* columnist James Hogans vividly recalled the power of her "assertion of race" and the contagious "feeling of race pride" she exuded at public events. To Hogans, her charismatic leadership and unswerving commitment to uplift initiatives established her as "the ideal race woman."[1]

Hackley drew upon a variety of sources to assemble a composite and pioneering activist agenda. As a fusion of music making and New Thought fueled her activist momentum, we must view and evaluate her historical significance from interconnected and multiple viewpoints. The reclamation of her significance requires more specialized considerations and analytical approaches not often employed for the purpose of augmenting or reinterpreting our knowledge of racial uplift. It is also important to acknowledge the uniqueness of Hackley's approach as no precedence for widespread music education activism or New Thought spirituality prevailed within African American communities prior to her arrival on the racial uplift landscape. In contrast, her success on the concert stage owed much to the critically acclaimed virtuosity and courage of African American stage artists who came before her. Such luminaries as Marie Selika, Sissieretta Jones, and other Black concert singers defied US aesthetic and musical racism—a tradition of resistance Hackley inherited and perpetuated. Beyond racism, Hackley also had to contend with the overall lukewarm and inconsistent reception of classical music in the United States. Arguably, the US classical music world was and is confined to larger metropolitan areas and remains the domain of the financially comfortable. Additionally, readily accessible popular idioms, rather than the values and styles of European repertoire, have tended to mold US musical taste and preferences. A philosophical divide between the training of classical music performers and the pedagogical tenets of music education added to the complexity of the musical climate Hackley encountered. In the United States, music educators have traditionally embraced universality, and they approach music making as an avenue of expression deemed appropriate and beneficial for all citizens, regardless of innate or acquired capabilities or limitations. Conversely, artistic training usually requires private lessons and highly specialized instruction, along with requisite financial resources. Hackley struggled with this dichotomy as she attempted to meld the methodologies of music education with artistic performance and more challenging European repertoire. The former holds out the potential for generalized application and broad appeal, while the latter is associated with elitism and exceptionality, along with hierarchical propensities. As an activist, Hackley explored areas of commonality between classical repertoire and music education, and she presented to her public an empowering compromise between these two seemingly disparate worlds.

However unique and innovative her teaching and activist methods, Hackley did not remain philosophically insular. She identified with, adopted, and put into practice salient aspects of African American activist philosophies prominent in her era, especially those associated with Booker T. Washington and W. E. B. Du Bois. As a supporter of some of Washington's principles, she promoted policies of pragmatism and lectured on the virtues of thrift, a strong work ethic and the acquisition of employable skills. She also adhered, substantially, to Washington's apolitical, accommodationist, and gradualist approaches. In addition, she favored the patriarchal and conservative role of wife/mother for women, as espoused upon throughout her etiquette book, *Colored Girl Beautiful*. But she did not and could not fulfill these roles herself. Of this realization, she wrote: "Every colored wife who has not borne children or a wife who has lost children, owes a duty to the children of others."[2] She resolutely followed her own advice as she promoted African-derived traditions of communal caring, education, and spiritual engagement. Her philosophy of racial uplift, infused with the ethics of morality, respectability, and race allegiance, complemented and enhanced the values of Black communities' institutions, namely benevolent societies, schools, and churches. Yet even as racist denigration and violence raged unchecked during Hackley's career, she generally shunned political agitation. Although she did not become embroiled in the fight to abolish

Jim Crow segregation, she joined other activists who initiated legal action in protest of the unclean and unsafe travel accommodations forced upon Blacks, particularly girls and women. Regardless of political acquiescence, Hackley's unprecedented popularity attests to her extraordinary and widespread allure and effectiveness as a race leader.

So, too, Hackley articulated and exhibited philosophical contradictions, especially noticeable in her adherence to principles associated with W. E. B. Du Bois and the Talented Tenth. She sometimes manifested elitist and classist attitudes, especially in her own sense of personal exceptionality and her occasional insensitivity toward the general Black population. Her pursuit of music studies in Europe reflected Du Bois's influence and yielded her a compelling credential with which to expound upon the virtues of artistic training. She sought out and associated with well-heeled Blacks while in Paris and cultivated an image of an elegantly attired and expensively coiffed prima donna. Her light skin hue and wavy hair—characteristics associated with many members of the Talented Tenth—allowed her to travel on whites-only train cars in the South and thus to sidestep, however temporarily, the humiliations of Jim Crow regulations. Although she did not employ passing as a means of denying her African heritage and identity and its attendant restrictions, she did occasionally take advantage of light skin privilege as a strategy of protest and defiance.

The extraordinary popularity of Hackley's mediatory public persona calls into question the very existence of an intractable and unbridgeable philosophical chasm between the viewpoints and strategies of Washington and Du Bois. Hackley did not, however, lay claim to, or clearly articulate, a definitive philosophical middle ground as an alternative to the reputed Washington-Du Bois divide. Perhaps unexpectedly, her conciliatory posture did not taint her relationship with either Washington or Du Bois, both of whom admired her talent and appreciated her uplift efforts. Du Bois frequently mentioned her in the pages of the *Crisis* while the Tuskegee administration welcomed her to their campus. The *New York Age*, a newspaper largely under Washington's proprietary control, followed Hackley's career quite closely. However unusual her seemingly noncommittal stance regarding certain hot-button racial issues, such a stance was not entirely unique in her day.[3] In fact, one of her influential contemporaries, Carrie W. Clifford, published an essay in which she disclosed a similar social and cultural ethos. Clifford opened with this observation: "I have closely followed the discussion which has waged so hotly concerning the manner of the solution of the [race] problem and the kind of education to be given to the Negro." She then boldly argued, "I deplore the fact we have, by internal disagreements and discussions, added to the already sadly confused state of affairs.... Both [Du Bois' and Washington's philosophies] are essential and each is indispensible to man's proper and well-rounded development. The result of such internal disagreements has been to leave on the public mind the impression that the race is divided into two schools of thinkers, . . . and that the ideas held by each are in direct opposition; that they are hopelessly antagonistic." In her article, Clifford advocated for what she construed to be the best result of this debate, attainable only when each approach "merges into the other." Ultimately, she refuted the supposed binary opposition assigned to Du Bois and Washington and their respective followings, and, instead, explored the possibilities of a rhetorical and philosophical bridge. Hackley put into action the mediatory narrative so eloquently expressed by Clifford.[4]

Looking beyond a correlation between the philosophies of Clifford and Hackley, the historiographical seduction to align Hackley's approach with more recent theoretical, analytical, or activist paradigms has been a constant presence during the writing of this book. Yet finding correspondences between her multiple talents and areas of expertise with those of more recent philosophical constructs presents numerous challenges. Womanism or nascent African American feminism might serve as starting points for such inquiry, yet there is little to justify a relationship between Hackley and the tenets of these theories. Ultimately, the many seemingly disparate facets of musical social uplift can be rendered more cohesive and interactive by exploring the contours of an open-ended analytical approach such as that offered by the lesser-known theory of "relational activism." A paradigm introduced by Sara O'Shaunghnessy and Emily Hudart Kennedy, relational activism foregrounds applications and strategies not often considered, or given credence, in philosophical discussions or analyses. I find the principles and values of relational activism to be useful tools in the effort to place Hackley's methodology in a more contemporary light. The theory, implementation, and effectiveness of relational activism depend upon several strategies and variables. Relational activists seek to do the following:

- forge networks of like-minded participants
- deemphasize conflict
- avoid militancy or heated rhetoric
- blur distinctions between public and private spheres
- pursue social change through modification of personal behavior
- promote incidental learning
- prioritize community relationships and values
- encourage maternal thinking[5]

Hackley blended public and private domains as she taught singing exercises to large crowds that could also be initiated in the intimacy of homes. The process of nurturing self-esteem and race pride involved engagement with the

New Thought strategies of thought concentration and telepathy—both highly personal pursuits. By replicating Hackley's instructions at home, audiences could actuate a component of relational activism by initiating social change within the practice of daily routines and thought processes. Relational activists also seek to deemphasize the centrality of conflict, and Hackley endeavored to downplay heated debate and rhetoric and political agitation throughout her career. Through musical uplift she validated incidental learning by harnessing music education as a tool for building race consciousness using strategies found outside the activist methodologies of her day. Her style and philosophy of music teaching and learning privileged social change and spiritual enlightenment over exclusive concentration on the acquisition of music skills. She exploited the use of highly visible and public activism and formed potent relationships with the innumerable communities she visited. In her advocacy of uplift eugenics and responsible procreation, she tapped into a dimension of contemporaneous maternal thinking that valorized the traditional and overlapping spheres of motherhood and domesticity.

However much Hackley intentionally sidestepped political agitation and overt militancy, she nonetheless occasionally engaged in resistance and defiance. Her lawsuits against the southern rail system should be recognized as significant manifestations of protest behavior. Additionally, she encountered and stalwartly resisted racist cultural and aesthetic barriers during the years she toured as a solo artist. Although she earned accolades from the Black press for her renditions of opera arias, art songs and virtuosic solo works, white newspapers paid comparatively little attention to her extraordinary vocal technique and acclaimed interpretations of classical repertoire. Her commitment to the reclamation of spirituals mandated an altogether different set of priorities and strategies in order to mediate the aesthetic and cultural divide between Black folk music and European-derived classics. For example, some Blacks of the postbellum-pre-Harlem period vociferously objected to the performance of spirituals and instead considered these songs as remnants of slavery's dehumanization and cruelty best allocated to obscurity. As whites tended to support a programming philosophy that confined Blacks to racially identified music, such as minstrelsy and spirituals, both genres bore the stamp of racist preference and taste. So, too, common reference to spirituals as "plantation songs" underscored their connection with slavery and ignored other invaluable cultural, performance, and aesthetic associations with this genre. Thus, in her effort to preserve spirituals, pursue a solo career, and perform Western classical repertoire, Hackley had to prove her *bona fides* as a multifaceted artist and teacher to both Black and white audiences and critics.

There has been insufficient attention given to the early history, foundational philosophy, and methodologies of African American education. Such an omission also persists in the more specialized field of music education as educators have tended to focus on teaching repertoire derived from global musics at the expense of seminal events in the postbellum-pre-Harlem era.[6] When Hackley began to teach singing techniques and music appreciation to large audiences, she had to assemble her own pedagogical approach as no methodology or philosophy for teaching music to Black students, *en masse*, had been formalized. Most Black music educators of the late nineteenth and early twentieth centuries employed methods established by pioneering US music teachers of the 1840s-90s, namely, Lowell Mason, William B. Bradbury and George F. Root. These and other early music educators taught music classes intended, for the most part, to improve singing in churches, to instill morality and to reinforce pious conduct.[7] To be sure, Hackley did not abandon these connections between music and spirituality, especially evident in her use of New Thought ideology in the teaching of singing. Otherwise, however, her approach to music teaching and learning deviated, considerably, from the fundamental methods and goals developed in the nineteenth century. To begin with, she assured students of the accessibility and racial relevance of her methods, and she configured her music lessons with the needs of African Americans at the forefront of her teaching strategies. Even as she, herself, participated in the highly competitive world of the concert stage, she refused to allow competition and its resultant hierarchy to enter into her lessons or vocal demonstrations before large audiences. Instead, her methods of music teaching and learning served as pillars of an uplift agenda supportive of self-esteem, race pride, positive thinking, and individual confidence. She believed in the universality of African-derived musical gifts and the uniqueness of Black interpretive powers, whether in the singing of spirituals or in classical works. When teaching spirituals, she celebrated African American performance practices and considered them to be essential for authentic interpretations of these songs. This aspect of her philosophy allowed students to cultivate the spontaneity and improvisation characteristic of Black music, quite in contrast to the methods of early white music educators who tended to adhere, strictly, to the pitches, harmonies, dynamics, and other elements dictated by music notation. And finally, contrary to the philosophy of white music teachers, Hackley's classes served vital and far-reaching activist purposes that focused on positive change and racial justice.

Hackley's philosophy and methods presaged more recent contributions to educational innovation and liberative pedagogy. Her remarkable success as an educator becomes that much more compelling and noteworthy when we remember that she taught at hundreds of historically Black institutions and communities, coast to coast. She envisioned music making and music education as interconnected agencies for achieving social equality, building self-esteem, and enhancing racial solidarity. She also promoted aspects of her music pedagogy as conducive to wellness, especially as she believed New Thought–derived deep-breathing exercises and mental concentration could stave off the ravages of debilitating illnesses. As a pedagogue, she practiced what cultural critic bell hooks calls "transgressions." According to hooks, students and teachers "transgress" when they interrogate the very existence of pernicious philosophical, social, and cultural barriers and strive to dislodge, penetrate, or otherwise hobble such constraints. Among her pedagogical innovations, Hackley promoted the preservation of the cultural, expressive, and historical value of spirituals—an initiative she justifiably ascertained lay largely dormant in her era. In so doing, she routinely disseminated what hooks describes as "the messages of resistance that emerged in the music created by slaves."[8] In another of her transgressions, Hackley performed and taught in many venues access to which whites often denied Blacks. Her methodology helped to disrupt the tyranny of stereotypes of Black musical inferiority and to decenter white aesthetics, performance practices, pedagogy and repertoire. She approached teaching as a performative act in which she engaged audiences to join her in focusing on change, hope, and positive thinking. Acknowledging the commonalities between Hackley's activist strategies and philosophy with those of contemporary educators allows her accomplishments—to borrow the words of renowned pedagogue Paulo Freire—"to enter the historical process," thereby confirming that recent and current trends and debates regarding repertoire and methodology in education owe much to pioneering teachers such as Hackley. Decades before Freire wrote of the political, personal, and social significance to a people of "their word, their expressiveness, and their culture," Hackley's leadership in the promotion of African American music yielded a compelling alternative voice to the devastating effects of racism. Freire's account of his now classic "pedagogy of the oppressed" details the transformation of education from a "practice of dominance" to a "practice of freedom" based on methods and materials "forged with, not for, the oppressed." His pedagogy fosters "the emergence of consciousness"—a process that recalls the goals of Hackley's agenda of musical social uplift, especially evident in her choice of African American–centered repertoire and performance practices.[9]

As a New Thought advocate, Hackley helped establish the legitimacy of a more supple, metaphysical, and ecumenical response to racism. Marcus Garvey's public declamations of New Thought aphorisms extended Hackley's efforts to nurture African American self-determination and an abiding sense of optimism. Of more recent Black New Thought leaders, several were ordained clergy, and some founded places of worship dedicated to New Thought practices. Those of particular prominence include Rev. Garland Anderson, Father Divine, Rev.

Johnnie Colemon, and Rev. Ike. Rev. Anderson, a writer and playwright, became an ordained New Thought clergyman, wrote extensively about transcendent spirituality, and lectured widely. Father Divine infused his Peace Mission movement with New Thought principles, especially those related to the pursuit of abundant living, positive thinking, and mental healing. He often delivered sermons about the power of telepathy and thought concentration. Colemon enhanced New Thought's visibility in African American communities with the formation of mega churches and centers devoted to its study. Recent scholarship has added Oprah Winfrey to the list of prominent African Americans who espouse New Thought ideology.

Many of Hackley's protégées continued to work as professional musicians or achieved success in their teaching careers. Among these, Denver resident and baritone Clarence Carroll Clark and Michigan native and contralto Daisy Robinson Tapley became the first African Americans to make commercial recordings. Soprano Mary Saunders Patterson (1882–1951), a student of Hackley and subsequently a respected instructor of singing in the Philadelphia area, was Marian Anderson's first voice teacher. Some of the musicians in Hackley's circle taught or served influential administrative posts at various institutions' music departments. For example, composer R. Nathaniel Dett benefitted enormously from his association with Hackley, and she persuaded Hampton Institute to appoint him as the director of their music department and choral program. In addition, Clarence Cameron White taught at the Washington Conservatory of Music, West Virginia State College, and Hampton Institute, and Carl Rossini Diton held positions at Paine and Talladega Colleges and at New York's celebrated Juilliard School.

A few of Hackley's protégées founded influential and enduring community music schools. Among these, contralto Pauline James Lee established the Chicago Conservatory of Music around 1918. In an advertisement for her institution, Lee promised prospective students they could look forward to being taught the "Azalia Hackley Method."[10] Lee hired esteemed musicians to serve on her faculty, including Hackley's friend, concert pianist and composer Hazel Harrison (1883–1969); Clarence Cameron White; and yet another Hackley protégée, soprano Florence Cole Talbert (1890–1961). Hackley also mentored Mary L. Fitzhugh (later Fitzhugh-Valentine, 1888–1946), a well-known blind soprano, and helped her establish a successful stage career. The two women toured extensively together from 1910 through 1912. In 1921, Fitzhugh-Valentine founded the Fitzhugh-Valentine College of Music in Indianapolis, and her institution remained open for some two decades. As an expression of gratitude to her mentor, Fitzhugh-Valentine named a concert space and meeting room the "Azalia Hackley Assembly Hall."[11] Finally, in 1925, pianist Bertha A. Hansbury, who benefitted enormously from Hackley's assistance, established a music school in Detroit. Her school also featured art classes, an employment agency, and a kindergarten, referred to by her, affectionately, as a "Little Folks School."[12]

Although many memories of Hackley's career faded after her death, the People's Chorus, founded by her in Philadelphia, continued to rehearse and perform. Later known variously as the "Hackley Choral Society" or the "Azalia Hackley Choral Club," the ensemble remained active until the mid-1930s. Institutions and individuals also created tributes to Hackley's accomplishments. On 18 October 1933, Hampton Institute dedicated a performance space, the Azalia Hackley Recital Hall, in her honor. Hackley's protégé, Clarence Cameron White, then the director of Hampton's School of Music, led the effort to name this performance venue in her memory.[13] In 1938, two acquaintances of Hackley, A. Merral Willis and Edith E. Baker, founded the Azalia Hackley School of Music in New York City. Shortly after opening its doors, the school experienced financial difficulties. After hearing of the institution's budget shortfall, tenor Roland Hayes performed a benefit recital and donated the proceeds to the school. The Hackley School of Music remained open into the mid-1960s.[14] In 1943 the Detroit Public Library established the E. Azalia Hackley Collection of African Americans in the Performing Arts as a lasting and significant memorial to Hackley's life and career. The collection preserves rare archival materials of African and African American heritage, including music scores, instruments, recordings, books, pamphlets, photographs, artifacts, and personal, unpublished documents. At the time of its founding, the collection was the first of its kind in the world. The collection's staff continues to sponsor an annual concert of performances by Black musicians to commemorate Hackley's legacy.[15]

Unfortunately, frustratingly few recollections of persons who knew Hackley well have been located. Among those close to Hackley, R. Nathaniel Dett wrote this poignant tribute to his mentor: "I consider her to have been one of America's remarkably gifted educators.... There is probably no name in America which should be more honored for having stimulated respect for Negro music and musicians than Madame E. Azalia Hackley.... Mrs. Hackley, by going all through the country, especially the South, and personally organizing mammoth Negro choruses to sing spirituals in the largest available halls, before large audiences, not only dramatically focused attention on Negro native musical ability, but gave the Negroes themselves a thrill of pride" in their "racial inheritance."[16] Hackley's student and friend Kate Johnson provided this tribute at the unveiling of a portrait of her mentor at the Bertha Hansbury School of Music:

> I am sure there is nothing that gives me more pleasure, although mingled with sadness at this time, than to say a few words about our own beloved Azalia Hackley.

Associated with her as a girl and then as a woman, it brings to my mind some of the pleasant memories; an inspiration she always was to me. We were closely associated musically. She was a wonderful promoter and lover of her Race of people, and her greatest plea was to members of her Race to improve and cultivate their wonderful God-given vocal talent. She was a passionate lover of nature in all its manifestations, and of the beautiful in art and artistic in everything. She gave to us a new standard of Race musician and carried love in her heart for her people.

She had a vision for Race Progress and many she has helped to fulfillment. She was a woman of the highest ideal and a born leader. Her personality was one of her strongest points, admired by everyone, and while honors were showered upon her everywhere, yet she was simplicity itself. Then came her vision of folk song festivals to educate the masses of the people through mammoth entertainments, planned along the lines of logical musical development. . . . It is a pleasure to look over some of the press comments [about her] and the many splendid compliments of our greatest critics. She was a musical wonder, a musical genius and finished artist. . . . So, words fail to describe this gifted woman of our race. . . . She made many sacrifices to help others who were struggling for a chance in the arena of life.[17]

By 1961, late in his life, Carl Rossini Diton knew full well the tenuous nature of Hackley's historical reputation. Accordingly, he wrote to W. E. B. Du Bois, reiterating her activist and musical significance. As Diton reminded Du Bois, "credit rightfully belongs to the musical uplift worker" for the surge in popularity of Black music in the 1920s. Yet, he expressed frustration that Hackley had yet to receive due acclaim, from the Black "musical intelligentsia" for her contribution to the recognition of African American musical accomplishments. Hoping to set the record straight and to establish for Hackley a deserved place in the historiography of American music, Diton offered this explanation: "I hold that E. Azalia Hackley was our first national musical uplift worker, in that our present Negro vocal renaissance is due to the periods . . . she used to allot in her concert appearances to training whole audiences in vocal production, having them sing at first without training, and then [again] after training, point out the difference, which they eagerly saw." Diton also admired Hackley for her ability to resist cultural and aesthetic racism, especially as "in those days she was fighting white propaganda." He applauded the unprecedented efforts she put forth to create scholarships, when she "took $500 from her earnings and sent Clarence Cameron White to London [in 1908], and a year later $400 to me for study in Munich, Germany." Clearly, Diton realized Hackley's career had long slipped from public memory, and he informed Du Bois, "I am hereby submitting this record for future Negro music historians."[18]

Hackley, too, was ever mindful of historical precedence and its implications for receptivity to African American music making. Accordingly, she opened *Colored Girl Beautiful* with a chapter entitled "The Future." She noted, optimistically, "the beautiful part about the colored race in America is the future." Even as she remained convinced the prospects of improved race relations appeared "veiled," she nonetheless refused to abandon her belief in the power of music to heal and to encourage interracial cordiality. Ultimately, she contemplated the possibilities of a world in which African Americans valued performance, music education, and music of European origin as she did. She looked to music "futurists" to continue the essential dual missions of the preservation of spirituals and the teaching of singing: "It is my belief that to do things that really count in race progress we must have an inner vision which looks forward and sees effects at least half a century ahead.... It is also my belief that each musician in a generation must create something original to be improved upon by the next generation.... We need more self-sacrificing musicians who are futurists, ... with real love for the race, and real love of good music, who have a vision which cannot be commercialized."[19]

Hackley's call to safeguard the future of African American musical achievements did not go unheeded, even if her name rarely appears in the historiographies of US music and the Harlem Renaissance. Although memories of Hackley as a musician-activist lingered in obscurity for decades, the results of her tireless advocacy exerted profound influence on music making in the Harlem Renaissance. Beginning in the early 1920s, African American music drew increasingly frequent accolades from whites, especially evident in the rise of jazz in the years following the end of World War I. Music theater productions, written, produced, and directed by classically trained, well-educated Black musicians, became a hallmark of the Harlem Renaissance. Particularly noteworthy among these, works by Will Marion Cook, along with Hackley associates J. Rosamond Johnson and James Weldon Johnson, amassed critical acclaim. Harriet Gibbs Marshall, founder of the Washington Conservatory of Music, helped sustain the tradition of Black pageantry popularized by Hackley. The compositions and performances of Harry T. Burleigh, another Hackley associate, continued to receive favorable reviews. Several notable African American composers who wrote music in the European classical tradition soon followed, including Camille Nickerson, Nora Douglas Holt, Florence Price, and the "Dean of African American composers," William Grant Still. Hackley's protégée Marian Anderson led a concert career of astounding success, highlighted by her ground-breaking and activist-imbued performances at Washington, DC's Lincoln Memorial in 1939 and the Metropolitan Opera in 1955. These legacies, and others, confirm Hackley's incontrovertible influence in African American music making that followed during the Harlem Renaissance and beyond. When viewed in its totality, Hackley's story becomes, then, not a historical aberration or exception and instead should be afforded a place in the histories of racial uplift and musical, spiritual, and pedagogical African American activism.

NOTES

Introduction

1. Russell, "Madam Hackley Triumphs."
2. Logan (1897–1982) introduced the term "Nadir" in his book, *Negro in American Life*, 52, 79–96. It should be noted that Logan's "Nadir" spanned fewer years (1877–1901) in comparison to Chesnutt's "post-Bellum—pre-Harlem" period. In no way should my statement about Logan be construed as a rejection of his carefully wrought arguments. In fact, his book is one of three now classic resources I find indispensable when researching and writing about the complexities of the time period in African American history under consideration in this book. The other requisite sources are Meier, *Negro Thought*; and Levine, *Black Culture*.
3. Chesnutt, "Post-Bellum." Chesnutt (1858–1932), a founding member of the NAACP and a political activist, became a celebrated author of the Harlem Renaissance. For the most thorough analysis of Chesnutt's designation, "post-Bellum—pre-Harlem," see Barbara McCaskill and Caroline Gebhard, "Introduction," in McCaskill and Gebhard, eds., *Post-Bellum, Pre-Harlem*, 1–14.
4. My summary of Hackley's approach to racial uplift here, as well as my consideration of uplift activism throughout this book, benefitted enormously from the following sources: Gaines, *Uplifting*; Moore, *Booker T. Washington*; and Schenbeck, *Racial Uplift*.
5. Trotter, *Music*, 4. Trotter (1842–92), an early proponent of the potential role music could assume in racial uplift, served in the administration of President Grover Cleveland and also wrote about African American music history. For an excellent analysis of Trotter's contributions to US music historiography, see Schenbeck, *Racial Uplift*, 15–70.
6. Hackley's article series appeared in the widely circulating newspaper, *New York Age*, 1914–15. I discuss this series in chapter 6.
7. Karpf, "Emma Azalia Hackley."
8. Even so, some materials had disappeared by the time Davenport began her work on a biography of Hackley, and she lamented that "many of her [Hackley's] diaries and records were [already] lost" (*Azalia*, Foreword).
9. My own disappointments and occasional setbacks as I worked to recover Hackley's historical reputation bring to mind the research undertaken by musicologist Jane Bowers and her quest to write a biography of African American blues singer Estelle "Mama" Yancey

(1896–1986). After exhaustive searching and interviews with several persons who knew Yancey well, Bowers was nonetheless forced to admit that "there were too many holes for a continuous narrative" about Yancey's life (Bowers, "Writing," 158–59).

10. Campbell, "Vocal Teacher."

Chapter One. Formative Years and Early Career

1. The KKK launched its Murfreesboro campaign in February 1868, and the organization claimed to have amassed a few thousand members and sympathizers in the area not long after its founding; see McFarlin, "Ku Klux Klan." Other useful sources, consulted for this discussion, include Alexander, "Kukluxism"; and Parsons, *Ku-Klux*.

2. "Corilla Beard Smith," online. For more on African American schools in central Tennessee during this era, see Jarmon, *Arbors*, 27–31; and Phillips, "Education."

3. Very little information about Azalia's family survives. Azalia's sister (and only sibling), Marietta Smith, remains an elusive figure, especially as her given name was sometimes misspelled as "Maryetta." Further complicating matters, she married three times and assumed each of her husband's surnames. Her husbands were George Philip Gray (ca. 1869–1916, married to Marietta in 1908), Joseph Johnson (1860–1934), and William C. Boston (1873–1969, married to Marietta in 1934). Corilla A. Beard Smith (1845–1908), originally from Detroit, moved to Murfreesboro with her husband shortly after marrying. Azalia's father, Henry B. Smith (1841–after 1908), a Tennessee native, worked as a blacksmith in Murfreesboro. Her maternal grandfather, Wilson Beard (1820–95), a former enslaved man in Kentucky, moved to Michigan after the death of his wife (Azalia's grandmother), Deborah Howard Beard (1822–65). No documentation has been located about Azalia's paternal grandparents. Sources of information about Azalia's family include the following: Ancestry.com; Davenport, *Azalia*, 19–25; *Detroit Plaindealer* 18 July 1890, 4; *Detroit Plaindealer* 13 March 1891, 3; *Detroit Free Press* 19 April 1895, 5; and Jones, "What Madame."

4. McCaughan, "Detroit's Historically," online. This church is now known as St. Matthew's and St. Joseph's Episcopal Church.

5. "An Old Curiosity Shop," *Detroit Free Press* 17 August 1890, 10.

6. Davenport, *Azalia*, 31.

7. Davenport, *Azalia*, 30–31, 39.

8. Marietta Smith Boston, quoted in Davenport, *Azalia*, 51. In assembling information for her biography, Davenport interviewed Boston, Edwin Henry Hackley, and several of Azalia Hackley's friends, protégées and former students.

9. [Marie A. D. Madre], *E. Azalia Hackley*, 2, pamphlet, Special Collections and Archives, Johnston Memorial Library, Virginia State University, Petersburg, VA. Around 1915, Hackley shared information about her formative years with her friend Marie Ardena Duvall Madre (1865–1938). I attribute the authorship of this pamphlet (*E. Azalia Hackley*) to Madre (hereafter cited as "[Madre]") based on these considerations: Madre (later Marshall), a Washington, DC resident, issued a pamphlet she described as a "book of Madame Hackley's life" with "pictures of the artiste [sic] from her sixteenth year to date." Newspaper advertisements promised a copy of this pamphlet to those who purchased tickets in advance for upcoming Hackley concerts (see, for example, "Hackley Recital-Demonstration," *Philadelphia Tribune* 7 October 1916, 3). Activist Hallie Quinn Brown (ca. 1848–1949) included much of this pamphlet's text, retitled as "Madam Emma Azalia Hackley," in her anthology, *Homespun* (231–36).

However, Brown retained only one of the fifteen photographs Madre had included in her pamphlet. Brown listed the author of the essay about Hackley as "M. M. Marshall"; Madre used the names "M. M. Marshall" or "M. Madre Marshall" after her marriage to Rev. James H. Marshall in 1918 ("News of the Nation's Capitol," *Savannah Tribune* 17 August 1918, 4).

10. Kate Johnson, quoted in Maude Roberts George, "News of the Music"; and [Madre], 1–2.

11. Hackley, "Conference."

12. Note, written by Azalia Smith, quoted in Davenport, *Azalia*, 29, 96.

13. Davenport, *Azalia*, 29. Davenport, undoubtedly echoing remarks made to her by Edwin Hackley and Marietta Smith Boston, described Corilla Smith as "ill-tempered" and Henry B. Smith (Azalia's father) as largely "absent" from Azalia's life (*Azalia*, 96).

14. "Detroit's Most Exclusive Social Clique, the Cultured Colored 40," *Detroit News-Tribune* 27 April 1902, 7. See also, Gatewood, *Aristocrats*, 141; and Katzman, *Before*, 136–37.

15. At commencement, Azalia's predominantly white high school graduating class processed to a march she composed for the occasion; see *Detroit Free Press* 29 January 1886, 5; and [Madre], 2.

16. Reid, "Career," 1–27; *Cleveland Gazette* 12 February 1887, 2; *New York Freeman* 19 February 1887, 2; and "These Go to School," *Detroit Plaindealer* 15 May 1891, 3.

17. In his study of African racial characteristics and Black identity, Reuter categorized the Smith family as "mulatto" (Reuter, *Mulatto*, 220).

18. Carter (later Brooks, 1867–1951) trained as an architect and taught school for a number of years in New Bedford, Massachusetts. She also held various offices in the National Association of Colored Women, was a member of the NAACP, and garnered considerable respect in activist circles. The Elizabeth Carter Brooks School, an elementary school in New Bedford, was named in her honor.

19. The Chandler Lodge honored Zachariah Chandler (1813–79), a white Bedford, New Hampshire, native, one-time Detroit mayor, ardent abolitionist, member of the US Senate, and cabinet member during President Ulysses S. Grant's administration.

20. Azalia Smith, quoted in *Detroit Tribune* 28 September 1887, 4; and *Detroit Tribune* 26 October 1887, 4.

21. *Detroit Plaindealer* 13 June 1890, 5; *Indianapolis Freeman* 23 May 1891, 4; "Detroit City Band," *Detroit Plaindealer* 6 October 1891, 5; and *Detroit Plaindealer* 1 January 1892, 5.

22. *Detroit Plaindealer* 27 December 1889, 5.

23. *Detroit Plaindealer* 18 April 1890, 5.

24. *Detroit Plaindealer* 5 December 1890, 5.

25. *Cleveland Gazette* 20 August 1892, 2. See also *Detroit Plaindealer* 24 January 1890, 5; *Detroit Plaindealer* 20 May 1892, 5; and *Detroit Plaindealer* 3 June 1892, 5.

26. "The Dress Rehearsal," *Detroit Plaindealer* 22 April 1892, 5.

27. For more on Bradbury's *Esther*, see Karpf, "If it's"; and Karpf, "Opportunity."

28. "The Cantata Christmas Night," *Detroit Plaindealer* 2 January 1891, 4.

29. *Indianapolis Freeman* 19 August 1893, 1.

30. *Indianapolis Freeman* 16 September 1893, 2.

31. Information about Edwin Hackley's extended family and ancestors can be found in these sources: "The Hackleys," online; and Brevard, *Biography of Edwin Henry Hackley*. Among Edwin Hackley's family members who lived in Michigan, his mother, Susan Belmore Hackley (1828–1910), resided in Howell, Michigan, a township located near Detroit.

32. A Michigan resident, J. Frank Rickards (1850–1920) accompanied Azalia Smith when she attended an event for teachers affiliated with the National Education Association, held

in 1888 in San Francisco; see, "A Teachers' Reception," *San Francisco Chronicle* 23 July 1888, 6. The *Chronicle* incorrectly reported Rickards's surname as "Richardson." Davenport also mentioned "Uncle Frank" but offered no information about him (*Azalia*, 55, 70). Rickards was married to Corilla A. Beard Smith's sister (Azalia Smith's maternal aunt and Corilla's only sibling), Emma S. Beard Rickards (1849–1924). J. Frank Rickards was a onetime barber, served as one of the first Black letter carriers in Michigan, and was the Great Eminent Grand Commander of Scottish Rite Masons in the jurisdiction encompassing Michigan and Canada's Ontario Province. For more information about Rickards, see Warren, *Michigan Manual*, 298; "Colored Knights Templar," *Detroit Free Press* 10 August 1886, 8; "Our Masonic Department," *Cleveland Gazette* 26 February 1887, 2; "Colored Knights Celebrate the Anniversary of the Emancipation Proclamation," *Kalamazoo Gazette* 14 September 1898, 1; "Event in Colored Society," *Detroit Free Press* 1 February 1903, 12; obituary notice for Corilla A. Beard Smith, *Detroit Times* 4 September 1908, 9. Rickards's page on the *Find-a-Grave* database includes two photographs of him.

33. Davenport, *Azalia*, 69.

34. *Cleveland Gazette* 10 February 1894, 3.

35. "Miss Smith Married," *Detroit Free Press* 30 January 1894, 2. According to Davenport, on the day of the Smith-Hackley nuptials, Azalia taught school and returned home afterward to gather up her belongings. Marietta Smith agreed to keep the sisters' mother distracted by playing the piano for her. This ploy permitted Azalia to slip out of the house, apparently unnoticed (*Azalia*, 73). The two friends in attendance at the wedding ceremony were Annie Miller and George Duncan, both residents of Detroit (Ancestry.com). For more on Joshua Bowdon Massiah (1856–1916) and his importance in the history of Black Detroit, see Beard, *Higher*, 43–47.

36. Geraldine J. Clifford, *Those Good Gertrudes*, 128–37; and Mungazi, *Evolution*, 206–7. For another overview of the "marriage bar" and female teachers, see Thomas, *Marriage*, 20–40.

37. "Miss Smith Married."

38. Basch, "Five Points," online.

39. The newspaper article "Dunbar's 'Poet and His Song'" (*Denver Post* 29 January 1900, 5), mentions a program at which Dunbar presented poetry recitations and Hackley performed solo selections. Wells (later Wells-Barnett, 1862–1931) described Edwin Hackley as "one of the finest young men it has been my good fortune to meet" (Wells, quoted in DeCosta-Willis, ed., *Memphis Diary*, 91–92).

40. Edwin H. Hackley, "Your Opportunity."

41. For example, Edwin Hackley filed a lawsuit against a Denver restaurant owner for refusing to serve him; see "The Color Line," *Rocky Mountain News* (Denver, CO) 17 March 1886, 2; and Rhodes, "Restaurant Rights." See also Hackley, "Colored Brother."

42. "The Negro Editors," *Kansas City* [KS] *Gazette* 24 August 1897, 1; *Kansas City Gazette* 26 August 1897, 4; "These Were Chosen," *Afro-American Sentinel* (Omaha, NE) 27 August 1898, 1; "Colored Editors Meet," *Fair Play* (Fort Scott, KS) 9 September 1898, 1; and "Our Western Editors," *Iowa State Bystander* (Des Moines, IA) 8 September 1899, 4.

43. Wilborn, "Wickedest City." Born into slavery in Georgia, David Wilborn (1856–1940) eventually settled in Ohio after Emancipation and wrote for several newspapers. For an autobiographical essay by Wilborn and a photograph of him, see Ancestry.com.

44. "A Gratifying Success: Afro-Americans in National Conference Organize a National League," *Detroit Plaindealer* 24 January 1890, 1; and "An Afro-American League," *Cleveland*

Gazette 25 January 1890, 1. Activist T. Thomas Fortune (1856–1928), one-time editor of the *New York Age*, is credited with founding the league.

45. *Aspen* [CO] *Union Era* 24 December 1891, 3; and McMurry, *To Keep*, 348.

46. Hackley, "Constitutional Union"; and "Constitutional Union: A Substitute for the Working Plans of the Afro-American League," *Times-Observer* (Topeka, KS) 20 February 1892, 1.

47. "Republican Women's Club," *Rocky Mountain News* 4 May 1894, 5; *Rocky Mountain News* 11 April 1895, 8; and "Statesman and Its Editors," *Denver Evening Post* 6 April 1899, 3.

48. "Colored People's Society," *Denver Evening Post* 16 December 1897, 3; and Hackley, "Bond." Most white fraternal organizations practiced racist membership restrictions, and thus Blacks formed their own societies.

49. *Rocky Mountain News* 11 April 1895, 8.

50. John W. Jacks, letter to Florence Belgarnie, 6 March 1895, Mary Church Terrell Papers, Moorland-Spingarn Research Center, Howard University, Washington, DC; and "A Timely Call," *Indianapolis Freeman* 22 June 1895, 4. Jacks (1845–1921), a prominent journalist, served as president of the Missouri Press Association. The recipient of Jacks's infamous letter, Florence Belgarnie (1857–1923) campaigned as a radical suffragist and held various offices in England's Anti-Lynching League.

51. "A Timely Call."

52. Peterson, "Truth."

53. Terrell, *Colored Woman*, 149–52. Hackley maintained membership in the NACW, but touring often precluded a more active role in the organization. Newspapers occasionally mentioned her presence at NACW meetings; see, for example, *Indianapolis Freeman* 23 July 1910, 4. She occasionally provided musical entertainment at NACW conferences but did not hold an office. Additional sources on the early years of the NACW, consulted for this discussion, include the following: Shaw, "Black Club Women"; Silone-Yates, "National Association"; and Terrell, "Duty."

54. "The Late Madam E. Azalia Hackley," *Chicago Broad Ax* 12 December 1922, 1.

55. Azalia Hackley, quoted in Davenport, *Azalia*, 93. See also "Statesman and Its Editors." Very few issues of the *Denver Statesman* survive, so it is impossible to offer much in the way of analysis of Azalia Hackley's editorials.

56. "God Bless the Women," *Leavenworth* [KS] *Herald* 20 April 1895, 2.

57. Carrie Melvin Lucas, eventually a multi-instrumentalist, toured as a musical comedy performer. Maude Cuney (later Cuney-Hare, 1874–1936), a prolific writer during the Harlem Renaissance, is best remembered for her important historical study, *Negro Musicians*.

58. Hackley's article content quoted in Davenport, *Azalia*, 92–93.

59. "Colored Chorus Sings [Felix Mendelssohn's] 'Elijah,'" *Denver Evening Post* 21 October 1899, 8; and Baker, "Stage."

60. *Detroit Free Press* 28 August 1898, 26.

61. *Denver Post* 5 September 1900, 5. No other information about this performance has been located.

62. "Colored Opera Troupe on Road," *Denver Evening Post* 14 June 1899, 7; and *Colored American* (Washington, DC) 29 July 1899, 7.

63. *Kansas Blackman* (Topeka) 9 November 1894, 1. No information survives to indicate that Azalia Hackley ever pursued employment for which this credential would have been advantageous or required.

64. "The Teacher," *Denver Evening Post* 27 December 1899, 8.

65. *Indianapolis Freeman* 27 October 1894, 5; "Colored Chorus Sings 'Elijah'"; and "Mrs. Hackley's Recital," *Denver Post* 23 October 1900, 2. In the early years of the twentieth century, Black Denver residents renamed their largest community chorus the "Azalia Hackley Choral Club" in her honor; see, for example, *Denver Statesman* 11 December 1909, 13.

66. "Bachelor of Music," *Denver Post* 9 June 1900, 8; and "DU Adds New Chapter to Its Black History," online.

67. "Song Recital," *Topeka* [KS] *Plaindealer* 18 January 1901, 3. The aria, "Thou Brilliant Bird" ("Charmant Oiseau" in the original French), is from *La Perle du Brézil* (*The Pearl of Brazil*, 1851), a comic opera written by Félicien-César David (1810–76).

68. Sir George Henschel (1850–1934) wrote "Spring" as part of his incidental music for *Summer's Last Will and Testament*, a satirical Elizabethan stage comedy by Thomas Nash (1567–1647), premiered about 1592 and published in 1600. "La Villanelle" is the first of six songs in the cycle *Les Nuit d'été* (*Summer Nights*), Op. 7 (1841), a setting of poetry by Théophile Gautier (1811–72), composed by Hector Berlioz (1803–69).

69. *Indianapolis Freeman* 16 February 1901, 8.

70. [Madre] confirmed that this photograph was taken in Denver; photograph located between pages two and three in [Madre].

71. [Lewis], "New Star." The song "Unless" is a setting of a poem by Elizabeth Barrett Browning with music written by Luigi Caracciole (1847–88). "Comin' Thro' the Rye" is a Scottish air with lyrics supplied by Robert Burns's 1782 poem of the same title. The word "when" in Lewis's review refers to this song's lyrics in the refrain: "Yet all the lads they smile on me / when comin' thro' the rye." Hackley performed both these songs throughout her career.

72. Southern, *Music*, 244–48; Graziano, "Early Life."

73. Wilborn, "Wickedest City." Wilborn's reference to "opera houses" included any venue used for entertainment purposes as most performance spaces were called by the generic term "opera house" during the nineteenth and early twentieth centuries.

74. Azalia Hackley's name appears in the church registry in an entry dated 3 April 1903 (Ancestry.com). Ultimately, Azalia Hackley did not pursue employment with the *Philadelphia Tribune*, nor is it certain that Edwin Hackley ever worked for the paper. However, given Edwin Hackley's reputation among the Black press, it seems quite likely that he assumed some sort of position with the *Tribune*.

75. Du Bois, *Philadelphia*, 117.

76. *Colored American* (Washington, DC) 1 November 1902, 9. The People's Chorus underwent various name changes over the years and remained active well into the 1930s (Davenport, *Azalia*, 114–15).

77. Taylor, "In Retrospect," 129–33.

78. Azalia Hackley, quoted in Keiler, *Marian Anderson*, 22.

79. Hackley, quoted in Davenport, *Azalia*, 111; and in Arsenault, *Sound*, 12–13.

80. "Washington Conservatory of Music Opens," *Cleveland Gazette* 17 October 1903, 1; and "The Washington Conservatory of Music," *Colored American* 7 November 1903, 11.

81. [Gibbs], "Washington Conservatory." A full-page portrait of Hackley appears opposite Gibbs's announcement. Additional sources on the early years of the Washington Conservatory, consulted for this discussion, include: McGinty, "Washington Conservatory," 59–74; Schmalenberger, "Shaping Uplift," 73–75; and Terrell, "Washington Conservatory," 525–30.

82. Azalia Hackley, letter to Harriet A. Gibbs, 15 September 1903. Washington Conservatory of Music Papers, Moorland-Spingarn Research Center, Howard University, Washington, DC; hereafter cited as "WCM Papers."

83. Azalia Hackley, letter to Gibbs, 30 September 1903, WCM Papers.
84. Azalia Hackley, letter to Gibbs, 17 June 1904, WCM Papers.
85. Edwin H. Hackley, letter to Harriet A. Gibbs Marshall, 2 September 1906, WCM Papers. Gibbs married Harvard graduate and Washington, DC, lawyer Napoleon Bonaparte Marshall (1873–1933) on 23 June 1906.
86. Edwin Hackley's death certificate lists him as a widower and, thus, still legally married to Azalia Hackley (Ancestry.com).
87. Dodson, "Noted Songster."
88. Hackley, "Musical Progress"; and Marshall, "Madam Emma Azalia Hackley," 235. Hackley often referred to her activist agenda simply as "musical uplift."
89. *Chicago Broad Ax* 2 September 1911, 2. Scurlock's photograph of Hackley appeared in nationally circulating newspapers, especially the *Philadelphia Tribune*. After retirement, Addison N. Scurlock (1883–1964) sold his business to his sons, and it remained open in Washington, DC until the 1990s. During its operation, the Scurlock Studio photographed many prominent African Americans. Within the extensive bibliography of the Scurlocks, these sources proved particularly helpful for my purposes: Fearing, "Addison Scurlock," online; Gardulla, *Scurlock Studio*; Levey, "Scurlock Studio," 40–57; and "Scurlock Studio Records, ca. 1888–1995," Smithsonian Institution website, online.
90. Russell, "Madame Hackley Triumphs." Russell (1860–1930) was the first African American arts critic to achieve national recognition.
91. Peter P. Jones, best known as a pioneering filmmaker, also served as an official photographer for the *Chicago Defender*. Jones opened his Chicago studio in 1908 and photographed such notables as W. E. B. Du Bois, Booker T. Washington, painter Henry O. Tanner, and musical comedy stars Bert Williams and Aida Overton Walker. For more on Jones, see Everett, *Returning*, 112–14; and Field, *Uplift Cinema*, 207–13.
92. Skillern (1869–1943) created gowns for well-heeled African Americans in Colorado; see "Madame A. M. Skillern," *Denver Star*, ca. 1913, Denver Public Library Digital Collection, online. Unfortunately, the only surviving image from Hackley's session with Jones is not clear enough to reproduce here. The image was printed in the *Pittsburgh Courier* 28 June 1912, 5.
93. "Negro Soprano Heard in Classical Numbers," *Pittsburgh Post-Gazette* 2 July 1912, 3; "Mrs. Hackley's Recital," *Pittsburgh Press* 2 July 1912, 12; and Randolph, "Some Comments."
94. A. R. Taylor, "Madame Hackley's Retiring."

Chapter Two. Travel, Domestic and Abroad

1. Hackley submitted this itinerary to the press; see *New York Age* 3 February 1910, 6.
2. Hackley, "Madam E. Azalia Hackley Relates"; and Hackley, "Experience in 'Jim Crow' Cars." See also Terrell, *Colored Woman*, 295–307.
3. "Texas Jim Crow Cars: Mme. Hackley a Race Woman," *Philadelphia Tribune* 16 March 1912, 3.
4. Hackley, "Madam E. Azalia Hackley Relates"; and Hackley, "Experience in 'Jim Crow' Cars."
5. Hackley, "Madam E. Azalia Hackley Relates."
6. Hackley, "Madam E. Azalia Hackley Relates"; and Hackley, "Experience in 'Jim Crow' Cars." The regulations regarding "smoking" and "ladies" cars (the latter off limits to tobacco users) were mutable and varied from one location to the next. For example, in certain

locales, a Black woman who paid first-class fare might be permitted to occupy a ladies' car but would be forced to move to another car in order to make room for a white female passenger should the ladies' car fill to capacity. More often than not, however, a ladies' car was, in fact, reserved exclusively for white women. Furthermore, regulations usually did not require a white woman to purchase a first-class ticket for a seat in a ladies' car. Ultimately, Black travelers could never expect tobacco-free travel accommodations. For an excellent discussion of these matters and their intricacies, see Mark, "Law, Society," 377–409.

7. For more on the meningitis epidemic to which Hackley referred, see O'Leary, *Texas*.

8. Hackley, "Experience in 'Jim Crow' Cars." Tuberculosis was the single greatest cause of death in the United States between 1870 and 1910. Hackley's Denver acquaintance, Paul Laurence Dunbar, died of the disease in 1906 at age 33. For an excellent discussion of how tuberculosis, often formerly referred to as "consumption," disproportionately affected African Americans, see Snyder, et. al., "Who Died."

9. Hackley, "Madam E. Azalia Hackley Relates."

10. Hackley, "Queen of Song."

11. Cooper, "Woman versus," 93.

12. Terrell, *Colored Woman*, 296–99.

13. Terrell, *Colored Woman*, 337; and Cooper, *Beyond Respectability*, 81–82.

14. Clifford, "Plea." Clifford (1862–1934), an Ohio native and longtime Washington, DC, resident, published poetry and essays. As an uplift activist, she maintained membership in the NACW and the NAACP. Fannie Barrier Williams also chastised Black men for their lack of protection of Black females; see Williams, "Colored Girl," 403.

15. Cooper, "Negro," 134.

16. "Club and Social Notes," *New York Tribune* 4 December 1910, 57. See also, "Lecture Recital: Mrs. Mary Church Terrell and Mme. E. Azalia Hackley," *Chicago Broad Ax* 10 December 1910, 2.

17. "Texas Jim Crow Cars: Mme. Hackley a Race Woman," *Philadelphia Tribune* 16 March 1912, 3.

18. "Mme. Hackley Sues Southern Railroad for Jimcrowism," *Philadelphia Tribune* 23 May 1914, 3.

19. Cooper, "Womanhood," 64.

20. "Mme. E. Azalia Hackley Will Return to Chicago," *Chicago Defender* 18 April 1914, 6.

21. For more on Black travelers, especially those who ventured to Europe, see Totten, *African American Travel*. See also Foster, "In the Face," 130–49; Mason, "Travel as Metaphor," 337–56; and Totten, "Embodying," 47–60.

22. Famous African American musicians who traveled overseas prior to Hackley's trips include the following: Philadelphia band leader and composer Francis Johnson (1781–1860), who performed before Queen Victoria in 1838; soprano Elizabeth Taylor Greenfield (1820–76), who sailed to England in 1854 and also performed for Queen Victoria; the Fisk Jubilee Singers, who first toured Great Britain in 1873; soprano Marie Selika, who sang in Europe 1882–85; and soprano Sissieretta Jones, who first toured overseas in 1895.

23. E. Azalia Hackley, letter to Bert Williams and George Walker, 7 March 1907; entire letter printed in *Alexander's Magazine* 3, no. 6 (15 April 1907): 272–73. Williams (1874–1922) and Walker (1873–1911), a renowned musical comedy and vaudeville duo, performed throughout the United States and toured England.

24. Charles W. Chesnutt, letter to Edwin J. Chesnutt, 5 February 1906; entire letter reprinted in Crisler, Leitz, and McElrath, eds., *Exemplary Citizen*, 5. Edwin J. Chesnutt

(1883–1939), a Harvard University graduate, served, at one time, as Booker T. Washington's secretary and also practiced dentistry in the Chicago area.

25. Brooks, "Negro Travelers," 15. Brooks (1859–1940), a Kentucky native and nephew of Booker T. Washington, taught school, traveled widely, and studied law at Howard University. For related points of view, see "The Race Question in France," *Appeal* (St. Paul, MN) 21 November 1903, 2; and "Negro in Europe," *Independence* [KS] *Daily Reporter* 19 October 1900, 2.

26. Simmons, "European."

27. Fauset (1882–1961) studied at the Sorbonne in Paris. Warrick (later Fuller, 1877–1968), a protégée of venerated sculptor Auguste Rodin (1840–1917), was well-known in Parisian artistic circles and among Harlem Renaissance intellectuals. In addition to her friendship with Hackley, Warrick also associated with Henry O. Tanner and W. E. B. Du Bois. Tanner (1859–1937), a native of Pittsburgh, Pennsylvania, spent nearly his entire artistic career in Paris.

28. Ford, "Across." Rev. John Elijah Ford (1862–1943) studied at the University of Denver and traveled to Europe in 1907 ("Will Visit the Old World," *Nashville Globe* 22 February 1907, 4). Ford's wife, Dr. Justina Laurena Ford (1871–1951), was Colorado's first Black female physician; see Varnell, *Women*, 78–81. Dr. Sumner Alexander Furniss (1874–1953), a prominent resident of Indianapolis, became the first Black physician to join the staff of a local white hospital; see "Dr. S. A. Furniss," *Colored American Magazine* 11, no. 2 (1 August 1906): 140–41; and "Dr. Sumner A. Furniss, 78, Negro Physician, Succumbs," *Indianapolis Star* 19 January 1953, 4.

29. Henry O. Tanner, quoted in Lester, "Henry O. Tanner," 73. For other useful contemporaneous sources on Tanner, consulted for this discussion, see "Henry O. Tanner, the Artist: A Distinguished Negro Artist Attracting Attention," *Indianapolis Freeman* 4 January 1902, 1; and Cole, "Henry O. Tanner." More recent sources consulted for my purposes include Woods, *Henry Ossawa Tanner: Art*; Marley, ed., *Henry Ossawa Tanner: Modern*; Boime, "Henry O. Tanner's Subversion"; and Winter and Reymond, "Henry Ossawa Tanner."

30. Terrell, "International Congress."

31. Many newspapers and periodicals carried announcements about de Reszke's studio, including the following: "Jean de Reszke to Quit Stage: Famous Operatic Tenor Has Decided to Turn Professor," *Atlanta Constitution* 24 April 1904, 3; "A New Teacher," *Sheffield* [England] *Daily Telegraph* 8 April 1904, 8; Baughan, "Music and Musicians"; and "A New School for Singers," *Musician* 9, no. 6 (June 1904): 208.

32. Finck, *Success*, 388. Finck (1854–1925) authored a number of books on music and was a leading US arts critic.

33. De Reszke's better-known students, some of whom studied with him after Hackley's Parisian residency, included the following singers: upstate New York native and French opera star Bessie Abott (1878–1919); Kansas tenor Joseph Horace Benton (1898–1975); British baritone Clive Carey (1893–1968); Boston soprano Edith de Lys (1886–1961); Canadian soprano Louise Edvina (1878–1948); New York City native and soprano Lucille Marcel (1877–1921); Indiana soprano Minnie Saltzmann-Stevens (1874–1950); Brazilian soprano Bidu Sayão (1902–99); Tennessee baritone Oscar Seagle (1877–1945); Austrian tenor Leo Slezak (1872–1946); and British soprano Maggie Teyte (1888–1976).

34. "De Reszke's Music Studio," *Oshkosh* [WI] *Daily Northwestern* 21 May 1904, 10. See also Leiser, *Jean de Reszke*, 265–66.

35. MacDonald, "Jean de Reszke at Home." MacDonald (1846–1926), a well-known London journalist, served on the staff of the *Daily News* for nearly fifty years.

36. Douglas, "Lesson," 209–10. Douglas (1886–1972), an accomplished pianist and singer, served as one of de Reszke's accompanists for several years.

37. Jean de Reszke, quoted in "Jean de Reszke Praises American Voices and Tells What Is Lacking," *Musical America* 8, no. 17 (September 1908): 23; and de Reszke, quoted in "Is Like One Long Opera: De Reszke Makes All His Pupils Do Their Work in a Little Theater of His Own," *Des Moines Register* 22 May 1904, 10.

38. P[arker], "Jean de Reszke Today." Henry Taylor Parker (1864–1934), a leading Boston arts critic, typically signed articles with only his initials.

39. Jean de Reszke, quoted in *Inter Ocean* (Chicago) 8 May 1904, 31.

40. Hackley often performed the aria "Plus Grand dans Son Obscurité" ("Greater in Your Obscurity") from Goldmark's *Queen of Sheba*; see, for example, Adams, "Musical and Dramatic." Hackley undoubtedly studied this aria with de Reszke. She later confirmed that she was de Reszke's only Black student during the years 1906–07 ("Madame E. Azalia Hackley, the Greatest Queen of Song," *Chicago Broad Ax* 31 December 1910, 5). However, Hackley was not the only African American to study with de Reszke. At some point, soprano Abbie Mitchell (later Cook, 1884–1960) studied voice in Paris, although exactly when she did so is not known. Most likely Mitchell spent time in de Reszke's studio when she toured Europe in 1919. Her training in opera roles under the tutelage of de Reszke proved enormously beneficial to her career as she was selected to perform the role of Clara in the world premiere of George Gershwin's *Porgy and Bess* in 1935. As Clara, Mitchell introduced to the world the celebrated aria, "Summertime."

41. Accounts of just how much de Reszke charged for lessons varied. See, for example, "Expensive Singing Lessons," *Topeka* [KS] *State Journal* 18 June 1904, 14; and "How Jean de Reszke Teaches His Singing Classes," *New York Times* 30 October 1904, SMA3.

42. "Near View of Jean de Reszke: A Young Girl's Experience as His Pupil," *San Francisco Chronicle* 21 May 1905, 9.

43. Hackley, "Hints . . . Demonstration in Voice Culture (No. 1)," 5.

44. Douglas, "Lesson."

45. di Sala, "Fertile Soil," 419. Maurice [de] Noufflard (1874–ca. 1933), a one-time de Reszke student, served as his mentor's secretary and as one of his piano accompanists.

46. Jean de Reszke, quoted in "Jean de Reszke to Quit Stage."

47. Cécil, "Singer's," 14.

48. The description of de Reszke's descent to his front parlor was supplied by American soprano Marguerite Chapin Caetani (1880–1963), a one-time de Rezske student (Dennett, *American Princess*, 47–48).

49. Jean de Reszke, quoted in "Is Like One Long Opera." For a photograph of de Reszke's theater, see Teyte, *Star*, 48.

50. This photograph appeared in the following: *Buffalo Morning Express* 23 August 1908, 10; *New York Age* 9 November 1908, 8, and again 24 December 1908, 1; *Colored American Magazine* 1 March 1909, 5; *The Philadelphia Colored Directory: A Handbook of the Religious, Social, Political, Professional, Business and other Activities of the Negroes of Philadelphia* (Philadelphia: Philadelphia Colored Directory Co., 1910), 12; and in the *Philadelphia Tribune* 17 February 1912, 4. It was undoubtedly printed elsewhere as well.

51. Rosseau, "Madame Hackley."

52. "Race Gleanings," *Indianapolis Freeman* 25 May 1907, 7.

53. Rosseau, "Madame Hackley."

54. Guthrie, *Letters*, 62.

55. "A Haven for Girls Who Go to Paris to Study," *San Francisco Call* 25 August 1907, 1. See also, Delcomyn, "Holy Trinity"; and Whiting, *Paris*, 394–95.

56. Rosseau, "Madame Hackley." Gounod (1818–93) wrote *Gallia* (1871) to commemorate the French defeat of 1870, in the Franco-Prussian War. For this work, he used excerpts from the biblical Book of Lamentations.

57. "Paris," *Musical Courier* 8 May 1907, 92. Henry White (1850–1927) served with distinction as a government official in various capacities during the administrations of US presidents William McKinley, Theodore Roosevelt, Howard Taft, and Woodrow Wilson.

58. *American Register* (London) 27 April 1907, 3. The *American Register* published news items of interest to English-speaking tourists and residents of Paris.

59. "Fourth of July in Paris," *American Register* 29 June 1907, 1.

60. *L'Aurore: Politique, Littéraire, Sociale*, 21 October 1906, 2; my translation and paraphrase. The concert was also publicized in "Théâtres et Concerts," *Le Journal* 21 October 1906, 6; and "Matinée musicale et littéraire du 21 octobre," *Bulletin de la Société pour la Propagation des Langues Étrangères en France* 14, no. 12 (December 1906): 148–49.

61. Rosseau, "Madame Hackley."

62. Three other African American sopranos also frequently performed the infamously difficult "Staccato Polka": Sissieretta Jones, Mary Saunders Patterson, and Marie Selika. Patterson (1882–1951), a student of Hackley, studied this song with her. The rendition of "Staccato Polka" by coloratura soprano Marie Selika earned her the press sobriquet "Queen of Staccato"; see, for example, "The Selika Concert," *Cleveland Gazette* 5 March 1887, 3; "Selika the Artist," *Cleveland Gazette* 11 August 1888, 1; Southern, *Biographical*, s.v., "Selika, Marie," 28–32; and Gable-Wilson, *Let Freedom Sing*, 77–87.

63. Rosseau, "Madame Hackley." Other than a probable location on Avenue d'Eylau, a fashionable district in the 16th arrondissement, no information has been located about "Salle Eylau" or Hackley's performance at this venue.

64. Hackley, "How the Color," 210–15.

65. Hackley, "Foreign Musical."

66. Hackley, "Foreign Scholarship." Thompson (1874–1933) taught, for a time, at Tuskegee Institute and was an associate of Marcus Garvey.

67. Shakespeare (1849–1931) was born John William Thomas Shakespeare. Unlike de Reszke, who did not memorialize his instructional methodology and philosophy, Shakespeare left behind a treasure trove of information about his pedagogy, so we know a great deal about his teaching philosophy and methodology. Contemporary teachers of singing still consult his many books and articles. Among the myriad publications by Shakespeare, the following are still highly regarded: *Singing for Schools*; *Art of Singing*; *Plain Words*; and *Speaker's Art*. See also, Greene, "More about Shakespeare"; "Mr. William Shakespeare," *Hendon and Finchley Times* (London) 6 November 1931, 7; and "Mr. William Shakespeare," *Times* (London) 4 November 1931, 14.

68. William Shakespeare, quoted in "Mr. William Shakespeare," *Musical Herald and Tonic Sol-Fa Reporter* 1 March 1891, 68.

69. Greene, "More about Shakespeare."

70. "William Shakespeare Here," *New York Sun* 3 January 1900, 7.

71. Greene, "More about Shakespeare"; "Mr. Shakespeare's Recital," *New York Times* 31 December 1899, 18; "To Lecture on Singing," *New York Times* 4 January 1900, 6; *Hartford* [CT] *Courant* 13 January 1900, 10; and "William Shakespeare Here," *New York Sun* 3 January 1900, 7.

72. "Mr. William Shakespeare," *Musical Herald and Tonic Sol-Fa Reporter* 1 March 1891, 67–69.

73. Green, *Black Edwardians*, 189–90. These sources enhanced my knowledge and appreciation of Toynbee Hall and its mission: Briggs and McCartney, *Toynbee Hall*; Meacham, *Toynbee Hall and Social Reform*; Picht, *Toynbee Hall and the English*; and Reinders, "Toynbee Hall."

74. *Cleveland Gazette* 23 January 1909, 4; and *Colorado Statesman* (Denver, CO) 30 January 1909, 4.

75. "Old World News," *Topeka* [KS] *Plaindealer* 12 March 1909, 3.

76. *Kensington News*, quoted in "The Stage," *Indianapolis Freeman* 13 March 1909, 5. See also "Famous Singer Madame E. Azalia Hackley Sings Friday Night," *Savannah* [GA] *Tribune* 5 March 1909, 5.

77. *Bystander* (Des Moines, IA)12 February 1909, 1.

78. Anonymous letter, quoted in Lewis, "Current News . . . Brilliant Affair."

79. "Negro Natural Singers, So Says Azalia Hackley, the Noted Negro," *Wichita* [KS] *Searchlight* 21 May 1910, 1. The best contemporaneous source of information on Henschel (1850–1934) is still his autobiography, *Musings*. During the years 1881–84, Henschel served as the first conductor of the Boston Symphony Orchestra.

80. McGinty, "That You Came So Far." Coleridge-Taylor (1876–1912) drew international acclaim as a composer and conductor. His works elicited unstinting praise from several music luminaries, most notably venerated British composer Sir Edward Elgar (1857–1934). News about Coleridge-Taylor appeared frequently in the press, and hence he was well known among the US music-loving public. He was a close friend of Frederick J. Loudin (1836–1904) of the Fisk Jubilee Singers and of Paul Laurence Dunbar, whose poetry he set to music. Both W. E. B. Du Bois and Booker T. Washington admired Coleridge-Taylor and considered his status and accomplishments to be of considerable significance for African Americans. Coleridge-Taylor published many arrangements of spirituals, all of which garnered much attention in the press and on stage. Still one of the best sources on Coleridge-Taylor is the contemporaneous biography by Sayers. See also Terrell, "Samuel Coleridge-Taylor"; Storer, "S. Coleridge-Taylor"; and Tunnell, "Samuel Coleridge-Taylor."

81. Hackley, quoted in Walton, "Music and the Stage."

82. Hackley, quoted in Walton, "Music and the Stage."

83. Racism continued to plague the US classical music world long after Hackley's death. New York's Metropolitan Opera desegregated its stage only in 1955 when Marian Anderson appeared in the role of Ulrica in Giuseppe Verdi's *Un ballo en maschera* (1859). For more on how class hierarchy influenced the reception history of classical music, and the arts more generally, see Levine, *Highbrow, Lowbrow*.

84. Hackley, "How the Color Question Looks," 210–15.

85. "Argent Archer," National Portrait Gallery, London, website, online.

86. Although a respected photographer in his day, Archer (1860–1932) remains largely forgotten. Information about him can be found in "Automobile Photography," *Commercial Motor* 30 July 1908, 513; and Archer, "How Military."

87. Ships records, Ancestry.com.

88. Hackley, "Madam Azalia Hackley Talks," 6. See also Hackley, "Madam Azalia Hackley Talks . . . (continued from last week)," 3; and "In Chicago and Its Suburbs," *Chicago Defender* 22 February 1913, 3.

89. Hackley, "Queen of Song"; and Hackley, "Madame E. Azalia Hackley Visits."

90. Hackley, "Madame E. Azalia Hackley Visits."

91. Hackley, "Madame E. Azalia Hackley Visits."

92. For contemporaneous press sources regarding the annexation debate, see, for example, "European Vindication of Our Course in Cuba," *Literary Digest* 33, no. 15 (13 October 1906): 497–98; "[Benjamin] Tillman on the Negro Question," *Deseret News* (Salt Lake City, UT) 28 November 1906, 4; and "Resolution to Annex Cuba," *Deseret News* 6 February 1902, 5. South Carolina's virulently racist one-time governor and US Senator Benjamin Ryan Tillman (1847–1918) strenuously and loudly opposed annexation of Cuba owing to fears of racially mixed marriages and a general increase in the size of the Black population. For the most recent and comprehensive source on Cuban race relations as they affected African Americans, see Horne, *Race to Revolution*, 176–200.

93. *Chicago Defender* 22 February 1913, 3.

94. Hackley, "Second Trip."

95. *Indianapolis Freeman* 1 May 1909, 5.

96. "Mme. Hackley en Route to Europe," *Indianapolis Freeman* 4 July 1914, 5.

97. Hackley informed Du Bois that one of her students, soprano Annis Hutchinson Hackley (ca. 1869–after 1921), was present at the recording session. Annis Hackley sang with the Williams Jubilee Singers, a popular professional touring ensemble. The Williams Jubilee Singers concertized throughout the United States and in Europe. Whether or not Annis Hackley, married to Frank Hackley, was an in-law of Azalia Hackley, cannot be determined.

98. E. Azalia Hackley, letter to W. E. B. Du Bois, 20 July 1916, W. E. B. Du Bois Papers, University of Massachusetts, Amherst, MA.

99. Baritone Clarence Carroll Clark (1885–after 1924), Denver resident and Hackley associate, became the first African American to make commercial recordings in the United States. One of Hackley's students, contralto Daisy Robinson Tapley (1870–1925), also made recordings in the early twentieth century (Brooks, *Lost Sounds*, 159–72, 254–58).

100. Although Hackley never left Paris, she had related her plans to tour Europe to the Black press; see Austin, "Madame Hackley Touring."

101. E. Azalia Hackley, postcard message, quoted in *Cleveland Gazette* 29 August 1914, 3.

102. *Indianapolis Freeman* 12 September 1914, 1.

103. *Indianapolis Freeman* 28 September 1914, 3.

104. Passenger lists, Ancestry.com. The SS *Rochambeau*'s manifest gives Hackley's address as Philadelphia.

105. One colorized image of Hackley survives, confirming not only her light skin and hair texture, but also that her hair was dark auburn in color; see Resource ID hk000058, E. Azalia Hackley Collection of African Americans in the Performing Arts, Detroit Public Library, Detroit, MI.

106. Williams, "Perils," 421. See also Chesnutt, "What Is."

107. Marshall, "Madam Emma Azalia Hackley," 233.

108. Hackley, "Madam E. Azalia Hackley Relates"; and Hackley, "Experience in 'Jim Crow' Cars."

109. "'Jim Crow' Car Law," *Detroit Plaindealer* 24 March 1893, 1.

110. Hackley, "Hints . . . Being Introduced."

111. Hackley, "Hints . . . Reducing the Ego (No. 1)."

112. "She Says the Negro Is a Natural Singer," *Indianapolis Freeman* 1 July 1911, 6.

113. Hogans, "Pullman." Hogans (1877–1960), a railroad employee, regularly contributed columns to the *Age* for decades.

114. "The Musical Critic for the Sunday *Dispatch* of Columbus, Ohio Praises the Musical Ability of Madam E. Azalia Hackley," *Chicago Broad Ax* 27 May 1911, 1; and "About Madam Hackley," *Colorado Statesman* 17 June 1911, 1.

115. "Great Contralto Star of Approaching Festival," *Spartanburg* [SC] *Herald-Journal* 20 March 1910, 1. Gerville-Réache (1882–1915) earned press accolades when she sang with the Metropolitan Opera in New York and with the Chicago Grand Opera. Thus, US audiences were quite familiar with her.

116. Baker, *Following the Color*, 151; see also "Pass as White People," *Cleveland Gazette* 2 December 1911, 2. A Michigan native, Baker (1870–1946) was a prolific author and Pulitzer Prize laureate, noted for his publications about US president Woodrow Wilson.

117. Baker, *Following the Color*, 151.

118. "Musical Missionary Will Lecture Here," *Times* (Philadelphia) 24 April 1901, 5.

119. [Madre], 3; and Marshall, "Madam Emma Azalia Hackley," 233.

120. W[illiam Milton] Lewis, *Indianapolis Freeman* 30 March 1901, 4. Lewis (1863–1925) was a nationally respected arts critic for the Black press.

121. Kate Johnson, quoted in George, "News of the Music."

122. "Texas Jim Crow Cars." For recent conjecture regarding the ways Hackley navigated through the stormy waters of racial identity, see Dineen-Wimberly, *Allure of Blackness*, especially 188–94.

123. Hackley, quoted in Siwel, "Rambling"; and Hackley, quoted in Walton, "Music and the Stage." Several well-known contemporaries of Hackley passed as white. Cleveland, Ohio, native and soprano Rachel Walker (1873–194?), known as the "Creole Nightingale," passed and concertized in Europe in the late 1890s under the stage name "Lucie Lenoir" (Billie, "Madame"). Author Alice Dunbar-Nelson (1875–1935), Mary Church Terrell, and Fannie Barrier Williams also occasionally passed, at least for short time periods. In addition, Anita Florence Hemmings (later Love, 1872–1960) passed as white for an extended length of time and, by so doing, became the first African American, in 1897, to graduate from Vassar College. The matter attracted considerable national press coverage, including these articles: "Beautiful Anita Hemmings," *Record-Union* (Sacramento, CA) 24 September 1897, 6; "How a Negro Girl Slipped through Vassar College," *Bryan* [TX] *Daily Eagle* 7 October 1897, 2; "Vassar's Colored Graduate," *Wilmington* [DE] *Messenger* 28 August 1897, 10; "Vassar's Colored Graduate: Her Name Is Hemmings and Her Home Is in Boston," *Washington* [DC] *Evening Star* 17 August 1897, 9; and "That Colored Girl: Miss Hemmings Tells How She Got through College," *Oshkosh* [WI] *Daily Northwestern* 28 August 1897, 6.

124. Hackley, *Colored Girl*, 193.

125. Cooper, *Beyond Respectability*, 81–82.

126. Terrell, *Colored Woman*, 115, 305, 427.

127. "Texas Jim Crow Cars."

128. Hackley must have sung spirituals in London, but no documentation has surfaced to confirm this assertion.

Chapter Three. New Thought Activism

1. Hackley, "Being."

2. Henry Louis Gates Jr. writes, of noncollective uplift efforts: "Unable to overcome the structures of oppression, black leaders embraced individual agency, will, and achievement as the most potent way to fight back against this tidal wave of antiblack racism" (*Stony*, 200).

3. Quimby's publications appear in Annetta Gertrude Dresser, ed., *Philosophy*; and in Horatio W. Dresser, ed., *History*.

4. The denomination of Christian Science also derived many of its principles from Quimby's work. However, the founder of Christian Science, Mary Baker Eddy (1821–1910), insisted on a singular allegiance to biblically derived beliefs and shunned practices associated with non-Christian texts and those traditions based on Asian practices. Within the immense and rich bibliography of New Thought, useful sources on its history, consulted for this discussion, include the following: Anderson and Whitehouse, *New Thought: A Practical American*; Atkins, *Modern Religious*, 165–90; deChant, "American New Thought"; Horatio W. Dresser, ed., *History*; Griswold, "New Thought: A Cult"; Mosley, *New Thought, Ancient*; Wood, *New Thought Simplified*; and "'New Thought' and What It Teaches," *Rochester* [NY] *Democrat and Chronicle* 9 December 1899, 8.

5. Evans, *Mental Cure*, preface.

6. "Growing Interest in 'New Thought,'" *New York Times* 20 November 1904, 4.

7. New Thought authors often became quite popular, and their works sold well. For example, New Thought leader Ralph Waldo Trine's book, *In Tune with the Infinite*, reputedly sold more than 2 million copies.

8. Dresser, "What Is the New Thought?" 33–34.

9. The history of New Thought among African Americans, especially prior to the Harlem Renaissance, remains elusive and largely unchronicled. While historian Beryl Satter acknowledges the presence of "separate networks" of New Thought in Black communities in the 1920s, she deems these networks substantially unrecoverable (Satter, *Each Mind*, 16). In her work on contemporary African American New Thought churches, Darnise C. Martin presents a ground-breaking introduction to the history of African American New Thought, but begins her discussion with events of the 1920s; see Martin, *Beyond Christianity*, 37–59; and Martin, "New Thought Religions."

10. Hackley, *Colored Girl*, 33; Hackley, "Hints . . . How a Professional Achieves Success"; and Hackley, "Lesson IV," 114.

11. Hackley, *Colored Girl*, 104, 125, 135, 162.

12. Woodson, *History*, 248–52.

13. Cooper, "Women versus," 194.

14. Du Bois, *Souls*, 142–45.

15. Du Bois, *Autobiography*, 285.

16. Du Bois, *Souls*, 142–45. For a related viewpoint, see Williams, "Religious Duty."

17. Martin, *Beyond Christianity*, 143, 148.

18. Hackley, *Colored Girl*, 128.

19. Hackley, *Colored Girl*, 128. The New Thought advocacy of self-reliance originated with transcendentalist philosopher Ralph Waldo Emerson and his essay "Self Reliance" (1841).

20. Patterson, *What Is New Thought*, 14–16.

21. Dresser, *History*, 261.

22. Gatewood, *Aristocrats*, 136–37.

23. "Only Woman Bishop in the World Now Lives in Los Angeles and Will Teach New Thought," *Los Angeles Herald* 24 August 1909, 3. La Grange (later Althouse, 1876–1938) left Detroit in 1909 and established a New Thought church in Los Angeles. Her name appeared in national and international newspapers; see, for example, the following: "Church of the New Thought," *Detroit Free Press* 29 November 1903, 27; "New Thought Folk Open Services," *Los Angeles Herald* 23 May 1910, 5; "A Woman Bishop," *Globe* (London) 6 August 1912, 4; "Woman Bishop," *New Zealand Herald* (Auckland) 12 October 1912, 19; and *Church Times* (London) 24, no. 10 (June 1914): 156–57.

24. Among the sources by and about Nona Brooks consulted for this discussion, Brooks, *Short Lessons*, and Deane, *Powerful* proved most helpful.

25. Gaze, *My Personal*, 8. New Thought continues to thrive in London; see website for "The Centre for Positive Living," online.

26. Russell, "Madame Hackley Triumphs."

27. Harley, *Emma Curtis Hopkins*, 35–91. Hopkins (1849–1925) published a weekly New Thought column in the Chicago *Inter Ocean*, where advertisements for her lectures also appeared.

28. Braden, *Spirits*, 140–47.

29. Hackley, "Hints . . . Reducing the Ego (No. 1)."

30. Hackley, "Hints . . . Demonstration in Voice Culture (No. 2)."

31. For example, William Walker Atkinson (1862–1932) likened Marconi's telegraph to the process of thought transference; see Atkinson, *Nuggets*, 89–90; and Atkinson, *Thought Vibration*, 13–14.

32. Hackley, "Hints . . . Demonstration in Voice Culture (No. 2)."

33. "The Hackley Song Recital-Demonstration," *Philadelphia Tribune* 28 October 1916, 3.

34. Adams, "Musical and Dramatic."

35. Hackley, *Colored Girl*, 24–25, 56–58.

36. Hackley, "Lesson IV," 112, 114–15. As Henry Louis Gates, Jr. writes, "there was a sound and look of respectability as requisite as its other components" (*Stony*, 200).

37. Hackley, "Hints . . . Demonstration in Voice Culture (No. 1)," 5; and Hackley, *Guide*, 2.

38. Hackley, "Foundation."

39. Hackley, *Colored Girl*, 55, 82, 106.

40. Hackley, "Hints . . . Demonstration in Voice Culture (No. 1)."

41. Ramacharaka, *Hindu-Yogi*, 16–19.

42. Hackley, "Hints . . . Demonstration in Voice Culture (No. 1)"; and Hackley, *Colored Girl*, 79.

43. Ramacharaka, *Hindu-Yogi*, 25. See also Dumont, *Solar Plexus*.

44. Towne, *Just How*, 10–12.

45. Hackley, "Hints . . . Demonstration in Voice Culture (No. 1)."

46. Hackley, "Hints . . . Demonstration in Voice Culture (No. 2)." The concept "thoughts are things" originated with New Thought philosopher Prentice Mulford (1834–91), especially his *Thoughts Are Things*. See also Atkinson, *Thoughts Are Things*; and Walker, *Thoughts Are Things*.

47. Hackley, *Colored Girl*, 21–33, 103.

48. Hackley, *Colored Girl*, 17. See also Haddock, *Power of Will*, 3–96; and Towne, *Joy Philosophy*, 51–53.

49. Hackley, *Colored Girl*, 42, 45, 65, 106, 185.

50. Dineen-Wimberly draws attention to the relationships among racial uplift, Black identity, and eugenics, referring to this network as an "eugenic aesthetic" (*Allure of Blackness*, 160–61).

51. Gaines, *Uplifting*, 80–83. For more on uplift eugenics, and the history of US eugenics more generally, see Chresfield, *To Improve*; English, *Unnatural Selections*, 35–64; Selden, "Transforming"; and Sherman, *In Search of Purity*, 35–84.

52. Du Bois, "Black North."

53. Hackley, *Colored Girl*, 197.

54. Du Bois, "Black North."

55. Du Bois, "Conservation," 25.

56. Du Bois, *Philadelphia*, 310–11. Du Bois elaborated on the term "submerged tenth" in *Souls*, 94–113.

57. Hackley, *Colored Girl*, 197.

58. Dorr and Logan, "Quality," 70–71.

59. English, *Unnatural Selection*, 35–64.

60. "Prize Babies Will Get Cups: Twelve Beautiful Silver Cups Awarded in the Better Babies' Contest," *New York Age* 6 July 1916, 1. See also "*Age* Contest for Better Babies," *New York Age* 15 July 1915, 1.

61. Thompson, "Better."

62. Hackley, *Colored Girl*, 193.

63. Hackley, *Colored Girl*, 197.

64. Hackley, *Colored Girl*, 18.

65. Hackley, *Colored Girl*, 29.

66. Du Bois, "Conservation," 23.

67. Dorr and Logan, "Quality," 70–71.

68. As the twentieth century dawned, the number of mixed-race persons in the United States increased. The *Philadelphia Tribune* issued this report regarding racial identity: "In the continental United States there are 9,827,763 full-blooded Negroes and 2,000,686 mulattoes or 20.9 percent of the total Negro population. This is an increase of 8.8 percent of mulatto blood since 1870. . . . [T]he figures, taken at face value, show that about one-fifth of all Negroes in 1910 had some admixture of white blood as against about one-eighth in 1870" ("Statistics Show Mulattoes Increasing: Addition of 8.9 Percent of Half Breeds Since 1870," *Philadelphia Tribune* 2 November 1912, 1).

69. Crummell, *Race Problem*, 7–8, 11.

70. Hackley, *Colored Girl*, 199.

71. Hackley, *Colored Girl*, 182.

72. Hackley, *Colored Girl*, 181, 197.

73. Hackley, *Colored Girl*, 26. Hackley's stance confirms her familiarity with at least a sampling of contemporaneous sources about New Thought parenting. Some of these sources include, for example: Gibson, *Golden Thoughts*; Grenside, *Little Builders*; Partlow, *Training*; and Towne, *How to Train*.

74. Hackley, *Colored Girl*, 32.

75. Hackley, *Colored Girl*, 14.

76. Hackley, *Colored Girl*, 82–84.

77. Hackley, *Colored Girl*, 185.

78. Thoreau, *Walden*, 238.

79. Wood, *New Thought Simplified*, 180. Other references to the New Thought concept of an inner, or mind, sculptor include the following: Marden, *Peace, Power*, 78; Wood, *New Thought Simplified*, 21, 180; and James, *Truth and Health*, 204–5.

80. Hackley, *Colored Girl*, 51.

81. Hackley, *Colored Girl*, 49.

82. Hackley, *Colored Girl*, 18.

83. Dixon's *Leopard's Spots* was the first installment in a series of three novels, the other two titles are *Clansman: A Historical Romance*, and *Traitor*. Known as the "Klan Trilogy," the plots and characters of these novels coalesced in a staged drama entitled *The Clansman*, a work that appeared in theaters coast to coast. His fiction also provided the basis for the screenplay of the film *Birth of a Nation*, released in 1915. Dixon published a total of twenty-eight novels.

84. Dixon, *Leopard's Spots*, 459–60. See also Murphy, *Shadowing*, 60–61; and Gates, 104–06.

85. Arguably the most widely read and publicized reaction to Dixon among Black spokespersons came from Howard University professor Kelly Miller (1863–1939), who issued an elegant rebuttal in 1905. In his pamphlet *As to the Leopard's Spots*, Miller painstakingly deconstructed Dixon's novel, laying bare his incendiary rhetoric, prejudices, fallacious arguments, and total denial of empirical evidence. Other notable reviews of and commentaries on Dixon's fiction include the following: "An Infamous Book," *Washington, DC Bee* 11 February 1905, 4; "Blatant Tom Dixon," *Cleveland Gazette* 28 February 1903, 2; Clem, "Launching"; Clifford, "Reply to Thomas Dixon," in *Race Rhymes*, 11; Du Bois, "Problem," 1324–25; "Leopard's Spots," *Washington, DC Bee* 13 December 1902, 4; and Thorne, "Mr. Thomas Dixon."

86. Hackley, *Colored Girl*, 26, 32–36, 47.

87. For example, see Lomax, *Physiognomy*; Stanton, *Encyclopedia*; and Vaught, *Vaught's Practical*.

88. Hassin and Trope, "Facing Facts." Hassin and Trope conclude: "We are not necessarily 'trapped' by our faces; verbal and nonverbal information might change the physiognomic information conveyed by one's face and hence 'untrap' it" (850).

89. Du Bois, "Conservation," 27. In this essay, Du Bois elaborated on this point, citing the imperative to "keep black boys from loafing, gambling and crime; . . . [and] to guard the purity of black women and to reduce the vast army of black prostitutes" (25).

90. "Mme. Hackley's New Method," *New York Age* 20 July 1911, 6; Gross, "Impressions"; and "Woman to Give Entertainment," *Daily Telegram* (Clarksburg, WV) 30 September 1911, 11.

91. Russell, "Madame Hackley Triumphs."

92. Hackley, *Colored Girl*, 26, 34–36. For criticism of Hackley's comments about racial characteristics, see Smith, "Childhood," 798. Smith reads Hackley's comments as racial self-mockery and derision of African Americans. However, Smith did not acknowledge, or appear to know about, the role New Thought played in Hackley's various interpretations of "objectionable racial characteristics," and the ways she believed the inward sculptor could be engaged to confront racist interpretations of "spots."

93. *Chicago Defender* 8 October 1911, 3.

94. Hackley, *Colored Girl*, 33.

95. Hackley, *Colored Girl*, 28, 31.

96. Walton, "Mme. Hackley's Recital."

97. Billie, "Madame E. Azalia Hackley."

98. "The Hackley Song Recital-Demonstration," *Philadelphia Tribune* 28 October 1916, 3.

99. Hackley, *Colored Girl*, 33; and Hackley, "Lesson IV," 114. With her mention of Samson's hair, Hackley referenced Judges, chapters 13–16, in the Hebrew Bible.

100. Hackley, *Colored Girl*, 35–36.

101. Hackley, "Lesson IV," 115.

102. "'The Leopard's Spots': Dixon's Damnable Book Scored [reviewed] by the [Chicago newspaper] *Epworth Herald*"; rpt., *Appeal* (St. Paul, MN) 4 October 1902, 4.

103. Emerson, "Sovereignty," 409.

104. Hackley, "Hints . . . How a Professional Achieves Success."

105. Hackley, *Colored Girl*, 57; and Hackley, "Hints . . . How a Professional Achieves Success."

106. "Hints . . . How a Professional Achieves Success."

107. Hackley, quoted in Walton, "Music and the Stage."

108. Hackley, letter to Bert Williams and George Walker.

109. Diton (1886–1962) became the first African American concert pianist to tour the United States coast to coast. He eventually held important positions at various colleges, most notably New York's Juilliard School; see Samet, "Diton, Carl Rossini"; Hackley, "Some Colored"; and Hackley, "Foreign Scholarship," 3. Diton and White were the only musicians who received funding from Hackley's Foreign Scholarship program. However, she mentored or otherwise assisted innumerable other musicians, including: sopranos Cleota Collins (1893–1976), Eliza Tompkins Dishman, Francis E. Robinson and Florence Cole Talbert (1890–1961); violinists W. Harrison Emanuel (1889–1948) and Bessie Williams (1891–1985); contralto and pianist Bertha A. Hansbury (1888–?); and pianist Myrtle Mae Williams; see Hackley, "Foreign Scholarship," 3–10. In addition, Hackley toured with and mentored blind soprano Mary L. Fitzhugh (later Fitzhugh-Valentine, 1880–1946); see, for example, "Hackley-Fitzhugh Tour," *New York Age* 3 November 1910, 6; "Madame E. Azalia Hackley and Miss Mary Fitzhugh Left for Indianapolis, Indiana," *Chicago Broad Ax* 19 November 1910, 1; and "Madam Hackley and Miss Fitzhugh Arrive in St. Louis, MO, from Southern Tour," *Chicago Broad Ax* 21 January 1911, 1.

110. Baker, "Stage."

111. *Chicago Broad Ax* 23 May 1908, 2.

112. Baker, "Stage."

113. Letter from Rev. Henry Hugh Proctor (1863–1933) to W. E. B. Du Bois, 23 May 1908, W. E. B. Du Bois Papers, Special Collections, University of Massachusetts Amherst Libraries. Hackley's letter to Proctor has been lost.

114. Du Bois, *Efforts for Social Betterment*, 107–8.

115. Hackley, "Foreign Scholarship."

116. Anderson (1888–1939) published numerous books, articles, and at least one play. His books include *From Newsboy*, *Hows and Whys*, and *Uncommon Sense*.

117. For example, see Hill and Bair, eds., *Marcus Garvey*, xxv–xxix, xlix–li; Martin, *Beyond Christianity*, 37–59; Martin, "New Thought Religions," 273–82; Prentiss, "Full Realization"; and Travis, "'It Will Change.'"

Chapter Four. Music Education and Racial Uplift

1. Hackley, quoted in "She Says."
2. Hackley, "Concert Conditions."
3. Hackley, quoted in "She Says."
4. Baker, "Madam E. Azalia Hackley."
5. E. Azalia Hackley, letter to George Foster Peabody, 4 August 1918, Manuscript Division, Library of Congress, Washington, DC.
6. "Mme. Hackley to Give Recital," *Pittsburgh Post-Gazette* 23 June 1912, 40; and "Celebrated Colored Vocalist," *Wilmington* [NC] *Morning Star* 13 April 1913, 5. See also untitled letter, *New York Age* 14 August 1920, 5.
7. Adams, "Musical and Dramatic"; and Adams, "Musical and Dramatic: Mme. Hackley Recital." Hackley offered some information about her "vocal demonstrations" in "Hints . . . Demonstration in Voice Culture (No. 1)" and "Hints . . . Demonstration in Voice Culture (No. 2)."
8. Hackley, "Concert Conditions."
9. *Indianapolis Freeman* 13 November 1909, 6.

10. Comment originally printed in the *St. Louis Palladium* and quoted in the *Indianapolis Freeman* 13 November 1909, 6.

11. Hackley, "Musical Progress."

12. Hackley, letter to George Foster Peabody, 4 August 1918.

13. Taylor, *Psychology*, x.

14. *Catalogue of the University of Denver and Colorado Seminary, 1892–93* (Denver: University of Denver, 1892), 121. In addition to his appointment as the university's instructor of singing, Brierley (1842–1920) served as the institution's choral director and as dean of its Conservatory of Music.

15. Taylor, *Psychology of Singing*, x.

16. Henry Holbrook Curtis, *Voice Building and Tone Placing*, v. Curtis (1856–1920) was a friend of Jean de Reszke and regularly consulted with him regarding singing instruction. Curtis dedicated *Voice Building and Tone Placing* to de Reszke ("Care of the Voice," *Chicago Tribune* 11 April 1896, 10).

17. Carter, "Forging," 12.

18. Shaftsbury, *Lessons in Voice Culture*, 10.

19. Wheeler, "Vocal Methods."

20. Gunn, "Voice Culture of To-day." Lutie A. Baker Gunn (1868 -1928), a pianist and singer, and noted clubwoman, studied voice in Europe and taught singing in several locations including Carthage College, in Kenosha, WI.

21. Hackley, *Guide*, introduction.

22. Hackley, quoted in Russell, "Madame Hackley Triumphs"; and in "She Says the Negro Is a Natural Singer: Mrs. Hackley Explains Requisites Necessary to Become a Singer," *Indianapolis Freeman* 1 July 1911, 6. See also, Hackley, "Foundation," 1.

23. Hackley, *Colored Girl*, 28.

24. Hackley, "Lesson IV," 112.

25. Hackley, quoted in Lewis, "Current News of Chicago: The Hackley Recital to Be Greatest Ever."

26. Hackley, *Colored Girl*, 66, 71–82.

27. Hackley, *Colored Girl*, 9.

28. Hackley, "Hints . . . Demonstration in Voice Culture (No. 2)."

29. Hackley, "Hints . . . Demonstration in Voice Culture (No. 2)."

30. Hackley, *Guide*, 2.

31. Hackley, "Foundation."

32. Hackley, *Guide*, 13.

33. Hackley, "Hints . . . Demonstration in Voice Culture (No. 2)."

34. Hackley, "Foundation," 2.

35. Hackley, "Foundation," 2.

36. Hackley, *Guide*, 1, 13.

37. Hackley, "Hints . . . Demonstration in Voice Culture (No. 2)."

38. Hackley, *Guide*, 1.

39. Hackley, "Hints . . . Demonstration in Voice Culture (No. 2)."

40. Zelma Watson George, 207, online. George (1903–94), a well-known Cleveland resident, was a philanthropist, sociologist, and opera singer.

41. Greene, "More about Shakespeare," 110.

42. Dooly, "Negro Festival"; rpt., "Teaching the Old Plantation Melodies," *New York Age* 3 August 1918, 6. Dooly (1884–1955) was the arts critic for Atlanta's *Journal and Constitution* for a number of years.

43. Dykema, "Spread," 218–23.

44. Farwell, "Community," 418. In addition to composing, Farwell (1872–1952) was an ethnomusicologist and publisher with a particular interest in Native American music. He also served as president of the New York Community Chorus (Hackley, "Conference").

45. Hackley, "Conference."

46. Hackley, "Concert Conditions."

47. Hackley, "Concert Conditions."

48. Hackley, "Some Colored Community Music."

49. Hackley, "Conference." See also "Musical Festivals: Community Idea to Be Shown in National Conference," *New York Times* 27 May 1917, 77; and, "Chorus of 1,500 Sings 'Creation,'" *New York Times* 2 June 1917, 7.

50. Hackley, letter to George Foster Peabody, 4 August 1918.

51. Hackley, "Being a Somebody."

52. Campbell, "Vocal Teacher."

53. Hackley, letter to George Foster Peabody, 4 August 1918. Hackley's estimate of the number of African Americans reflected the *Philadelphia Tribune*'s claim that the US population included "9,827,763 full-blooded Negroes and 2,000,686 mulattoes." Hackley combined these numbers to arrive at her estimate of "12,000,000 colored people" ("Statistics Show Mulattoes Increasing: Addition of 8.9 Percent of Half Breeds Since 1870," *Philadelphia Tribune* 2 November 1912, 1).

54. Lewis, "Current News of Chicago: The Hackley Recital to Be Greatest Ever."

55. "Return of Madame E. Azalia Hackley to the Capital City," *Washington, DC Bee* 10 May 1913, 5.

56. Hackley, "Lesson IV," 110.

57. Thompson, "Madame Hackley in Los Angeles." Eloise Bibb Thompson (1886–1928), a teacher, activist, philanthropist, poet, and playwright, was married to the well-known journalist Noah D. Thompson.

58. Hackley, "Hints . . . Reducing the Ego (No. 2)."

59. Hackley, letter to George Foster Peabody, 4 August 1918.

60. Hackley, "Hints . . . Demonstration in Voice Culture (No. 1)," 5; "Mme. Hackley as Director," *Chicago Defender* 23 May 1914, 6; *Indianapolis Freeman* 6 June 1914, 5; "Negro Folk Song Festival Held at Dallas, Texas under the Direction of Mrs. E. Azalia Hackley," 13 June 1914, 1; Thompson, "Mme. Hackley Wins"; "Music and Art," *Crisis* 8, no. 4 (August 1914): 164; "Washington['s] First Folksong Festival," *Washington, DC Bee* 11 March 1916, 1; and White, "Music Notes."

61. "Interest Aroused for Folk Song Festival: Over Two Hundred Voices Being Trained by Madame Hackley for the Event," *Baltimore Afro-American Ledger* 10 March 1917, 1.

62. White, "Music Notes."

63. "Mme. Hackley, Singer, Dies in Detroit," *St. Paul Appeal* 23 December 1922, 3.

64. Hackley, "Hints . . . Demonstration in Voice Culture (No. 1)."

65. John C. Freund, quoted in J. A. H. [sic], "Serious." In addition to his advocacy of Hackley's work, Freund (1848–1924) was a longtime ally of Booker T. Washington and an advisor and financial supporter for the *New York Age*. The photograph of Hackley's Harlem chorus (figure 4.1) also appeared in the *New York Age* 8 March 1917, 7. The *New York Age* distinguished the Harlem Chorus as "the result of Mme. Hackley's efforts to attract attention to the musical hunger of a musical people" ("Mrs. Hackley to Give Folk Song Festival," *New York Age* 8 November 1917, 6). For more on the ways music instruction and concepts of community interact in a mutually beneficial constellation, see Jorgensen, "Music Education as Community."

66. White, "Music Notes."

67. James Weldon Johnson, letter to E. Azalia Hackley, 27 August 1915, James Weldon Johnson and Grace Nail Johnson Papers, Beinecke Rare Book and Manuscript Library, Yale University, New Haven, Connecticut, hereafter cited as "Johnson Papers."

68. The article, "Normal Vocal Institute" (*Indianapolis Freeman* 8 January 1916, 6) includes a photograph of the building Hackley acquired. Unfortunately, the image is too grainy to reproduce here. In a letter to James Weldon Johnson, Hackley mentioned she carried "a note of $700" on the building (Hackley, letter to James Weldon Johnson, 21 October 1915, Johnson Papers). As an interesting side note, Hackley purchased the building from the estate of multimillionaire Hetty Green (*née* Henrietta Howland Robinson, 1834–1916) (see White, "Music Notes"). At the time of her death, Green was the richest woman in the United States and, possibly, in the world. Green became infamous as the "Witch of Wall Street" for her miserly, shrewd, and cutthroat investment practices that augmented her inherited wealth many fold; see, for example, "Hetty Green Dies, Worth $100,000,000," *New York Times* 4 July 1916, 1.

69. Jones, "What Madame."

70. "Gave Concert in Mt. Zion Church," *Trenton* [NJ] *Evening Times* 3 March 1916, 7; "Big Negro Chorus to Give Festival," *Detroit Free Press* 13 August 1918, 5; "Do We Appreciate the Efforts of Our Classical Musicians?" *Philadelphia Tribune* 16 October 1915, 3; and Hackley, letter to James Weldon Johnson, 21 October 1915, Johnson Papers.

71. Hackley, letter to James Weldon Johnson, 21 October 1915, Johnson Papers.

72. *Indianapolis Freeman* 9 September 1916, 5.

73. *New York Age* 20 October 1916, 6.

74. Hackley, letter to George Foster Peabody, 4 August 1918.

75. White, "Music Notes"; and "Mme. E. Azalia Hackley Will Return to Chicago."

76. *Chicago Broad Ax* 30 December 1922, 1. See also *Indianapolis Freeman* 9 September 1916, 7.

77. Hackley, *Guide*, 5–9.

78. "Marian Anderson in Mississippi," *Enterprise-Journal* (McComb, MS) 21 October 1941, 2; "Better Race Relations," *Enterprise-Journal* 5 November 1941, 2; and Bronson, "Story," 3. Soprano Anna Medah Hyers (ca. 1855–1929) and contralto Emma Louise Hyers (ca. 1857–1901) pioneered musical theater performances that did not resort to blackface makeup, demeaning antics, or buffoonery.

79. Hackley, "Musical Progress," 12.

80. Thompson, "Mme. Hackley Wins New Laurels."

81. Krehbiel (1854–1923), a Michigan native, became a nationally respected music critic. He authored many books and articles on music appreciation and teaching. His *Afro-American Folksongs* is one of the earliest comprehensive analyses of the music of Black Americans. Hackley must have known of this landmark publication, although I have not located any mention of it by her.

82. Some of the well-known composers represented in Krehbiel's collection include J.S. Bach, Beethoven, Brahms, Dvořák, Grieg, Haydn, Liszt, Massenet, Mendelssohn, Mozart, Purcell, Scarlatti, Schubert, Schumann, Tchaikovsky, and Wagner.

83. Both *Etude* and *Musician* were published in Philadelphia, 1883–1957 and 1896–1948, respectively.

84. Hackley, *Guide*, 13–14.

85. Hackley, quoted in Davenport, *Azalia*, 108.

86. "Folk Song Festival," *Washington, DC Bee* 26 February 1916, 5; Thompson, "Mme. Hackley Wins New Laurels"; and "Helping the Race: Mrs. Azalia Hackley Cultivates the Musical Talents of Colored People and Sets Example to White Folks," *Oak Leaves* (Oak Park, IL) 16 September 1916, 44.

87. Hackley, quoted in "Negro Folk Song Festival Planned," *Berkeley* [CA] *Daily Gazette* 31 December 1920, 11; and Hackley, quoted in "Great Chorus to Sing Negro Folk Songs in Oakland," *San Francisco Chronicle* 2 January 1921, 56.

88. "Negro Folk Songs," *Cleveland Gazette* 18 March 1911, 5.

89. Work, *American*, 15. Work (1871–1935), a pioneering collector and anthologist of African American folk music, also served as conductor of the Fisk Jubilee Singers.

90. Dett, *Religious Folk-songs*, xv.

91. Cuney-Hare, *Negro Musicians*, 240. In his study of Black cultural identity, Levine notes that spirituals did not altogether disappear, but they went through periods when they were sung far less often and in fewer locales (Levine, *Black Culture*, 162–67). See also Cruz, *Culture*, 167–81.

92. "The Real American Folksong," *Crisis* 14, no. 4 (August 1917): 179.

93. "Folk Song Festival at Lincoln Jubilee," *New York Age* 2 September 1915, 2; and Hackley, letters to James Weldon Johnson, 17 August 1915, and 21 October 1915, Johnson Papers.

94. Willis, quoted in Davenport, *Azalia*, 153. See also, "Oppose Singing Plantation Melodies," *New York Age* 30 December 1909, 1; and *Washington, DC Bee* 26 February 1916, 5.

95. Ganaway, "Approves." G[eorge] H[enry] P[erry] Ganaway (1875–1940?) served the Black Boston population as a funeral director for decades.

96. "Mme. Hackley Scores a Triumph," *Washington, DC Bee* 5 February 1916, 1.

97. Judge, "Savannah Hears." For other accounts of similar Hackley events, see, for example, "Folk Song Festival," *Los Angeles Times* 7 March 1915, 42; and "Colored Folk-Song Festival a Success," *Chicago Broad Ax* 19 August 1916, 4; and "Song Festivals among Negroes: Notable Work Being Done in the South by Colored Singers under the Direction of Mme. E. Azalia Hackley," *Musical America* 29, no. 22 (29 March 1919): 16. In addition to her prominence in journalism, Jane Judge (1871–1948) supported Black musicians, worked as a teacher, held public office, and served greater Savannah as a child welfare activist; see "Miss Jane Judge Dies in Savannah," *Southern Cross: The Bulletin of the Catholic Laymen's Association of Georgia* 23 February 1948, 10; and "Miss Jane Judge, Retired Georgia Editor, Dies," *Atlanta Constitution* 16 February 1948, 18.

98. Wilson's analyses of African American performance practices can be found in these sources: "Black American Composer," 33–36; "Significance," 3–22; "Black Music," 1–22; "Heterogeneous," 327–40; "Composition," 43–51; and "'It don't mean a thing,'" 153–68.

99. Hackley, unpublished memo, "For Mr. [R. Nathaniel] Dett and Miss [Bessie L.] Drew," September 1913, Hampton Special Collections and Archives, Hampton University, Hampton, Virginia. A contralto and occasional concert performer, Bessie L. Drew (1877–1934) taught singing and art at Hampton Institute for nearly thirty years.

100. Hackley, *Guide*, 14–15.

101. Jorgensen discusses the vibrant relationship between religion and music education that brings to mind Hackley's spiritually-grounded approach to teaching and the influence of New Thought in her pedagogy ("How Can," 156–63).

102. "Authority on Music," *Philadelphia Tribune*; rpt. *Western Outlook* (Oakland, CA) 6 March 1915, 2.

103. "Mme. Hackley to Give Recital," *Pittsburgh Post-Gazette* 23 June 1912, 40.

Chapter Five. World War I Activism

1. Chancellor Otto von Bismarck annexed Alsace and northern Lorraine to the new German Empire following the defeat of France in the Franco-Prussian War of 1870–71.

2. Hackley, "Paris under Military Government"; and Hackley, "Mme. Hackley Sends Letter."

3. Du Bois, "World War and the Color Line."

4. Du Bois, "Close Ranks." Useful analyses of Du Bois's viewpoint can be found in these sources, consulted for this discussion: Ellis, "'Closing Ranks' and 'Seeking Honors,'" 92–124; Ellis, "W. E. B. Du Bois and the Formation of Black Opinion," 1584–90; Shane A. Smith, "*The Crisis* in the Great War," 239–62; Williams, "World War I"; and Wolters, *Du Bois*, 108–42.

5. See Hicks, "Coverage of World," 57–82; Kornweibel, "Apathy and Dissent," 322–38; and Kornweibel, *"Investigate Everything,"* 37–49, 80–85, 118–31.

6. William Monroe Trotter, quoted in Fox, *Guardian*, 219. William Monroe Trotter (1872–1934), a radical crusader for racial justice and a successful Boston real estate developer, was the son of James Monroe Trotter.

7. Grimké, *Works*, 3:51, 3:26–27, 3:45–48. See also Ferry, "Patriotism and Prejudice," 86–94; and Weeks, "Racism," 471–88. Rev. Francis James Grimké (1850–1937), a graduate of Princeton University Theological Seminary and a founding member of the NAACP served as pastor of the influential Fifteenth Street Presbyterian Church, located in Washington, DC.

8. Jordan, "'Damnable Dilemma,'" 1565.

9. Grant, "Negro Patriotism," 343; Levine, *Black Culture*, 168; and "Place of Negro Music in War," *Topeka Plain Dealer* 18 April 1919, 1.

10. Burlin, "Preface." See also, Curtis (later Burlin), "Negro's Contribution," 660. Natalia Curtis Burlin (1875–1921), a pioneering ethnomusicologist, transcribed and published Native American music, along with African American folk songs.

11. "Hackley Song Recital-Demonstration," *Philadelphia Tribune* 23 October 1916, 3.

12. "Folk Song Festival at Lincoln Jubilee," *New York Age* 2 September 1915, 2.

13. "Lincoln Jubilee and National Half-Century Anniversary Exposition," *Chicago Defender* 22 May 1915, 5; and "Lincoln Jubilee Is a Big Success," *Chicago Defender* 28 August 1915, 1.

14. Hackley, "Queen of Song."

15. The other famous African American "wizard" of Hackley's day was Booker T. Washington, often referred to as the "wizard of Tuskegee."

16. "Washington['s] First Folk Song Festival," *Washington, DC Bee* 11 March 1916, 1. See also, Thompson, "Mme. Hackley Wins."

17. Hackley, "Pageants the Latest Form of Entertainment."

18. American Pageant Association, *Bulletin* 1 December 1917, 1.

19. Glassberg, *American Historical*, 131–32, 179–80, 224; Smith, "Constructing a Shared History," 40–43; and Gillman, "Pageantry, Maternity," 381, 405–7.

20. Goodson, *High Brows, Hillbillies*, 155–58; Du Bois, "Star of Ethiopia," 161–65; Schenbeck, *Racial Uplift*, 80–107; "Negroes to Give Music Festival," *Atlanta Constitution* 29 June, 1912, 9; and "Colored Music Festival at Auditorium this Week Will Feature Many Fine Voices," *Atlanta Constitution* 11 August 1912, 4.

21. Hackley, quoted in "A Patriotic Pageant by Madam Hackley," *Dallas Express* 22 March 1919, 1.

22. "News of the Nation's Capitol," *Savannah Tribune* 5 May 1917, 6. See also "Race's Patriotism Shown in Pageant," *Washington, DC Bee* 5 May 1917, 1; "Washington Letter," *New

York Age 3 May 1917, 5; and "Musical and Dramatic," *Half-Century Magazine* 2, no. 6 (June 1917): 8. Hackley graciously thanked the organizers of her DC pageant, who planned, in advance, to donate "the bulk" of the proceeds realized from this event to her Normal Vocal Institute (Hackley, letter, "Madame Hackley").

23. For biblical references to the Queen of Sheba, see I Kings (10:1–13) and II Chronicles (9:1–12).

24. Gillman, "Pageantry," 405–10.

25. Hazel MacKaye, "Wake up Woman!—To This Man-Made World," undated manuscript, Percy MacKaye Papers, Baker Library, Dartmouth College, Hanover, NH; quoted in Glassberg, *American Historical*, 135. Hazel MacKaye (1880–1944) was one of few women in the male-dominated field of pageantry. She wrote and produced many pageants, the most famous being *Pageant of Susan B. Anthony* (1915).

26. For example, Hackley produced subsequent Queen's Pageants in Washington, DC; see, "Mme. Hackley's Engagements for the Week," *Washington, DC Bee* 12 May 1917, 1. She also directed a Queen's Pageant at the Mt. Olivet Baptist Church in New York City on 12 July 1917 ("Queen's Rally Pageant a Success," *New York Age* 19 July 1917, 6).

27. Hackley, "Pageants." The Georgia and federal governments established Camp Gordon in 1917 as a temporary, segregated training facility to accommodate huge numbers of African American enlistees. A state historical marker, erected just inside the main entrance to Atlanta's DeKalb-Peachtree Airport, designates the former location of the camp.

28. For more on this pageant, see the following: *Chicago Defender* 6 July 1918, 5; "Madam Hackley Stages Big Pageant," *Cleveland Advocate* 27 June 1918, 5; "Atlanta Will Hear Folk Songs Tonight," *Atlanta Constitution* 1 July 1918, 5; "Madame Hackley Conducts a Chorus of 500 Voices," *Philadelphia Tribune* 13 July 1918, 1; and Dooly, "Negro Festival." See also Dittmer, *Black Georgia*, 181–202.

29. "Madam Hackley: Famous Musician and Teacher Has Great Success in Detroit," *Chicago Defender* 31 August 1918, 6. See also "Trains Chorus for Detroit Festival: Negroes Will Sing Saturday Evening," *Detroit Free Press* 24 August 1918, 5.

30. "Madam Hackley Stages Big Pageant," *Cleveland Gazette* 13 July 1918, 1; "Huge Crowd Expected at Auditorium to Hear Old-time Negro Songs," *Atlanta Constitution* 27 June 1918, 5; and "Atlanta Will Hear Folk Songs Tonight," *Atlanta Constitution* 1 July 1918, 5.

31. In her account of the singing of African American soldiers during World War I, American author and Parisian resident Helen Davenport Brown Gibbons (1882–1960) recalled the title of this song parody as "It Takes a Long, Tall Brown-Skin Man to Make a German Lay His Rifle Down" (*Little Gray*, 139). Duke University professor Newman Ivey White (1892–1948) recorded a slightly different title: "It Takes a Long, Tall, Slim Black Man to Make a German Lay His Rifle Down" (*American Negro*, 355).

32. For information about Will Marion Cook, see Riis.

33. "Exhortation" is the second song in the cycle entitled *Three Negro Songs*.

34. Matthew 5:39 reads: "But I say unto you, that ye not resist evil: but whosoever shall smite thee on thy right cheek, turn to him the other also" (KJV). For his version of Matthew 5:39, Alex Rogers wrote: "Remember, if a brudder smotes dee on de lef' cheek, turn roun' an' han' de odder! Kase, ef you kaint 'turn good 'fu evil, what's de good o' bein' a brudder? Dats right. All right! Amen."

35. Press references to performances of Burleigh's song at Hackley events include "Folk Song Festival Given at New Orleans," *New York Age* 18 May 1918, 6; and "Folk Song Festival Given at Louisville," *New York Age* 24 August 1918, 6.

36. Snyder, *Harry T. Burleigh*, 283–86.

37. *Fort Wayne* [IN] *Journal-Gazette* 8 July 1917, 8.

38. W. J. Nickerson (1865–1928), a life-long Louisiana resident, taught at Southern University (New Orleans) for a number of years and eventually chaired the institution's music department. A composer, performer, and amateur inventor, he tutored several aspiring young jazz musicians including the celebrated pianist and composer Jelly Roll Morton (1890–1941). Nickerson's daughter, Camille Nickerson (1888–1982), was an accomplished composer and pianist. Camille Nickerson played piano accompaniments for Hackley and other notable Black musicians, especially soprano Anita Patti Brown (ca. 1870–1960) and violinists Clarence Cameron White and Joseph H. Douglass (1871–1935), Frederick Douglass' grandson.

39. Camille Nickerson, quoted in McGinty, "Conversation," 81–83. See also Hamilton, *Beacon Lights*, 49–52.

40. Scott, *Scott's Official*, 313–14. Emmett Jay Scott (1873–1957), originally a journalist, was a close advisor of Booker T. Washington and the highest-ranking African American to serve in President Woodrow Wilson's administration.

41. For additional information about Newsom, see "Berean Choir Monthly Musical," *Chicago Defender* 10 May 1919, 12; and "New Song," *Chicago Defender* 12 April 1917, 8. Additional mention of Newsom, in the *Chicago Defender*, can be found on these dates: 30 August 1918, 8; 21 June 1919, 9; and 9 August 1919, 9.

42. Holt, "Music News." Singer, composer and author Nora Douglas Holt (1885–1974) served as an arts critic and columnist for the *Chicago Defender* for a number of years. The most useful and comprehensive source on Holt is Schenbeck, *Racial Uplift*, 171–208.

43. "New Song," *Chicago Defender* 12 April 1917, 8.

44. Tony L. Langston (1875–1938) served on the staff of the *Chicago Defender* for over thirty years and also contributed articles to other newspapers ("Tony Langston, Noted Critic, Dies in Chicago," *Pittsburgh Courier* 21 November 1938, 1).

45. Advertisements for Hackley's *Patriotic Pageant* appeared several times in both the *Chicago Defender* and the *Crisis*.

46. Hackley's *Patriotic Pageant* is listed in the *Catalogue of Copyright Entries* (Washington, DC: Government Printing Office, 1918), 1111.

47. Langston's comments about Hackley's book on pageantry can be found in the following: [Langston], "Music Victory Pageant"; [Langston], "Pageant Goes"; [Langston], "One Only to Each Pageant"; and "Victory Pageant Now!" See also "A Patriotic Pageant by Madam Hackley," *Dallas Express* 22 March 1919, 1.

48. [Langston], "Music Victory Pageant."

49. Scott, *Scott's Official*, 314.

50. [Langston], "Victory Pageant."

51. For information about pageantry during the Harlem Renaissance, see the following: Schmalenberger, "Harriet Gibbs Marshall," 210–36; Smith, *Children's Literature*, 53–106; Smith, "Constructing," 40–63; and Murray, *Development*, 43–61. Richardson included the complete text of four Harlem Renaissance pageants (*Plays and Pageants*, 297–373).

Chapter Six. Writing and Uplift

1. Hackley, letter to James Weldon Johnson, 6 June 1915, James Weldon Johnson and Grace Nail Johnson Papers, Beinecke Rare Books and Manuscript Library, Yale University, New Haven, Connecticut; hereafter cited as "Johnson Papers."

2. Hackley, letter to James Weldon Johnson, 6 June 1915, Johnson Papers. Hackley mentioned, in 1920, another essay she intended to publish, entitled, "Folk Song Experiences." This manuscript never appeared in print (White, "Mme. Hackley Gives Some Comments").

3. Hackley's "Catechism" was mentioned in the *Cleveland Gazette* 18 January 1913, 2.

4. "Lesson IV" was printed privately and never copyrighted. However, Black newspapers acknowledged receipt of copies of "Lesson IV"; see *Cleveland Gazette* 10 January 1914, 3; and *Indianapolis Freeman* 17 January 1914, 1.

5. "Echoes of Xmas from Race Leaders," *Indianapolis Freeman* 17 January 1914, 1. The French word "billet-deaux" should read "billet-doux," meaning, a "love note" or a "sweet" letter.

6. "Madame E. Azalia Hackley Completely Captivates Music Loving Afro-Americans in Chicago," *Chicago Broad Ax* 21 October 1911, 1.

7. Hackley, letter to George Foster Peabody, 14 August 1918.

8. Unfortunately, the issue of the *Philadelphia Tribune* in which Hackley's article about Paris was published is lost.

9. "Mme. Hackley Captivating California," *New York Age* 9 July 1908, 6.

10. Edwin Henry Hackley, quoted in Davenport, *Azalia*, 172–73.

11. E. Azalia Hackley, letter to James Weldon Johnson, 7 July 1915, Johnson Papers.

12. *Indianapolis Freeman* 3 July 1915, 3.

13. The titles of Hackley's twelve articles of her "Hints" series, published weekly between 17 December 1914 and 4 March 1915 follow: "How a Professional Achieves Success," "Demonstration in Voice Culture (No. 1)," "Demonstration in Voice culture (No. 2)," "Accompanists," "Conditions Where We Sing," "Reducing the Ego (No. 1)," "Reducing the Ego (No. 2)," "The Way of Aspirants," "Being Introduced," "Concert Annoyances and Interruptions," "Little Courtesies in the Musical Profession," and, "The Rosy Side of Professional Life."

14. Hackley, letter to James Weldon Johnson, 6 June 1915, Johnson Papers.

15. [Fred. R. Moore], *New York Age* 17 December 1914, 5. Fred R. (Frederick Randolph) Moore (1857–1943) owned and edited the *New York Age*, 1907–43. He received advice and financial backing from *Musical America* editor John C. Freund, and from Booker T. Washington.

16. *Indianapolis Freeman* 6 February 1915, 2.

17. *Indianapolis Freeman* 6 February 1915, 2.

18. Hackley, "Mme. Hackley Sends Letter."

19. For analyses of the relationships of Freund, Booker T. Washington, and Moore with the *Colored American Magazine* and the *New York Age*, consulted for this discussion, see Meier, "Booker T. Washington"; Chase, "Negro Publications"; and Moore, "Editorial."

20. Fred R. Moore, untitled item, *New York Age* 17 December 1914, 5.

21. Hackley, "Hints . . . How a Professional Achieves Success."

22. Hackley, "Hints . . . How a Professional Achieves Success."

23. Hackley, letter to James Weldon Johnson, 6 June 1915, Johnson Papers.

24. Hackley, letter to James Weldon Johnson, 17 August 1915, Johnson Papers.

25. Elbert Hubbard (1856–1915) and his wife, Alice Moore Hubbard (1861–1915), perished on board the *Lusitania*, torpedoed and sunk by a German U-boat on 7 May 1915. Alice Moore Hubbard, a noted feminist, writer, and suffragist, graduated from Boston's New Thought-oriented institution, Emerson College of Oratory.

26. Hackley, letter to James Weldon Johnson, 6 June 1915, Johnson Papers.

27. Hackley, letter to James Weldon Johnson, no date, but written in response to Johnson's letter of 7 July 1815, Johnson Papers.

28. Hackley, letter to James Weldon Johnson, 30 June 1915, Johnson Papers.
29. Hackley, letter to James Weldon Johnson, 27 August 1915, Johnson Papers.
30. Hackley, letter to James Weldon Johnson, 6 June 1915, Johnson Papers.
31. Hackley, letter to James Weldon Johnson, 2 July 1915, Johnson Papers.
32. Hackley, letters to Johnson, 6 June 1915, 7 July 1915, and 17 August 1915, Johnson Papers.
33. Hackley, letter to James Weldon Johnson, 13 August 1915, Johnson Papers.
34. Hackley, letter to James Weldon Johnson, 27 August 1915, Johnson Papers.
35. Hollis Burke Frissell (1851–1917) served as Hampton's second principal, assuming the position upon the death of the Institute's founding principal, General Samuel Chapman Armstrong (1839–93). Robert Russa Moton (1867–1940) left Hampton to assume the position of principal at Tuskegee Institute after the unexpected death of Booker T. Washington on 14 November 1915. Moton's sudden move to Tuskegee and the stress of his departure on Frissell explains why neither of them could assist Hackley with her search for a publisher.
36. Hackley, letter to James Weldon Johnson, 13 August 1915, Johnson Papers.
37. Hackley, letter to James Weldon Johnson, 17 August 1915, Johnson Papers.
38. Ollie (or Olly) David Burton (1868–1957) founded and owned Burton Publishing Company; see Sweeney, "Burton Publishing"; and "Olly D. Burton Dies," *Kansas City* [MO] *Times* 3 April 1957, 16.
39. "Do You Know the History?" *Kansas City* [MO] *Sun* 10 October 1914, 4; *Kansas City Sun* 24 October 1914, 3; and "Men and Women of Affairs," *Kansas City Sun* 19 September 1914, 3.
40. "Geo. W. Little," *Kansas City Sun* 24 October 1914, 5.
41. "A New History," *Kansas City Sun* 26 September 1914, 1.
42. Hackley, letter to George Foster Peabody, 1918. Johnson did not mention such an amount in his letters to Hackley.
43. *Pittsburgh Press* 2 July 1916, 40.
44. [Fred R. Moore], untitled item, *New York Age* 22 February 1917, 4.
45. *New York Age* 13 September 1917, 4.
46. Hackley, "Hints . . . How a Professional Achieves Success." Hackley credited advertising for attracting large audiences; see "Local News," *Pittsburgh Courier* 12 July 1912, 4.
47. Johnson, "Views and Reviews."
48. "Editorial Paragraphs," *Cayton's Weekly* (Seattle, WA) 11 August 1917, 1.
49. *Journal of the National Medical Association* 9, no. 3 (July–September 1917): 174. Members of the exclusively white American Medical Association barred African American medical practitioners from joining their organization or publishing in their *Journal of the American Medical Association*. Therefore, Blacks formed the National Medical Association and published their own journal.
50. *Negro World* 13 September 1924, 10.
51. Hackley, letter to George Foster Peabody, 14 August 1918.
52. Davenport, *Azalia*, 167.
53. Hackley, *Colored Girl*, 11.
54. For more on the currency of this verse among African Americans, see Barton, "I am Black," and Camp, "Black Is Beautiful."
55. For more on Washington's preoccupation with cleanliness, see Kowalski, "No Excuse," 181–96.
56. Hackley, *Colored Girl*, 11, 30–31.
57. Hackley, *Colored Girl*, 181–82.
58. Moton, introduction.

59. Many of the authors published in *Upward Path* were some of the best-known African American writers, including the following: Benjamin Brawley, William Wells Brown, Charles W. Chesnutt, John Wesley Cromwell, Frederick Douglass, W. E. B. Du Bois, Paul Laurence Dunbar, Jessie Redmon Fauset, Silas X. Floyd, Angelina Weld Grimké, James Weldon Johnson, Kelly Miller, Emmett J. Scott, Ralph W. Tyler, Booker T. Washington, and Phyllis Wheatley.

60. My discussion and consideration of "respectability" were informed by Higginbotham, *Righteous Discontent*, 185–229; and Gates, 193–96.

61. Williams, "After Many Days," 149.

62. Jones, "Greatest Needs," 38. Sarah Garland Boyd Jones (1866–1905) studied medicine at Howard University and co-founded a hospital for Black females in Richmond, Virginia; see "A Colored Female Doctor," *Owensboro [KY] Messenger* 21 May 1893, 5.

63. Hackley, *Colored Girl*, 88; and Hackley, "Hints . . . How a Professional Achieves Success."

Chapter Seven. Chronic Illness and New Thought

1. Hackley, letter to Harriet A. Gibbs, 14 May 1904, Washington Conservatory of Music Papers, Moorland-Spingarn Research Center, Howard University, Washington, D.; hereafter cited as "WCM Papers."

2. Hackley, comment to Lucille Tate (1874–1946), quoted in Davenport, *Azalia*, 113.

3. Edwin Henry Hackley, letter to Harriet A. Gibbs Marshall, 2 September 1906, WCM Papers.

4. Hackley, letter to Caroline M. S. Severance, 3 February 1909, Caroline Marie Seymour Severance Papers, Huntington Library, San Marino, California; hereafter cited as "Severance Papers." Severance (1820–1914) was a prominent and wealthy clubwoman, and a noted temperance and suffrage activist.

5. *Colorado Statesman* 8 May 1909, 4.

6. Hackley, letter to Caroline M. S. Severance, 3 February 1909, Severance Papers.

7. *Nashville Globe* 25 February 1910, 8.

8. "Madame Hackley Here," *Nashville Globe* 25 February 1910, 3.

9. *Chicago Broad Ax* 19 November 1910, 1.

10. "Madam Hackley and Miss Fitzhugh Arrive in St. Louis, Mo, from Their Southern Tour," *Chicago Broad Ax* 21 January 1911, 1; and *Chicago Broad Ax* 25 February 1911, 2. Hackley toured with Mary L. Fitzhugh (later Fitzhugh-Valentine, 1888–1946), a promising blind soprano, 1910–12.

11. "Mme. E. Azalia Hackley Will Return to Chicago," *Chicago Defender* 18 April 1914, 6.

12. "News of the Sick," *Chicago Broad Ax* 5 June 1915, 5. Influenza, a deadly and substantially untreatable disease in the 1910s, killed one million people in the pandemic of 1918. For more on influenza and African American healthcare, see Gamble, "There Wasn't."

13. Hackley, letter to James Weldon Johnson, 21 October 1915, Johnson Papers.

14. *Cleveland Gazette* 30 December 1916, 2. See also "Mme. E. Azalia Hackley," *Philadelphia Tribune* 23 December 1916, 1.

15. *Philadelphia Tribune* 23 December 1916, 1; and *Cleveland Gazette* 30 December 1916, 2.

16. *Savannah Tribune* 20 January 1917, 7.

17. "Chicago Singer Sick," *Chicago Defender* 27 January 1917, 13; and *Savannah Tribune* 3 February 1917, 1.

18. *Savannah Tribune* 10 February 1917, 7.

19. *Denver Star* 27 January 1917, 4.

20. *Savannah Tribune* 3 February 1917, 1.

21. Hackley, undated letter to Marietta Smith Johnson, quoted in Davenport, *Azalia*, 174.

22. *Washington, DC Bee* 3 February 1917, 5.

23. Hackley, letter to Berena Anderson Sogers, 21 February 1917, quoted in Davenport, *Azalia*, 175–76. Sogers (1880-ca. 1950), a Kentucky native, was a singer and may well have studied with Hackley.

24. Hackley, undated letter to Berena Anderson Sogers, quoted in Davenport, *Azalia*, 175.

25. *New York Age* 1 February 1917, 8; *Savannah Tribune* 3 February 1917, 1; and "Mme. Hackley Spends Week at Home of Dr. Lyman Abbott," *Kansas City* [MO] *Sun* 17 February 1917, 8. Rev. Lyman Abbott (1835–1922), a white liberal Congregationalist, Evolutionary Christian, and supporter of Progressive Era social reform, also endorsed Booker T. Washington's methods. Dr. Theodore Jacob Abbott (1872–1951), a Harvard University graduate, practiced in New York City and taught clinical medicine at New York University; see "Dr. Theodore J. Abbott," *New York Times* 3 March 1951, 13.

26. "Mrs. E. Azalia Hackley Is in Her Old Home, Philadelphia, Pennsylvania, at the Present Time," *Chicago Broad Ax* 31 March 1917, 1.

27. *Philadelphia Tribune* 31 March 1917, 5.

28. *Philadelphia Tribune* 7 April 1917, 5.

29. Davenport, *Azalia*, 175–76.

30. "Mrs. E. Azalia Hackley Is in Her Old home," *Chicago Broad Ax* 31 March 1917, 1; and "Mme. E. Azalia Hackley," *Philadelphia Tribune* 31 March 1917, 5.

31. "Mme. Hackley in Washington," *Philadelphia Tribune* 5 May 1917, 3.

32. "Mrs. Hackley to Give Folk Song Festival," *New York Age* 8 November 1917, 6.

33. Hackley, letter to George Foster Peabody, 14 August 1918.

34. "Madam E. Azalia Hackley," *Chicago Broad Ax* 15 November 1919, 2; and *Washington, DC Bee* 6 December 1919, 5.

35. "Mme. E. Azalia Hackley," *Philadelphia Tribune* 25 October 1919, 5.

36. Marie A. D. Madre married Rev. James H. Marshall in 1918 and used the surname "Marshall" while often retaining "Madre" as a middle name.

37. *Washington, DC Bee* 6 December 1919, 5.

38. Hackley, quoted in White, "Mme. E. A. Hackley."

39. Hackley, letter to Berena Anderson Sogers, 20 May 1920, quoted in Davenport, *Azalia*, 179.

40. Based on interviews with Hackley's sister and husband, Davenport stated that Hackley wanted to have several children (*Azalia*, 34).

41. Hackley, *Colored Girl*, 181.

42. Hackley, *Colored Girl*, 170.

43. Hackley, *Colored Girl*, 206.

44. White, "Mme. E. A. Hackley."

45. Hackley, *Colored Girl*, 56, 81.

46. Hackley's Seattle performance was, most likely, her final public appearance; see "About Colored Citizens," *Cayton's Weekly* (Seattle, WA) 4 December 1920, 2. Davenport claims that Hackley traveled to Tokyo in 1920 (*Azalia*, 180–81). Hackley delivered remarks at an AME Zion denomination conference in which she mentioned her hope to rebound from health problems and travel to Japan (*Missionary Seer* [New York] 20, no. 7 [July 1920]: 8). She also spoke to Lucien H. White of a possible trip to Japan (White, "Mme. E. A. Hackley").

No source has surfaced to confirm that Hackley ever traveled to Japan. Given her precarious health, it seems unlikely she could have undertaken such an arduous journey.

47. "Mrs. Hackley Found Unconscious," *New York Age* 16 July 1921, 5; and "Madam E. Azalia Hackley," *Chicago Broad Ax* 29 October 1921, 3.

48. "Singer Very Ill," *San Diego Union* 19 June 1921, 15.

49. White, "Mme. E. Azalia Hackley Is Dead."

50. *Washington, DC Bee* 5 November 1921, 5. See also "Mme. Hackley, Famous Producer of Pageants, Breaks Down in Health," *Chicago Defender* 20 August 1921, 7.

51. "Fear Mme. Hackley Is a Permanent Invalid," *New York Age* 30 September 1922, 6.

52. "Fear Mme. Hackley."

53. "Fear Mme. Hackley."

54. Notification of Hackley's death appeared in surprisingly few publications, including the following: *Buffalo American, Chicago Broad Ax, Crisis, Dallas Express, Negro World, New York Age, Phoenix Tribune, Savannah Tribune,* and *St. Paul Appeal.*

55. Garland-Thomas, Foreword, xiii.

56. So, too, age-related changes in her voice were undoubtedly factors. Her World War I activism also brought about changes in her repertoire.

57. For a discussion of the ways hearing-impaired musicians accommodate their loss, see Straus, *Extraordinary Measures*, 6–8, 26–29, 64, 67. After around 1914, Hackley conducted, accompanied, rehearsed, and taught, but performed far fewer solos.

58. Hackley, *Guide*, 13.

59. Hackley, *Colored Girl*, 18, 31, 125, 181.

60. For more on Black women's health issues and inferior medical treatment of Blacks during the nineteenth and early twentieth centuries, see Herndl, "Invisible," 131–45; and Parker, "Picture of Health," 165–207.

Coda

1. Hogans, "Pullman."

2. Hackley, *Colored Girl*, 178.

3. Britney Cooper discusses ways Mary Church Terrell and Fannie Barrier Williams also attempted to define and exploit commonalities in the Washington-Du Bois rift (*Beyond Respectability*, 25–26, 33–86).

4. Clifford, "Idealism and Materialism," 165–67.

5. O'Shaughnessy and Kennedy, "Relational," 551–72; and Dove and Fisher, "Why Relational Activism." O'Shaughnessy and Kennedy formulated their theory as a way to explain the uniqueness of certain contemporary approaches to environmental activism.

6. Dunn, "Educational Philosophies," 25. Historians Michael L. Mark and Charles L. Gary hardly mention the history of African American music education in their otherwise comprehensive survey, still considered the standard reference on the subject (Mark and Gary, *History*).

7. For more on the foundations of US music education and the careers of Mason, Bradbury, and Root, see Mark and Gary, *History*, 123–54. Bradbury (1816–68) studied with Mason (1792–1872); Root (1820–95) was a friend and associate of Mason and Bradbury. All three of these men promoted innovative music education strategies and were also prolific composers.

8. hooks, *Teaching*, 11, 40, 170.

9. Freire, *Pedagogy*, 18, 30, 62, 119. Hackley's choice of African American–centered teaching repertoire also manifested what Gloria Ladson-Billings identifies as "culturally relevant pedagogy" ("But That's Just Good Teaching").

10. Advertisement for Pauline James Lee's "School of Musical Arts," *Chicago Defender* 31 August 1918, 12.

11. *Indianapolis Recorder* 28 May 1932, 6.

12. Hansbury (1898–1974) pursued piano studies in Berlin. Her husband, William H. Phillips, ran the Household Guild, the first state-licensed employment agency for Blacks, out of the school's building as well. Unfortunately, the stress of the Great Depression forced the school to close in 1930. The elegant brick Queen Anne building that housed the Hansbury enterprises, built in 1885, now comprises part of the area's historic district.

13. "Hampton Dedicates Its Recital Hall to the Late Mme. E. Azalia Hackley," *New York Age* 28 October 1933, 6.

14. *New York Age* 25 November 1939, 4; "Music Notes," *New York Age* 10 August 1940, 4; *New York Age* 18 December 1943, 10; "Miss Ruth Baker Gives Recital," *Pittsfield* [MA] *Berkshire Evening Eagle* 10 May 1947, 16; and Davenport, *Azalia*, 195. Both Edith E. Baker and mezzo soprano Ruth Baker graduated from Oberlin College Conservatory of Music and taught at the Azalia Hackley School of Music.

15. Bulanda, "Detroit Public Library's." Aside from several photographs, Hackley's papers are not housed in the collection.

16. Dett, "Bell Stand," 78.

17. Kate Johnson, quoted in George, "News." The portrait of Hackley mentioned by Johnson was painted by African American artist and Detroit resident Jesse C. Stubbs (1876–1961). The whereabouts of this painting are unknown.

18. Carl Rossini Diton, "Biographical Notes," letter to W. E. B. Du Bois, 5 September 1961. Special Collections and University Archives, University of Massachusetts, Amherst, MA. Du Bois and Diton were friends, and they corresponded frequently. Diton died only three months after writing this letter to Du Bois.

19. Hackley, "Musical Progress."

BIBLIOGRAPHY

Adams, Minnie. "Musical and Dramatic," *Chicago Defender* 21 October 1911, 5.
Adams, Minnie. "Musical and Dramatic: Mme. Hackley Recital," *Chicago Defender* 17 May 1914, 6.
Alexander, Thomas B. "Kukluxism in Tennessee, 1865–69," *Tennessee Historical Quarterly* 8 (1949): 195–219.
Anderson, C. Alan, and Deborah G. Whitehouse. *New Thought: A Practical American Spirituality*, rev. ed. Bloomington, IN: First Books Library, 2003.
Anderson, Garland. *From Newsboy and Bellhop to Playwright*. San Francisco: Cathedral, 1925.
Anderson, Garland. *Hows and Whys of Your Success*. San Francisco: Geary, Meigs, 1925.
Anderson, Garland. *Uncommon Sense: The Law of Life in Action*. London: Fowler, 1933.
Anderson, Marian. *My Lord, What a Morning*. 1956; rpt., Madison: University of Wisconsin Press, 1992.
Archer, Argent. "How Military Photographs Are Taken: A Chat with Mr. Argent Archer," *New Penny Magazine* 7 (1900): 293–300.
Arsenault, Raymond. *The Sound of Freedom: Marian Anderson and the Concert That Awakened America*. New York: Bloomsbury Press, 2009.
Atkins, Gaius Glenn. *Modern Religious Cults and Movements*. Chicago: Revell, 1923.
Atkinson, William Walker. *Nuggets of New Thought*. Chicago: Psychic Research, 1902.
Atkinson, William Walker. *Thoughts Are Things*. London: Fowler, 1912.
Atkinson, William Walker. *Thought Vibration; or, the Law of Attraction in the Thought World*. Chicago: New Thought Publishing, 1906.
Austin, James. "Mme. Hackley Touring Europe," *Philadelphia Tribune* 13 July 1914, 3.
Baker, Henry E. "The Stage: Madam E. Azalia Hackley," *Indianapolis Freeman* 14 September 1907, 2.
Baker, Ray Stannard. *Following the Color Line: An Account of Negro Citizenship in the American Democracy*. New York: Doubleday, 1908.
Barton, Mukti. "I am Black and Beautiful," *Black Theology* 2, no. 2 (2004): 167–87.
Basch, Madison. "Five Points: The Heart and Soul of Denver," 11 February 2019. Colorado Virtual Library, online.
Baughan, E. A. "Music and Musicians," *London Daily News* 8 April 1904, 8.
Beard, Kathryn Lorraine. *"Higher than those of their race of less fortunate advantages": Race, Ethnicity and West Indian Political Leadership in Detroit's African American Community, 1885–1940*. Ph.D. diss., Wayne State University, Detroit, MI, 2011.

Billie. "Madame E. Azalia Hackley," *Indianapolis Freeman* 23 December 1911, 5.
Boime, Albert. "Henry O. Tanner's Subversion of Genre," *Art Bulletin* 75, no. 3 (September 1993): 415–42.
Bowers, Jane. "Writing the Biography of a Black Blues Singer," in Pirkko Moisala and Beverley Diamond, eds., *Music and Gender*. Urbana: University of Illinois Press, 2000, 140–65.
Braden, Charles S. *Spirits in Rebellion: The Rise and Development of New Thought*. Dallas: Southern Methodist University Press, 1963.
Brevard, Lisa Pertillar. *A Biography of E. Azalia Hackley (1867–1922), African American Singer and Social Activist*. Lewiston, NY: Edwin Mellen Press, 2001.
Brevard, Lisa Pertillar. *A Biography of Edwin Henry Hackley, 1859–1940: African American Attorney and Activist*. Lewiston, NY: Edwin Mellen Press, 2002.
Briggs, Asa, and Anne McCartney. *Toynbee Hall: The First Hundred Years*. London: Routledge, 1984.
Bronson, Arthur. "The Story of a Great Singer, Marian Anderson," *Negro* 4, no. 9 (1 September 1946): 3–7.
Brooks, Charles H. "Negro Travelers in Europe," *Indianapolis Freeman* 29 December 1900, 15.
Brooks, Nona L. *Short Lessons in Divine Science*. Denver: Welch-Haffner, 1923.
Brooks, Tim. *Lost Sounds: Blacks and the Birth of the Recording Industry, 1890–1919*. Urbana: University of Illinois Press, 2004.
Brown, Hallie Quinn. *Homespun Heroines and other Women of Distinction*. Xenia, OH: Aldine, 1929.
Bulanda, George. "The Detroit Public Library's Hackley Collection Promotes African American Performing Artists," *Hour Detroit* (24 January 2012), online.
Burlin, Natalie Curtis. Preface, "Hymn of Freedom." New York: G. Schirmer, 1918, n.p.
Camp, Stephanie M. N. "Black Is Beautiful: An American History," *Journal of Southern History* 81, no. 3 (August 2015): 675–90.
Campbell, Gladys B. "The Vocal Teacher of Ten Thousand," *Half-Century Magazine* 1, no. 2 (September 1916): 2.
Carter, Scott A. "Forging a Sound Citizenry: Voice Culture and the Embodiment of a Nation, 1880–1920," *American Music Research Center Journal* 22 (January 2013): 11–34.
Cécil, George. "The Singer's Life Luxurious," *Town and Country* 15 July 1905, 14–16.
Chase, W. E. H. "Negro Publications," *Colored American Magazine* 9, no. 1 (July 1905): 491–95.
Chesnutt, Charles W. "Post-Bellum—Pre-Harlem," *Colophon* (February 1931); rpt., *Crisis* (June 1931): 193–94.
Chesnutt, Charles W. "What Is a White Man?" *Independent* 41 (30 May 1889): 5–6.
Chresfield, Michell. *To Improve the Race: Eugenics as a Strategy for Racial Uplift, 1900–1940*. MA thesis, Vanderbilt University, Nashville, TN, 2013.
Clem, Charles D. "Launching of a New Enterprise," *Vindicator* (Coffeyville, KS) 1 September 1905, 1.
Clifford, Carrie W. "Idealism and Materialism," *Colored American Magazine* 10, no. 3 (1 March 1906): 21–23.
Clifford, Carrie W. "A Plea to Colored Men," *Indianapolis Freeman* 11 January 1908, 2.
Clifford, Carrie W. *Race Rhymes*. Washington, DC: Pendleton, 1911.
Clifford, Geraldine J. *Those Good Gertrudes: A Social History of Women Teachers in America*. Baltimore: Johns Hopkins University Press, 2014.
Cole, Helen. "Henry O. Tanner, Painter," *Brush and Pencil* 6, no. 3 (June 1900): 97–107.

Cooper, Anna Julia. "The Negro as Presented in American Literature" (1892), in Lemert and Bhan, eds., 134–60.
Cooper, Anna Julia. "Womanhood: A Vital Element in the Regeneration and Progress of a Race" (1886), in Lemert and Bhan, eds., 53–71.
Cooper, Anna Julia. "Woman versus the Indian" (1891–92), in Lemert and Bhan, eds., 88–108.
Cooper, Brittney C. *Beyond Respectability: The Intellectual Thought of Race Women*. Urbana: University of Illinois Press, 2017.
Crisler, Jesse S., Robert C. Leitz, III, and Joseph R. McElrath, Jr., eds. *An Exemplary Citizen: Letters of Charles W. Chesnutt, 1906–32*. Redwood City, CA: Stanford University Press, 2002.
Crummell, Alexander. *The Race Problem in America*. Washington, DC: Morrison, 1889.
Cruz, John. *Culture on the Margins: The Black Spiritual and the Rise of American Cultural Interpretation*. Princeton: Princeton University Press, 1999.
Cuney-Hare, Maude. *Negro Musicians and Their Music*. Washington, DC: Associated, 1936.
Curtis, H[enry] Holbrook. *Voice Building and Tone Placing*, 2nd ed. New York: Appleton, 1902.
Curtis (later Burlin), Natalie. "The Negro's Contribution to the Music of America: The Larger Opportunity of the Colored Man of Today," *Craftsman* 23, no. 6 (1 March 1913): 660.
Davenport, M. Marguerite. *Azalia: The Life of Madame E. Azalia Hackley*. Boston: Chapman and Grimes, 1947.
Deane, Hazel. *Powerful Is the Light: The Story of Nona Brooks*. Denver: Divine Science College, 1945.
DeChant, Dell. "The American New Thought Movement," in Eugene V. Gallagher and W. Michael Ashcraft, eds., *Introduction to New and Alternative Religions in America*, 5 vols. Westport, CT: Greenwood Press, 2006. Vol. 3: *Metaphysical, New Age, and Neopagan Movements*, 67–91.
DeCosta-Willis, Mariam, ed. *The Memphis Diary of Ida B. Wells*. Boston: Beacon Press, 1995.
Delcomyn, Marion. "Holy Trinity Lodge, Paris," *Churchman* 14 February 1914, 213.
Dennett, Laurie. *An American Princess: The Remarkable Life of Marguerite Chapin Caetani*. Montreal: McGill-Queen's University Press, 2016.
Dett, R. Nathanial. "From Bell Stand to Throne Room," *Etude* 52 (February 1934); rpt. *Black Perspective in Music* 1, no. 1 (Spring 1973): 73–81.
Dett, R. Nathanial. *Religious Folk-Songs of the Negro as Sung at Hampton Institute*. Hampton, VA: Hampton Institute Press, 1927.
Dineen-Wimberly, Ingrid. *The Allure of Blackness among Mixed-Race Americans, 1862–1916*. Lincoln: University of Nebraska Press, 2019.
Di Sala, Countess. "A Fertile Soil for Millionaires," *Table Talk* 22, no. 11 (November 1907): 419–24.
Dittmer, John. *Black Georgia in the Progressive Era, 1900–1920*. Urbana: University of Illinois Press, 1980.
Dixon, Thomas, Jr. *The Clansman: A Historical Romance of the Ku Klux Klan*. New York: Doubleday, 1905.
Dixon, Thomas, Jr. *The Leopard's Spots: A Romance of the White Man's Burden—1865–1900*. New York: Doubleday, 1902.
Dixon, Thomas, Jr. *The Traitor: The Story of the Fall of the Invisible Empire*. New York: Doubleday, 1907.
Dodson, N. Barnett. "Noted Songster Begins Retiring Song Recitals," *Indianapolis Freeman* 29 October 1910, 1.

Dooly, Louise. "Negro Festival Monday and Tuesday to Provide Spellbinding Music," *Atlanta Constitution* 30 June 1918, 8; rpt., "Teaching the Old Plantation Melodies," *New York Age* 3 August 1918, 6.

Dorr, Gregory Michael, and Angela Logan. "'Quality, Not Mere Quantity, Counts': Black Eugenics and the NAACP Baby Contests," in Paul A. Lombardo, ed., *A Century of Eugenics in America: From the Indiana Experiment to the Human Genome Era.* Bloomington: Indiana University Press, 2010, 68–94.

Douglas, Walter Johnstone. "A Lesson with the Master," *Music and Letters* 6, no. 3 (July 1925): 209–13.

Dove, Becca, and Tim Fisher. "Why Relational Activism Might Bring Hope and Light to Social Change," 29 March 2019, online blog.

Dresser, Annetta Gertrude, ed. *The Philosophy of P. P. Quimby.* Boston: Ellis, 1895.

Dresser, Horatio Willis. *A History of the New Thought Movement.* New York: Crowell, 1919.

Dresser, Horatio Willis. "What Is the New Thought?" *Arena* 21, no. 1 (January 1899): 29–51.

Du Bois, W. E. B. *The Autobiography of W. E. B. Du Bois: A Soliloquy on Viewing My Life from the Last Decade of Its First Century.* New York: International, 1968.

Du Bois, W. E. B. "The Black North: A Social Study," *New York Times* 15 December 1901, 20.

Du Bois, W. E. B. "Close Ranks," *Crisis* 16, no. 3 (July 1918): 111.

Du Bois, W. E. B. "The Conservation of Races" (1897), in David Levering Lewis, ed., *W. E. B. Du Bois: A Reader.* New York: Henry Holt, 1995, 20–27.

Du Bois, W. E. B. *Efforts for Social Betterment among Negro Americans.* Atlanta, GA: Atlanta University Press, 1909.

Du Bois, W. E. B. *The Philadelphia Negro: A Social Study.* Philadelphia: University of Pennsylvania, 1899.

Du Bois, W. E. B. "The Problem of Tillman, Vardaman and Thomas Dixon, Jr.," *Central Christian Advocate* 49 (18 October 1905): 1324–25.

Du Bois, W. E. B. *The Souls of Black Folk.* 1903; rpt., New York: Bantam, 1989.

Du Bois, W. E. B. "*Star of Ethiopia*: A Pageant" (1915), in Herbert Aptheker, comp. and ed. *Pamphlets and Leaflets by W. E. B. Du Bois.* White Plains, NY: Kraus-Thomson, 1980, 161–65.

Du Bois, W. E. B. "World War and the Color Line," *Crisis* 9, no. 1 (November 1914): 28–30.

Dumont, Theron Q. (pseud. William Walker Atkinson). *The Solar Plexus or Abdominal Brain.* Chicago: Advanced Thought Publishing, 1920.

Dunn, Frederick. "The Educational Philosophies of Washington, Du Bois, and Houston: Laying the Foundations for Afro-Centrism and Multiculturalism," *Journal of Negro Education* 62, no. 1 (Winter 1993): 24–34.

Dykema, Peter W. "The Spread of the Community Music Idea," *Annals of the American Academy of Political and Social Science* 67 (September 1916): 218–23.

Ellis, Mark. "'Closing Ranks' and 'Seeking Honors': W. E. B. Du Bois in World War I," *Journal of American History* 79, no. 1 (June 1992): 92–124.

Ellis, Mark. "W. E. B. Du Bois and the Formation of Black Opinion in World War I: A Commentary on 'The Damnable Dilemma,'" *Journal of American History* 81, no. 4 (March 1995): 1584–90.

Emerson, Ralph Waldo. "The Sovereignty of Ethics," *North American Review* 10, no. 12 (May-June 1878): 402–20.

English, Daylanne K. *Unnatural Selections: Eugenics in American Modernism and the Harlem Renaissance.* Chapel Hill: University of North Carolina Press, 2004.

Evans, Warren Felt. *The Mental Cure.* Boston: Carter, 1869.
Everett, Anna. *Returning the Gaze: A Genealogy of Black Film Criticism, 1909–1914.* Durham, NC: Duke University Press, 2001.
Farwell, Arthur. "Community Music-Drama," *Craftsman* 26, no. 4 (July 1914): 418–24.
Fearing, Jeffrey John. "Addison Scurlock and the Scurlock Studios of Washington, D.C.," online.
Ferry, Henry Justin. "Patriotism and Prejudice: Francis J. Grimke [sic] on World War I," *Journal of Religious Thought* 32 (1975): 86–94.
Field, Allyson Nadia. *Uplift Cinema: The Emergence of African American Film and the Possibilities of Black Modernity.* Durham, NC: Duke University Press, 2001.
Finck, Henry Theophilus. *Success in Music and How It Is Won.* New York: Scribner, 1909.
Ford, [John Elijah]. "Across the Briny Deep," *Colorado Statesman* 11 October 1907, 8.
Foster, Mark S. "'In the Face of Jim Crow': Prosperous Blacks and Vacations, Travel and Outdoor Leisure, 1890–1945," *Journal of Negro History* 84, no. 2 (Spring 1999): 130–49.
Fox, Stephen R. *The Guardian of Boston: William Monroe Trotter.* New York: Atheneum, 1970.
Freire, Paulo. *Pedagogy of the Oppressed*, rev. ed., Myra Bergman Ramos, trans. New York: Continuum, 1993.
Gable-Wilson, Sonya R. *Let Freedom Sing!: Four African American Concert Singers in Nineteenth-Century America.* Ph.D. diss., University of Florida, Gainesville, 2005.
Gaines, Kevin K. *Uplifting the Race: Black Leadership, Politics and Culture in the Twentieth Century.* Chapel Hill: University of North Caroline Press, 1996.
Gamble, Vanessa Northington. "'There Wasn't a Lot of Comforts in Those Days': African Americans, Public Health, and the 1918 Influenza Epidemic," *Public Health Reports* (2010): 114–22.
Ganaway, G[eorge] H[enry] P[erry]. "Approves Plantation Melodies," *New York Age* 17 February 1910, 4.
Gardullo, Paul. *The Scurlock Studio and Black Washington: Picturing the Promise.* Washington, DC: National Museum of African American History and Culture, 2009.
Garland-Thomas, Rosemarie. Foreword, in Neil Lerner and Joseph N. Straus, eds., *Sounding Off: Theorizing Disability in Music.* New York: Routledge, 2007, xiii–xv.
Gates, Henry Louis, Jr. *Stony the Road: Reconstruction, White Supremacy, and the Rise of Jim Crow.* New York: Penguin, 2019.
Gatewood, Willard B. *Aristocrats of Color: The Black Elite, 1880–1920.* Fayetteville: University of Arkansas Press, 2000.
Gaze, Henry. *My Personal Recollections of Thomas Troward.* Privately published, 1958; rpt., *Thomas Troward: An Intimate Memoir of the Teacher and the Man.* Marina Del Rey, CA: DeVorss, 1992.
George, Maude Roberts. "News of the Music World," *Chicago Defender* 22 September 1928, 3.
George, Zelma Watson, interview. *The Black Women Oral History Project Interviews*, 297. Schlesinger Library, Radcliff Institute, Harvard University, Cambridge, MA, online.
Gibbons, Helen Davenport Brown. *A Little Gray Home in France.* New York: Century, 1919.
[Gibbs, Harriet A.] "The Washington Conservatory of Music," *Negro Music Journal* 2, no. 14 (October 1903): 28.
Gibson, J. W. *Golden Thoughts on Chastity and Procreation including Heredity, Prenatal Influences, Etc.* Washington, DC: Jenkins, 1904.
Gillman, Susan Kay. "Pageantry, Maternity, and World History," in Susan Kay Gillman and Alys Eve Weinbaum, eds., *Next to the Color Line: Gender, Sexuality, and W. E. B. Du Bois.* Minneapolis: University of Minnesota Press, 2007, 378–416.

Glassberg, David. *American Historical Pageantry: The Uses of Tradition in the Early Twentieth Century*. Chapel Hill: University of North Carolina Press, 1990.
Goodson, Steve. *High Brows, Hillbillies and Hellfire: Public Entertainment in Atlanta, 1880–1930*. Athens: University of Georgia Press, 2007.
Grant, Francis R. "Negro Patriotism and Negro Music," *Outlook* 26 February 1919, 343.
Graziano, John. "The Early Life and Career of the 'Black Patti': The Odyssey of an African American Singer in the Late Nineteenth Century," *Journal of the American Musicological Society* 53, no. 3 (Autumn 2000): 549–62.
Green, Jeffrey. *Black Edwardians: Black People in Britain, 1901–14*. London: Taylor and Francis, 1998.
Greene, H[erbert] W. "More about Shakespeare," *Etude* 18, no. 3 (1 March 1900): 110.
Grenside, Dorothy. *Little Builders: New Thought Talks to Children*. New York: Dodge, 1916.
Grimké, Francis James. *The Works of Francis James Grimké*, 4 vols. Carter G. Woodson, ed. Vol. 3: *Thoughts and Meditations*. Washington, DC: Associated, 1942.
Griswold, Alfred Whitney. "New Thought: A Cult of Success," *American Journal of Sociology* 40, no. 3 (November 1934): 390–18.
Gross, William E. "Impressions of Mme. E. Azalia Hackley, Soprano, and Three of Her Pupils," *New York Age* 10 August 1911, 7.
Gunn, Lutie A. Baker. "Voice Culture of To-day," *Etude* 23, no. 1 (January 1905): 25.
Guthrie, Arthur. *Letters from France and Italy*. Chicago: McClung, 1909.
Hackley, E. Azalia. "Being a Somebody," *Chicago Broad Ax* 14 January 1911, 1.
Hackley, E. Azalia. *The Colored Girl Beautiful*. Kansas City, MO: Burton, 1916.
Hackley, E. Azalia. "Concert Conditions," *New York Age* 5 July 1917, 6.
Hackley, E. Azalia. "Conference on Community Music," *New York Age* 12 July 1917, 6.
Hackley, E. Azalia. "English in England," *Colored American Magazine* 15, no. 3 (March 1909): 175–76.
Hackley, E. Azalia. "An Experience in 'Jim Crow' Cars in the State of Texas," *Philadelphia Tribune* 16 March 1912, 1, 4.
Hackley, E. Azalia. "Foreign Musical Scholarship," *New York Age* 30 May 1907, 5.
Hackley, E. Azalia. "The Foreign Scholarship Bulletin," 1908; rpt., "The Foreign Scholarship," in Arthur Randolph LaBrew, comp., *Documentary: Negro Music and Musicians*. Detroit: LaBrew, 1969, n.p.
Hackley, E. Azalia. "The Foundation of Voice Building," *Chicago Broad Ax* 9 September 1911, 1–2.
Hackley, E. Azalia. *Guide in Voice Culture*. Philadelphia: E. Azalia Hackley, 1909.
Hackley, E. Azalia. "Hints to Young Colored Artists: Being Introduced," *New York Age* 1 February 1915, 5.
Hackley, E. Azalia. "Hints to Young Colored Artists: Demonstration in Voice Culture (No. 1)," *New York Age* 24 December 1914, 5.
Hackley, E. Azalia. "Hints to Young Colored Artists: Demonstration in Voice Culture (No. 2)," *New York Age* 31 December 1914, 5.
Hackley, E. Azalia. "Hints to Young Colored Artists: How a Professional Achieves Success," *New York Age* 17 December 1914, 5.
Hackley, E. Azalia. "Hints to Young Colored Artists: Reducing the Ego (No. 1)," *New York Age* 21 January 1915, 5.
Hackley, E. Azalia. "Hints to Young Colored Artists: Reducing the Ego (No. 2)," *New York Age* 28 January 1915, 5.

Hackley, E. Azalia. "The Home of the Colored Girl Beautiful," in Myron T. Pritchard and Mary White Ovington, comps., *The Upward Path: A Reader for Colored Children*. New York: Harcourt, Brace and Howe, 1920, 150–52.

Hackley, E. Azalia. "How the Color Question Looks to an American in France," *A.M.E.* [African Methodist Episcopal] *Church Review* 23, no. 3 (January 1907): 210–15.

Hackley, E. Azalia. "Lesson IV in Voice Culture Given in Colored Schools, Season 1913–14," privately printed by Hackley and included in Lisa Pertillar Brevard, ed., *Madame E. Azalia Hackley's The Colored Girl Beautiful*. Salem, VA: Monarch Baby, 2004, 109–22.

Hackley, E. Azalia. Letter, "Madame Hackley: It Is a Surprise, but She Accepts," *Washington, DC Bee* 21 April 1917, 8.

Hackley, E. Azalia. Letter to Bert Williams and George Walker, *Alexander's Magazine* 3, no. 6 (15 April 1907): 272–73.

Hackley, E. Azalia. "Madam Azalia Hackley Talks Interestingly on Cuba, the Garden Spot of the World," *Indianapolis Freeman* 30 March 1912, 6.

Hackley, E. Azalia. "Madam Azalia Hackley Talks Interestingly on Cuba, the Garden Spot of the World (continued from last week)," *Indianapolis Freeman* 6 April 1912, 3.

Hackley, E. Azalia. "Madam E. Azalia Hackley Relates Her Experience and Her Observations," *Chicago Broad Ax* 1 July 1911, 1–2.

Hackley, E. Azalia. "Madame E. Azalia Hackley Visits Cuba," *Philadelphia Tribune* 30 March 1912, 1, 4.

Hackley, E. Azalia. "Mme. Hackley Sends Letter from War Zone," *New York Age* 27 August 1914, 5.

Hackley, E. Azalia. "The Musical Progress of the Race during the Last Year," *Indianapolis Freeman* 23 December 1915, 12.

Hackley, E. Azalia. "Pageants the Latest Form of Entertainment," *New York Age* 19 April 1919, 6.

Hackley, E. Azalia. "Paris under Military Government—Blue Monday and Brilliant Tuesday—Colored People Caught in the Dragnet of War," *Indianapolis Freeman* 5 September 1914, 3.

Hackley, E. Azalia. "A Queen of Song Elated over Cuba," *Chicago Defender* 23 March 1912, 1.

Hackley, E. Azalia. "A Second Trip to Cuba," *New York Age* 19 June 1913, 4.

Hackley, E. Azalia. "She Says the Negro Is a Natural Singer: Mrs. Hackley Explains Requisites Necessary to Become a Singer," *Indianapolis Freeman* 1 July 1911, 6.

Hackley, E. Azalia. "Some Colored Community Music Missionaries," *New York Age* 19 July 1917, 6.

Hackley, E. Azalia. "Some Colored Community Music Missionaries," *New York Age* 26 July 1917, 6.

Hackley, E. Azalia. "Some Colored Community Music Missionaries," *New York Age* 2 August 1917, 6.

Hackley, E. Azalia. "Through Cuba with Madame Hackley," *Chicago Defender* 13 April 1912, 1.

Hackley, Edwin Henry. "The Bond of Libya," *Denver Evening Post* 9 February 1898, 3.

Hackley, Edwin Henry. "A Colored Brother Speaks," *Denver Evening Post* 12 March 1897, 2.

Hackley, Edwin Henry. "Constitutional Union: Plans for Local and National Organization as Given in the Denver Statesman," *Parsons* [KS] *Weekly Blade* 17 December 1892, 2.

Hackley, Edwin Henry. "Your Opportunity," *Atchison* [KS] *Blade* 4 March 1893, 4.

Haddock, Frank Channing. *Power of Will* (1907), 2nd ed. Meridian, CT: Pelton, 1914.

Hamilton, Green Polonius. *Beacon Lights of the Race*. Memphis: Clarke, 1911.

Harley, Gail M. *Emma Curtis Hopkins: Forgotten Founder of New Thought*. Syracuse: Syracuse University Press, 2002.

Hassin, Ran, and Yaacov Trope, "Facing Faces: Studies on the Cognitive Aspects of Physiognomy," *Journal of Personality and Social Psychology* 75, no. 5 (2000): 837–52.

Henschel, George. *Musings and Memories of a Musician*. London: Macmillan, 1918.

Herndl, Diane Price. "The Invisible (Invalid) Woman: African American Women, Illness, and Nineteenth-century Narrative," in Judith Walzer Leavitt, ed., *Women and Health in America*, 2nd ed. Madison: University of Wisconsin Press, 1999, 131–45.

Hicks, Mary. "The Coverage of World War I and the Radical Black Press, 1917–1919," *Iowa Historical Review* 1 (2007): 57–82.

Higginbotham, Evelyn Brooks. *Righteous Discontent: The Women's Movement in the Black Baptist Church, 1880–1920*. Cambridge: Harvard University Press, 1993.

Hill, Robert A., and Barbara Bair, eds. *Marcus Garvey: Life and Lessons*. Berkeley: University of California Press, 1987.

Hipkins, Julian, III, and David Busch. "Transportation Protests: 1844–1992," online.

Hogans, James H. "Pullman Porter News," *New York Age* 13 January 1923, 7.

Holt, Nora Douglas. "Music News," *Chicago Defender* 19 April 1919, 12.

hooks, bell. *Teaching to Transgress: Education as the Practice of Freedom*. New York: Routledge, 1994.

Horne, Gerald. *Race to Revolution: The United States and Cuba during Slavery and Jim Crow*. New York: Monthly Review Press, 2014.

J. A. H. "Serious Purpose Is Revealed in Work of Colored Singers," *Musical America* 26 (December 1917): 13.

James, Fannie B. *Truth and Health: Science of the Perfect Mind and the Law of Its Expression*, 4th ed. Denver: Colorado College of Divine Science, 1911.

Jarmon, Laura C. *Arbors to Bricks: A Hundred Years of African American Education in Rutherford County Tennessee, 1865–1965*. Murfreesboro: Middle Tennessee State University Press, 1994.

Johnson, James Weldon. "Views and Reviews," *New York Age* 13 September 1917, 4.

Jones, Elizabeth. "What Madame E. Azalia Hackley Accomplished," *Pittsburgh Courier* 14 June 1912, 1.

Jones, Sarah G. "The Greatest Needs of the American Negro Woman," in Carrie W. Clifford, ed., *Sowings for Others to Reap*. Boston: Alexander, 1900, 33–40.

Jordan, William. "'The Damnable Dilemma': African American Accommodation and Protest during World War I," *Journal of American History* 81, no. 4 (March 1995): 1562–83.

Jorgensen, Estelle R. "How Can Music Education Be Religious?" *Philosophy of Music Education Review* 19, no. 2 (Fall 2011): 155–63.

Jorgensen, Estelle R. "Music Education as Community," *Journal of Aesthetic Education* 29, no. 3 (Autumn 1995): 71–84.

Judge, Jane. "Savannah Hears Folk Song Festival," *Savannah Morning News*; rpt. *New York Age* 18 January 1919, 6.

Karpf, Juanita. "Emma Azalia Hackley," in Jessie Carney Smith, ed., *Notable Black American Women*. Detroit: Gale Research, 1992, 429–34.

Karpf, Juanita. "'If it's in the Bible, it can't be opera': William Bradbury's *Esther, the Beautiful Queen*, in Defiance of Genre," *American Music* 29, no. 1 (Spring 2011): 1–34.

Karpf, Juanita. "'An Opportunity to Rise': Reinterpreting *Esther, the Beautiful Queen*," *Black Music Research Journal* 30, no. 2 (Fall 2010): 241–72.

Katzman, David M. *Before the Ghetto: Black Detroit in the Nineteenth Century*. Urbana: University of Illinois Press, 1973.
Keiler, Allan. *Marian Anderson: A Singer's Journey*. New York: Scribner, 2000.
Kornweibel, Theodore, Jr. "Apathy and Dissent: Black America's Negative Response to World War I," *South Atlantic Quarterly* 80, no. 3 (Summer 1981): 322-38.
Kornweibel, Theodore, Jr. *"Investigate Everything": Federal Efforts to Compel Black Loyalty during World War I*. Bloomington: Indiana University Press, 2001.
Kornweibel, Theodore, Jr. *Railroads in the African American Experience: A Photographic Journey*. Baltimore: Johns Hopkins University Press, 2010.
Kowalski, Philip J. "No Excuse for Our Dirt: Booker T. Washington and a 'New Negro' Middle Class," in McCaskill and Gebhard, eds., 181-96.
Krehbiel, Henry Edward. *Afro-American Folksongs: A Study in Racial and National Music*. New York: G. Schirmer, 1913.
Krehbiel, Henry Edward, ed. *Famous Songs*. Cincinnati: Church, 1902.
Ladson-Billings, Gloria. "But That's Just Good Teaching: The Case for Culturally Relevant Pedagogy," *Theory into Practice* 34, no. 3 (Summer 1995): 159-65.
[Langston, Tony]. "Music Victory Pageant," *Chicago Defender* 3 May 1919, 6.
[Langston, Tony]. "One Only to a Pageant," *Chicago Defender* 5 April 1919, 16.
[Langston, Tony]. "The Pageant Goes," *Chicago Defender* 17 May 1919, 16.
[Langston, Tony]. "Victory Pageant Now!" *Chicago Defender* 10 May 1919, 9.
Leiser, Clara. *Jean de Reszke and the Great Days of Opera*. New York: Minton, Bulch, 1934.
Lemert, Charles, and Esme Bhan, eds., *The Voice of Anna Julia Cooper*. New York: Rowman and Littlefield, 1998.
Lester, William R. "Henry O. Tanner, Exile for Art's Sake," *Alexander's Magazine* 7, no. 2 (15 December 1908): 69-73.
Levey, Jane Freundel. "The Scurlock Studio," *Washington History* 1, no. 1 (Spring 1989): 40-57.
Levine, Lawrence W. *Black Culture and Black Consciousness: Afro-American Folk Thought from Slavery to Freedom*. New York: Oxford University Press, 1977.
Levine, Lawrence W. *High Brow, Low Brow: The Emergence of Cultural Hierarchy in America*. Cambridge, MA: Harvard University Press, 1988.
Lewis, Cary B. "Current News of Chicago: Hackley Recital to Be Brilliant Affair," *Indianapolis Freeman* 14 October 1911, 1.
Lewis, Cary B. "Current News of Chicago: The Hackley Recital to Be Greatest Ever," *Indianapolis Freeman* 7 October 1911, 8.
[Lewis, William Milton]. "A New Star in the Musical Firmament," *Indianapolis Freeman* 9 March 1901, 4.
Logan, Rayford W. *The Negro in American Life and Thought: The Nadir, 1877-1901*. New York: Dial Press, 1954.
Lomax, Leila Holt. *Physiognomy*. Philadelphia: Penn, 1908.
MacDonald, John. "Jean de Reszke at Home," *London Daily News* 13 April 1904, 6.
Mack, Kenneth W. "Law, Society, Identity, and the Making of the Jim Crow South: Travel and Segregation on Tennessee Railroads, 1875-1904," *Law and Social Inquiry* 24, no. 2 (Spring 1999): 377-409.
Mark, Michael L., and Charles L. Gary. *A History of American Music Education*, 3rd ed. New York: Rowman and Littlefield, 2007.
Marley, Anna O., ed. *Henry Ossawa Tanner: Modern Spirit*. Berkeley: University of California Press, 2013.

Marshall, M[arie] M[adre]. "Madam Emma Azalia Hackley," in Hallie Quinn Brown, ed., *Homespun Heroines and other Women of Distinction*. Xenia, OH: Aldine, 1929, 231–36.
Martin, Darnise C. *Beyond Christianity: African Americans in a New Thought Church*. New York: New York University Press, 2004.
Martin, Darnise C. "New Thought Religions and the African American Experience," in Anthony P. Binn, ed., *African American Religious Cultures*, 2 vols. Santa Barbara, CA: ABC-CLIO, 2009, I:273–82.
Mason, Mary G. "Travel as Metaphor and Reality in Afro-American Women's Autobiography," *Black American Literature Forum* 24, no. 2 (Summer 1990): 337–56.
McCaskill, Barbara, and Caroline Gebhard, eds., *Post Bellum, Pre-Harlem: African American Literature and Culture, 1877–1919*. New York: New York University Press, 2006.
McCaughan, Pat. "Detroit's Historically Black St. Matthew's Added to 'Freedom Network,'" online.
McFarlin, Ben Hall. "The Ku Klux Klan" (1973). Rutherford County (TN) Historical Society Publications, online.
McGinty, Doris Evans. "Conversation with Camille Nickerson, the Louisiana Lady," *Black Perspective in Music* 7, no. 1 (1970): 81–94.
McGinty, Doris Evans. "'That You Came So Far to See Us': Coleridge-Taylor in America," *Black Music Research Journal* 21, no. 2 (Autumn 2001): 197–234.
McGinty, Doris Evans. "The Washington Conservatory of Music and School of Expression," *Black Perspective in Music* 7, no. 1 (Spring 1979): 59–74.
McMurry, Linda O. *To Keep the Waters Troubled: The Life of Ida B. Wells*. New York: Oxford University Press, 1998.
Meacham, Standish. *Toynbee Hall and Social Reform, 1880–1914*. New Haven: Yale University Press, 1987.
Meier, August A. "Booker T. Washington and the Negro Press: With Special Reference to the Colored American Magazine," *Journal of Negro History* 38, no. 1 (January 1953): 67–90.
Meier, August A. *Negro Thought in America, 1880–1915: Racial Ideologies in the Age of Booker T. Washington*. Ann Arbor: University of Michigan Press, 1966.
Miller, Kelly. *As to the Leopard's Spots: An Open Letter to Thomas Dixon, Jr*. Washington, DC: Howard University, 1905.
Moore, Fred R. "Editorial: Retrospection of a Year," *Colored American Magazine* 8, no. 6 (June 1905): 342–43.
Moore, Jacqueline M. *Booker T. Washington, W. E. B. Du Bois and the Struggle for Racial Uplift*. Wilmington, DE: Scholarly Resources, 2003.
Mosley, Glenn R. *New Thought, Ancient Wisdom: The History and Future of the New Thought Movement*. Philadelphia: Templeton Foundation Press, 2006.
Moton, Robert R. "Introduction," in Myron Thomas Pritchard and Mary White Ovington, comps., *The Upward Path: A Reader for Colored Children*. New York: Harcourt, Brace and Howe, 1920, ix–xi.
Mulford, Prentice. *Thoughts Are Things*. London: Bell, 1908.
Mungazi, Dickson A. *The Evolution of Educational Theory in the United States*. Westport, CT: Greenwood Press, 1999.
Murphy, Gretchen. *Shadowing the White Man's Burden: US Imperialism and the Problems of the Color Line*. New York: New York University Press, 2010.
Murray, Alana D. *The Development of the Alternative Black Curriculum, 1890–1940: Countering the Master Narrative*. New York: Palgrave Macmillan, 2018.

O'Leary, Margaret R. *The Texas Meningitis Epidemic, 1911-1913*. Bloomington, IN: iUniverse, 2018.
O'Shaughnessy, Sara, and Emily Hudart Kennedy. "Relational Activism: Reimagining Women's Environmental Work as Cultural Change," *Canadian Journal of Sociology* 35, no. 4 (2010): 551-72.
Parker, Allison M. "'The Picture of Health': The Public Life and Private Ailments of Mary Church Terrell," *Journal of Historical Biography* 13 (Spring 2013): 164-207.
P[arker], H[enry] T[aylor]. "Jean de Reszke Today," *Boston Evening Transcript* 20 August 1904, 18.
Parsons, Elaine Frantz. *Ku-Klux: The Birth of the Klan during Reconstruction*. Chapel Hill: University of North Carolina Press, 2015.
Partlow, Frances. *Training of Children in the New Thought*. Chicago: Psychic Research, 1903.
Patterson, Charles Brodie. *What Is New Thought?* New York: Crowell, 1913.
Peterson, Carrie. "The Truth Will Unite Us: Ida B. Wells and the Jacks Letter," online.
Phillips, Paul David, "Education of Blacks during Reconstruction, 1865-1870," in Carroll Van West, ed., *Trial and Triumph: Essays in Tennessee's African American History*. Knoxville: University of Tennessee Press, 2002, 145-67.
Picht, Werner. *Toynbee Hall and the English Settlement Movement*. London: Bell, 1914.
Prentiss, Craig R. "'The Full Realization of This Desire': Garland Anderson, Race, and the Limits of New Thought in the Age of Jim Crow," *Nova Religio* 17, no. 3 (February 2013): 84-108.
Ramacharaka, Yogi (pseud. William Walker Atkinson). *The Hindu-Yogi Science of Breath: A Complete Manual of the Oriental Breathing Philosophy of Physical, Mental, Psychic and Spiritual Development*. Chicago: Yogi Publication Society, 1904.
Randolph, William M. "Some Comments," *Pittsburgh Courier* 5 July 1912, 1.
Reid, John B., "'A Career to Build, a People to Serve, a Purpose to Accomplish': Race, Class, Gender, and Detroit's First Black Women Teachers, 1865-1916," *Michigan Historical Review* 18, no. 1 (Spring 1992): 1-27.
Reinders, Robert C. "Toynbee Hall and the American Settlement Movement," *Social Service Review* 56, no. 1 (March 1982): 38-54.
Reuter, Edward Byron. *The Mulatto in the United States*. Boston: Badger, 1918.
Rhodes, Ledru R. "Restaurant Rights," *Rocky Mountain News* 14 May 1886, 8.
Richardson, Willis, ed. *Plays and Pageants from the Life of the Negro* (1930). Rpt. Jackson: University Press of Mississippi, 1993.
Riis, Thomas L. "Cook, Will Marion." *Grove Music*, online.
Rosseau, Maurice. "Madame Hackley," *Cleveland Gazette* 18 May 1907, 3.
Russell, Sylvester. "Madame Hackley Triumphs in Orchestra Hall," *Indianapolis Freeman* 4 November 1911, 4.
Samet, Rachel. "Diton, Carl Rossini," *Grove Music*, online.
Satter, Beryl. *Each Mind a Kingdom: American Women, Sexual Purity and the New Thought Movement, 1875-1920*. Los Angeles: University of California Press, 1999.
Sayers, W. S. Berwick. *Samuel Coleridge-Taylor, Musician: His Life and Letters*. London: Cassell, 1915.
Schenbeck, Lawrence. *Racial Uplift and American Music, 1878-1943*. Jackson: University Press of Mississippi, 2012.
Schmalenberger, Sarah. "Harriet Gibbs Marshall and Three Musical Spectacles," in Eileen M. Hayes and Linda F. Williams, eds., *Black Women and Music: More than the Blues*. Urbana: University of Illinois Press, 2007, 210-36.

Schmalenberger, Sarah. "Shaping Uplift through Music," *Black Music Research Journal* 28, no. 2 (Fall 2008): 57–83.
Scott, Emmett J. *Scott's Official History of the American Negro in the World War*. Chicago: Homewood Press, 1919.
Selden, Steven. "Transforming Better Babies into Fitter Families: Archival Resources and the History of the American Eugenics Movement, 1908–1930," *Proceedings of the American Philosophical Society* 149, no. 2 (June 2005): 199–225.
Shaftsbury, Edmund (pseud. Albert Webster Eagerly). *Lessons in Voice Culture*. Washington, DC: Martyn College Press, 1889.
Shakespeare, William. *The Art of Singing*, 3 vols. London: Metzler, 1909.
Shakespeare, William. *Plain Words on Singing*. London: Putnam, 1924.
Shakespeare, William. *Singing for Schools and Colleges*. London: Boosey and Hawkes, 1907.
Shakespeare, William. *The Speaker's Art*. London: Putnam, 1931.
Shaw, Stephanie J. "Black Club Women and the Creation of the National Association of Colored Women," *Journal of Women's History* 3, no. 2 (Fall 1991): 11–25.
Sherman, Shantella Y. *In Search of Purity: Popular Eugenics and Racial Uplift among New Negroes, 1915–35*. PhD diss., University of Nebraska, Lincoln, 2015.
Silone-Yates, Josephine. "The National Association of Colored Women," *Voice of the Negro* 1, no. 7 (1 July 1904): 283–87.
Simmons, R[oscoe] C[onkling]. "European Reception to Negro Talent," *Colored American Magazine* (1 November 1905): 44.
Siwel, [Noel]. "Rambling," *Indianapolis Freeman* 31 July 1909, 11.
Smith, Katherine Capshaw. "Childhood, the Body and Race Performance: Early 20th-century Etiquette Books for Black Children," *African American Review* 40, no. 4 (Winter 2006): 795–811.
Smith, Katherine Capshaw. *Children's Literature of the Harlem Renaissance*. Bloomington: University of Indiana Press, 2006.
Smith, Katherine Capshaw. "Constructing a Shared History: Black Pageantry for Children during the Harlem Renaissance," *Children's Literature* 27 (1999): 40–63.
Smith, Shane A. "*The Crisis* in the Great War: W. E. B. Du Bois and His Perception of African American Participation in World War I," *Historian* 70 (2008): 239–62.
Snyder, Jean E. *Harry T. Burleigh: From the Spiritual to the Harlem Renaissance*. Urbana: University of Illinois Press, 2016.
Snyder, Rachel, et al. "Who Died of Consumption: Race and Disease in the United States," (2016), online.
Southern, Eileen. *Biographical Dictionary of African American and African Musicians*. Westport, CT: Greenwood Press, 1982.
Southern, Eileen. *The Music of Black Americans: A History*, 3rd ed. New York: W. W. Norton, 1997.
Stanton, Mary Olmstead. *Encyclopedia of Face and Form Reading*. 3rd ed. Philadelphia: Davis, 1913.
Storer, H[enry] J[ohnson]. "S. Coleridge-Taylor—A Sketch," *Negro Music Journal* 1, no. 1 (September 1902): 3–4.
Straus, Joseph N. *Extraordinary Measures: Disability in Music*. New York: Oxford University Press, 2011.
Sweeney, Michael. "Burton Publishing Company Collection," online.
Taylor, A. R. "Madame Hackley's Retiring Song Recital," *Indianapolis Freeman* 10 August 1912, 6.

Taylor, David Clark. *The Psychology of Singing: A Rational Method of Voice Culture Based on Scientific Analysis of All Systems, Ancient and Modern.* New York: MacMillan, 1908.

Taylor, Frederick Jerome. "In Retrospect: Black Musicians in the *Philadelphia Tribune*, 1912–20," *Black Perspective in Music* 18, nos. 1–2 (1990): 127–40.

Terrell, Mary Church. *A Colored Woman in a White World.* Washington, DC: Randsdell, 1940.

Terrell, Mary Church. "Duty of the National Association of Colored Women to the Race," *A. M. E.* [African Methodist Episcopal] *Church Review* 16, no. 3 (January 1900): 340–54.

Terrell, Mary Church. "The International Congress of Women Recently Held in Berlin, Germany," *Voice of the Negro* 1, no. 10 (1 October 1904): 454–61.

Terrell, Mary Church. "Samuel Coleridge-Taylor," *Voice of the Negro* 2, no. 1 (1 January 1905): 665–69.

Terrell, Mary Church. "The Washington Conservatory of Music for Colored People, and Its Teachers," *Voice of the Negro* 1, no. 11 (November 1904): 525–30.

Teyte, Maggie. *Star on the Door.* London: Putnam, 1958.

Thomas, Sabrina N. *Marriage Vows and Economic Discrimination: The Married Teacher Problem.* MA thesis, Marshall University, Huntington, WV, 2010.

Thompson, Eloise Bibb. "Madame Hackley in Los Angeles; Friend to Poor," *Chicago Defender* 6 March 1915, 4.

Thompson, Richard W. "Better Babies Insure a Better Race," *Indianapolis Freeman* 31 July 1915, 1.

Thompson, Richard W. "Mme. Hackley Wins New Laurels," *Indianapolis Freeman* 12 February 1916, 1.

Thoreau, Henry David. *Walden; or, Life in the Woods.* Boston: Ticknor and Fields, 1854.

Thorne, Jack. "Mr. Thomas Dixon, Jr., the Physiognomist," *Voice of the Negro* 11, no. 11 (November 1905): 789–91.

Totten, Gary. *African American Travel Narratives from Abroad: Mobility and Cultural Work in the Age of Jim Crow.* Amherst: University of Massachusetts Press, 2015.

Totten, Gary. "Embodying Segregation: Ida B. Wells and the Cultural Work of Travel," *African American Review* 42, no. 1 (Spring 2008): 47–60.

Towne, Elizabeth Jones. *How to Train Children and Parents.* Holyoke, MA: Towne, 1904.

Towne, Elizabeth Jones. *Joy Philosophy*, 3rd. ed. Chicago: New Thought, 1903.

Towne, Elizabeth Jones. *Just How to Wake the Solar Plexus.* Holyoke, MA: Towne, 1907.

Travis, Trysh. "'It Will Change the World If Everybody Reads This Book': New Thought in Oprah's Book Club," *America Quarterly* 59, no. 3 (September 2007): 1017–41.

Trine, Ralph Waldo. *In Tune with the Infinite, or Fullness of Peace, Power and Plenty.* New York: Dodd, Mead, 1897.

Trotter, James Monroe. *Music and Some Highly Musical People.* Boston: Lee and Shepard, 1878.

Tunnell, Rev. W[illiam] V. "Samuel Coleridge-Taylor," *Colored American Magazine* 8, no. 1 (January 1905): 43–47.

Varnell, Jeanne. *Women of Consequence: The Colorado Women's Hall of Fame.* Boulder: Johnson Books, 1999.

Vaught, L[ouis] A[llen]. *Vaught's Practical Character Reader.* Chicago: Vaught, 1902.

Walker, Edward. *Thoughts Are Things.* Chicago: Progress, 1909.

Walton, Lester A. "Mme. Hackley's Recital: Mme. Hackley's Talk Inspires Race Pride," *New York Age* 21 November 1912, 6.

Walton, Lester A. "Music and the Stage: Musical London," *New York Age* 1 July 1909, 6.

Warren, Francis H., comp. *Michigan Manual of Freedmen's Progress*. Detroit: Freedmen's Progress Commission, 1915.
Weeks, Louis B., III. "Racism, World War I and the Christian Life: Francis J. Grimke [sic] in the Nation's Capital," *Journal of Presbyterian History* 51 (1973): 471–88.
Wells, Ida B. *Crusade for Justice*, Alfreda M. Duster, ed. Chicago: University of Chicago Press, 1970.
Wheeler, J. Henry. "Vocal Methods," *Etude* 19, no. 4 (April 1901): 148.
White, Lucien H. "Mme. E. A. Hackley Gives Some Comments on Negro Music," *New York Age* 14 August 1920, 5.
White, Lucien H. "Mme. E. Azalia Hackley Is Dead after Months of Illness," *New York Age* 23 December 1922, 6.
White, Lucien H. "Mme. Hackley Presents Negro Song Festival in California," *New York Age* 1 January 1921, 1.
White, Lucien H. "Music Notes," *New York Age* 3 August 1916, 6.
White, Newman Ivey. *American Negro Folk-songs*. Hatboro, PA: Folklore Associates, 1928.
Whiting, Lillian. *Paris the Beautiful*. Boston: Little, Brown, 1909.
Wilborn, David. "The Wickedest City: Memphis Residents Fleeing to the Great West; Prejudice in Denver," *Detroit Plaindealer* 9 September 1892, 1.
Williams, Chad. "World War I in the Historical Imagination of W. E. B. Du Bois," *Modern American History* 1, no. 1 (March 2018): 3–22.
Williams, Fannie Barrier. "After Many Days: A Christmas Story," *Colored American Magazine* 5 (December 1902): 140–53.
Williams, Fannie Barrier. "The Colored Girl," *Voice of the Negro* 2, no. 6 (1 June 1905): 400–403.
Williams, Fannie Barrier. "Perils of the White Negro," *Colored American Magazine* 8, no. 6 (1 December 1907): 421–23.
Williams, Fannie Barrier. "Religious Duty to the Negro" (1893), in J. W. Hanson, ed., *The World's Congress of Religions*. Chicago: Conkey, 1894, 893–97.
Willison, Judith. "Supporting the Success of Students of Color: Creating Racial Justice through Student Activism," *Transformative Dialogues: Teaching and Learning Journal* 9, no. 2 (November 2016): 1–18.
Wilson, Ollie. "The Black American Composer," *Black Perspective in Music* 1, no. 2 (1973): 33–36.
Wilson, Ollie. "Black Music as an Art Form," *Black Music Research Journal* 3 (1983): 1–22.
Wilson, Ollie. "Composition from the Perspective of the African American Tradition," *Black Music Research Journal* 16, no. 1 (1996): 43–51.
Wilson, Ollie. "The Heterogeneous Sound Ideal in African American Music," in Josephine Wright, ed., with Samuel A. Floyd, Jr., *New Perspectives in Music: Essays in Honor of Eileen Southern*. Warren, MI: Harmonie Park Press, 1992, 327–40.
Wilson, Ollie. "'It don't mean a thing if it ain't got that swing': The Relationship between African and African American Music," in Sheila S. Walker, ed., *African Roots/American Cultures: Africa in the Creation of the Americas*. Lanham, MD: Rowman and Littlefield, 2001, 153–68.
Wilson, Ollie. "The Significance of the Relationship between Afro-American Music and West African Music," *Black Perspective in Music* 2, no. 1 (1974): 3–22.
Winter, Alice Crumpton, and Rhonsa Reymond, "Henry Ossawa Tanner and W. E. B. Du Bois: African American Art and 'High Culture' at the Turn into the Twentieth Century," in McCaskill and Gebhard, eds., 231–49.

Wolters, Raymond. *Du Bois and His Rivals*. Columbia: University of Missouri Press, 2002.
Wood, Henry. *New Thought Simplified*. Norwood, MA: Norwood Press, 1903.
Woods, Naurice Frank, Jr. *Henry Ossawa Tanner: Art, Faith, Race, and Legacy*. New York: Routledge, 2018.
Woodson, Carter. *The History of the Negro Church*. Washington, DC: Associated, 1945.
Work, John Wesley. *American Negro Songs and Spirituals*. New York: Bonanza Books, 1940.

INDEX

Abbott, Lyman, 154, 202n25
Abbott, Theodore J., 154, 202n25
abolitionism, 16, 43
Adams, Minnie, 34–35, 76
Anderson, Garland, 93, 167
Anderson, Marian, 14, 32, 107–8, 168, 171
Archer, Albert Argent, 61–62, 184n86
Atkinson, William Walker, 76, 78, 188n31

Baker, Edith E., 169, 204n14
Baker, Ray Stannard, 67, 186n116
Battles, Mabel A. Hill, 20
Berlioz, Hector, 27, 29
Boston, Marietta, 174n3, 174n8
Bradbury, William B., 20, 26, 166, 203n7; *Esther, the Beautiful Queen*, 20, 26
Brevard, Lisa P., 7
Brierley, George F., 97, 192n14
Brooks, Charles H., 45, 181n25
Brooks, Elizabeth C. Carter, 18–19
Brooks, Nona Lovell, 75
Burleigh, Harry T., 108, 126, 129–31, 171
Burlin, Natalie Curtis, 106, 120, 196n10

call and response, 112–13
Caracciolla, Luigi, 30
Carter, Elizabeth C., 18–19
Cayton, Horace, 147
Chesnutt, Charles W., 3–4, 45, 173n3
Chesnutt, Edwin J., 45, 180n24
Chicago, Illinois, 6, 22, 34, 35, 75, 76, 103, 106–7, 111, 120, 137, 143, 145, 153, 168, 179n91, 180n24

Clark, Clarence Carroll, 168, 185n99
Clifford, Carrie W., 43, 163–64, 180n14
Cole, Bob, 126, 129
Cole, Maggie Porter, 20
Colemon, Johnnie, 93, 168
Coleridge-Taylor, Samuel, 58–60, 108, 184n80
concert ("classical") music tradition, 4, 6, 8, 14, 30, 47, 59, 60, 61, 95, 98, 108, 113, 115, 128, 143, 162, 165, 166, 171
Cook, Will Marion, 126, 127, 128, 171
Cooper, Anna Julia, 25, 42, 43, 44, 73
Crummell, Alexander, 82–83
Cuba, 10, 36, 39, 62–63, 68, 121, 125, 185n92
Cuney-Hare, Maude, 25, 177n57
Curtis, Henry Holbrook, 97, 192n16
Curtis, Natalie. *See* Burlin, Natalie Curtis

Davenport, M. Marguerite, 6–7, 173n8
David, Félicien-César, 27, 36, 37, 178n67
De Goulaine, Countess Marie, 49
De Noufflard, Maurice, 49, 182n45
Denver, Colorado, 9, 13, 20, 21, 23–26, 27, 31, 35, 46, 75, 151, 153, 176n41; Church of the Redeemer (Episcopal), 75; Denver Choral Society, 26; *Denver Statesman*, 9, 23, 25, 140; Imperial Order of Libyans, 9, 24; racism in, 31; Republican Women's Club, 24; University of Denver, 9, 26, 39, 97, 98; Zion Baptist Church, 26
De Reszke, Jean, 10, 36, 45, 47–50, 51, 55, 56–57, 64, 68, 181n33, 182n40, 182n41

Detroit, Michigan, 9, 15–18, 125–26; Chandler Odd Fellows Lodge, 18, 175n19; Clinton Elementary School, 18, 22; Normal Training School, 9, 17; St. Matthew's Episcopal Church (St. Matthew's/St. Joseph's Episcopal Church), 16, 22, 75, 157, 174n4
Dett, R. Nathaniel, 108, 126, 168, 169
dialect, 110, 128, 129
Diton, Carl Rossini, 93, 108, 126, 168, 170
Divine, Major Jealous ("Father Divine"), 93, 167
Dixon, Thomas, Jr., 86, 87, 89, 90
Dooly, Louise, 102, 192n42
Douglas, Walter Johnstone, 48, 49, 182n36
Dresser, Horatio Willis, 72, 75
Du Bois, W. E. B., 4, 12, 32, 64, 73–74, 80, 81, 87, 92, 111, 118, 119, 123, 135, 138, 162, 163, 164, 170; *Star of Ethiopia*, 123; Talented Tenth, 4, 80, 81, 163
Dunbar, Paul Laurence, 23, 176n39, 180n8
Dykema, Peter, 102, 103

Eikerenkoetter, Frederick J. ("Rev. Ike"), II, 93, 168
Emancipation, 3, 110, 150
Emerson, Ralph Waldo, 91
Esther, the Beautiful Queen, 20, 26
eugenics, 11, 79–84, 188n50
Evans, Warren Felt, 72

Farwell, Arthur, 102, 103, 193n44
Fauset, Jessie Redmon, 46, 64, 181n27
Finck, Henry Theophilus, 47, 181n32
Fisk Jubilee Singers, 20, 107, 110, 142, 180n22, 184n80
Fisk University, 110, 113, 123
Fitzhugh-Valentine, Mary L., 168
Ford, John Elijah, 46, 181n28
Foster, Stephen, 107–8
Freire, Paulo, 167
Freund, John C., 105, 142, 193n65
Frissell, Hollis Burke, 145, 200n35
Furniss, Sumner Alexander, 46, 181n28

Ganaway, G. H. P., 111, 195n95
Garvey, Marcus, 10, 93, 147, 167

Gatewood, Willard B., 17
gender, 43, 65, 68, 103, 124, 150
George, Zelma W., 101, 192n40
Gerville-Réache, Jeanne, 67, 186n115
Gibbs, Harriet A., 33–34, 151–52, 179n85
Gilded Age, 3
Goldmark, Karl, 48
Gounod, Charles, 48, 51–52, 113, 114
Greene, Herbert W., 56, 102
Greenfield, Elizabeth Taylor, 107, 180n22
Grimké, Francis James, 118–19, 196n7
Gunn, Lutie A., 97–98, 192n20
Guthrie, Arthur, 51

Hackley, Edwin Henry, 9, 20–21, 31, 34, 44–45, 139, 152, 154, 155, 156, 175n31, 176n39, 176n41, 178n74, 179n86; Constitutional Union, 24; *Denver Statesman*, 23; *Honeymoon in Soudan*, 26; Iron Duke Mining Company, 23; National Afro-American League, 23; Northwestern Negro Press Association, 23
Hackley, Emma Azalia Smith: *Colored Girl Beautiful*, 6, 12–13, 86, 140, 143–50, 162, 171; Cuba, 62–63; Episcopalianism, 10, 16, 22, 31, 71–72, 75; eugenics, 79–84; folk song festivals, 120–22; *Guide in Voice Culture*, 30, 98, 107–8, 114, 138, 140; Harlem Chorus, 105; "Hints to Young Colored Artists," 140–43, 146, 147, 148; Holy Trinity Lodge, 51–52; Imperial Order of Libyans, 24; inward sculptor, 84–90; London, 3, 10, 11, 36, 45, 55–62, 75; marriage, 12, 17, 20, 21, 22, 34, 75, 81, 82, 83, 86, 155, 156; "marriage bar," 22; musical social uplift, 4–5, 34; National Association of Colored Women (NACW), 24–25; National Federation of Afro-American Women, 24; National League of Colored Women, 24, 25; Normal Vocal Institute, 6, 76, 106–7, 137, 143; pageantry, 119, 122–36; Paris, 45–55, 63–65; People's Chorus, 32, 169; relational activism, 164–65; Republican Women's Club, 24; respectability, 5, 149–50; spirituals, 6, 8, 14, 27, 69, 109,

110–13; Talented Tenth, 81, 163; Toynbee Hall, 57; University of Denver, 11, 97; voice culture, 96–101; Washington Conservatory of Music and School of Expression, 32–34
Hagan, Helen, 64
Hampton Institute, 82, 110, 113, 120, 139, 145, 168, 169, 200n35
Handel, George Frideric, 113, 114
Hansbury, Bertha A., 168–69
Harlem Renaissance, 3, 14, 46, 93, 136, 171–72
Harrison, Hazel, 168
Haydn, Franz Joseph, 113
Hayes, Roland, 14
Henschel, George, 27, 28, 30, 53, 57, 59, 64, 178n68
Hill, Mabel A., 20
Hogans, James, 66, 161
Holt, Nora Douglas, 171, 198n42
hooks, bell, 167
Hopkins, Emma Curtis, 76, 188n27
Howard University, 64, 82, 110, 111, 113
Hubbard, Elbert, 143, 199n25

Imperial Order of Libyans, 9, 24

Jacks, John W., 24–25, 177n50
Jim Crow, and segregation, 4, 6, 9, 13, 37, 39–44, 66, 69, 82, 89, 135, 138, 139, 163, 179n6
Johnson, James Weldon, 12, 106, 126, 130, 137–38, 143–44, 147, 171
Johnson, Joseph, 157, 174n3
Johnson, J. Rosamond, 106, 122, 126, 128–30, 171
Johnson, Kate, 17, 67–68, 169–70
Johnson, Marietta, 154, 157, 174n3
Jones, Peter P., 35, 179n91
Jones, Sissieretta, 31, 107, 161, 180n22
Jordan, William, 119
Judge, Jane, 112–13, 195n97

Kennedy, Emily Hubart, 164
Kramer, A. W., 130–31
Krehbiel, Henry, 108, 113, 194n81
Ku Klux Klan, 15–16

La Grange, Margaret C., 75, 187n23
Langdon, William Chauncey, 122–23
Langston, Tony, 133–35, 198n44
Lawrence, Mattie, 142
Lee, Pauline James, 107, 168
Lewis, Cary B., 99, 104
Lewis, William Milton, 67, 186n120
Little, George W., 145
Logan, Rayford W., 3
London, England, 3, 10, 11, 36, 45, 55–62, 75
Longfellow, Henry Wadsworth, 60
Lucas, Carrie Melvin, 25

MacDonald, John, 48, 181n35
MacKaye, Hazel, 125, 197n25
Madre, Marie A. D., 16, 67, 107, 124, 154, 155, 174n9
Manderville, James M., 23
Mannes, David, 106
Marconi, Guglielmo, 76
Marshall, Harriet Gibbs. *See* Gibbs, Harriet A.
Marshall, Marie A. D. *See* Madre, Marie A. D.
Massiah, Joshua Bowden, 22
Matthews, Victoria Earle, 25
Mendelssohn, Felix, 113
Metropolitan AME Church, Washington, DC, 122, 124
Meyerbeer, Giacomo, 48
Moore, Fred R., 138, 140, 141–42, 146, 199n15
Moten, Robert Russa, 139, 145, 149, 200n35
Mulder, Richard, 52–54
Murfreesboro, Tennessee, 9, 15–16, 156, 174n1, 174n3

NAACP, 80, 111, 118, 154, 173n3, 175n18, 180n14, 196n7
"Nadir" of race relations, 3
Newsom, Maude Dean, 132, 134
New Thought Movement, 6, 10, 71–94, 110, 153, 156; "give to get," 11, 91–94; history of, 71–73; inward sculptor, 84–90; telepathy, 10, 71, 76, 77, 78, 110, 168
Nickerson, Camille, 131, 171, 198n38
Nickerson, William Joseph "W. J.," 131–33, 198n38

O'Shaughnessy, Sara, 164
Ovington, Mary White, 149

Parker, Henry Taylor, 48, 182n38
Patterson, Charles Brodie, 75
Patterson, Mary Saunders, 168, 183n62
Peabody, George Foster, 95, 104, 147
performance practices, 112–13. *See also* call and response
Philadelphia, Pennsylvania, 9, 31–32, 33, 34, 55, 75, 92, 151, 152, 154, 155, 169; American Negro Historical Society, 32; Church of the Crucifixion, 31–32
Phillips, Henry Laird, 32
physiognomy, 85, 86, 90, 190n88
Pizzi, Emilio, 27
Porter, Maggie, 20
postbellum-pre-Harlem era, 3–4, 14, 161, 165
Price, Florence, 171
Pritchard, Myron T., 149
Proctor, Henry Hugh, 92, 123; *Up to Freedom*, 123
Progressive Era, 3

Quimby, Phineas Parkhurst, 72

racial identity, 65–69
Rickards, James Frank, 21, 175n32
Robeson, Paul, 14, 107
Rogers, Alex, 128
Rosseau, Maurice, 51
Rossini, Gioachino, 57
Russell, Sylvester, 3, 87–88

San Diego, California, 157
Sayres, Helen Abbott, 107
Scott, Emmett J., 131, 135, 198n40
Scurlock, Addison, 34–35, 179n89
segregation, 4, 12, 13, 42, 65, 66, 71, 73, 82, 118, 119, 151, 163
Selika, Marie, 31, 161
Severance, Caroline M. S., 152, 201n4
Shaftsbury, Edmund, 97
Shakespeare, William, 10, 56–57, 59, 68, 101–2, 183n67
Simmons, Roscoe Conkling, 45
Skidmore, Will E., 126, 127

Skillern, Anna M., 35, 179n92
Smith, Corilla, 15–17, 66, 174n3
Smith, Henry B., 16–17
Smith, Marietta, 16, 154, 174n3, 174n8, 175n13. *See also* Boston, Marietta; Johnson, Marietta
Sogers, Berena Anderson, 154, 155
spirituals, 6, 8, 14, 27, 69, 109, 110–13
Stainer, John, 113, 114
Stevens, Charles, 57
Still, William Grant, 171

Talbert, Florence Cole, 168
Tanner, Henry Ossawa, 46, 55, 64, 92, 179n91
Tapley, Daisy Robinson, 168
Tate, Lucille, 152
Taylor, A. R., 36
Taylor, David Clark, 96–97
Terrell, Mary Church, 25, 43, 46, 68–69
Thirteenth Amendment, 120
Thomas, Ambroise, 52
Thompson, Eloise Bibb, 104, 193n57
Thompson, Noah D., 55, 92, 193n57
Thompson, Richard W., 139, 140
Thoreau, Henry David, 84
Thrift, Mattie Lawrence, 142
Thyme, Grace, 57
Tibbs, Roy W., 64
Towne, Elizabeth, 78
Travis, Trysh, 93
Trotter, James Monroe, 5–6, 173n5
Trotter, William Monroe, 118, 196n6
Troward, Thomas, 75
Turner, Thomas Wyatt, 82
Tuskegee Institute, 82, 90, 110, 163, 183n66

Verdi, Giuseppe, 48
Victorian Age, 3, 159
voice culture, 11, 96–101

Walker, George, 45, 91
Walker, Madame C. J., 23
Walton, Lester A., 89, 142
Waring, Delia Martin, 107
Warrick, Meta Vaux, 46, 181n27
Washington, Booker T., 4, 25, 90, 118, 138, 148, 162, 163, 164

Washington Conservatory of Music and School of Expression, 9, 33
Wells, Ida B., 23, 24, 55, 92
Wheeler, J. Harry, 97, 98
White, Clarence Cameron, 92, 93, 126, 168, 169, 170
White, Lucien H., 105, 155
Wilborn, David, 23, 31, 176n43
Williams, Bert, 45, 91
Williams, Fanny Barrier, 25, 65, 66, 180n14
Willis, A. Merral, 111, 169
Wilson, Ollie, 113
Wilson, Woodrow, 12
Winfrey, Oprah, 93–94, 168
Wood, Henry, 84
Work, John Wesley, 110

Yoga, 11, 76, 78, 99, 156, 159

ABOUT THE AUTHOR

Photo by Lewis Nielson

Juanita Karpf played cello professionally, taught music in grades K–12 for many years, and has held positions at Case Western Reserve University, Middlebury College, Oberlin College, and the University of Georgia. Her research has appeared in numerous publications, including *American Music, Black Music Research Journal*, and *Popular Music and Society*. Now working as an independent scholar, she lives in a log cabin in the Vermont mountains with her husband and three rescued greyhounds.

www.ingramcontent.com/pod-product-compliance
Lightning Source LLC
Chambersburg PA
CBHW030621230426
43661CB00053B/2090